JAMES W. VON BRUNN

"KILL THE BEST GENTILES!"

"Tob Shebbe Goyim Harog!"

(THE TALMUD: Sanhedrin 59)

OMNIA VERITAS

"KILL THE BEST GENTILES!"

or

"Tob Shebbe Goyim Harog!"

(THE TALMUD: Sanhedrin 59)

THE RACIALIST GUIDE FOR THE PRESERVATION AND NURTURE
OF THE WHITE GENE POOL

by

JAMES W. VON BRUNN

PUBLISHED BY
OMNIA VERITAS LTD

ꝊMNIA VERITAS

www.omnia-veritas.com

Dedication

In Memory of:

REAR ADMIRAL JOHN G. CROMMELIN, USN.

"Now, there was a man!"

+ + +

John Geraerd Crommelin, Jr., Rear Admiral, USN, served in the Pacific Theater during WWII, as Executive Officer, and Air Officer, aboard the USS *Enterprise*, CV-6 (the most decorated ship in naval history). Crommelin, was acknowledged by the crew as the "heart and soul of the Big-E." Later, holding the Legion of Merit with a Gold Star; a Combat "V," a Presidential Unit Citation, a Letter of Commendation, and a Purple Heart, he was given Command of the then most advanced aircraft carrier in the world, the USS *Saipan* (CVL-48).

In 1949 Admiral Crommelin precipitated a Congressional investigation that prevented powerful Communist influence within the U.S. government from crippling the U.S. Navy and tipping the balance of military power in favor of the Soviet Union. In 1987, Rear Admiral Crommelin was elected to the Carrier Hall of Fame, located aboard the preserved USS *Yorktown* (CV-10), Patriot's Point, Charleston, S.C. His plaque, next to that of Secretary of the Navy James Forrestal, reads:

"In 1949 he sacrificed his 4.0 Naval career by precipitating the 'Admirals' Revolt' that saved Carrier Aviation."

A nation can survive its fools and even the ambitious. But it cannot survive treason from within. An enemy at the gates is less formidable for he is known and carries his banners openly. But the traitor moves among those within the gates freely, his sly whispers rustling through all the alleys, heard in the very halls of government itself... for the traitor appears no traitor: He speaks in accents familiar to his victims, and he wears their faces and their garments, he appeals to the baseness that lies deep in the souls of all men. He rots the soul of a nation; he works secretly and unknown in the night to undermine the pillars of the city; he infects the body politic so that it can no longer resist. A murderer is to be less feared.

— **Cicero**

PREFACE

The purpose of this book is to present to WHITE YOUTH factual information conventionally suppressed or distorted by the mass media, and denied them by schools and universities — which are forced to promulgate the Marxist line or lose their government subsidies. Appearing throughout the text are quotes from world authorities whose credentials appear in the bibliography. Upon reading TOB SHEBBE GOYIM HAROG! (KILL THE BEST GENTILES!) you will understand that — despite loud protests of denial — an age old CONSPIRACY does exist to destroy Western Civilization. At this moment we are engaged in a deadly war with the HISTORIC ENEMY to determine whether or not our Nation will endure. We are losing that war because an Iron Curtain of censorship has descended over the landscape abrogating the First Amendment to the Constitution of the United States. Without Freedom of Speech our system of government cannot function. The hour is late. You and your family are in grave danger. We will present the FACTS then discuss what actions must be taken.

Best wishes,

James W. von Brunn
Post Office Box 2821
Easton, Maryland 21601

8 June 1999 (Remember the U.S.S. *Liberty*.)

TABLE OF CONTENTS

ACKNOWLEDGEMENT

More than anything else this book is a compilation of research data, ideas, and writings of men and women whom I admire, whose words have inspired me, and from whose writings I have liberally borrowed. I have attempted to acknowledge and credit my sources throughout this work. Special acknowledgement must be given to Oswald Spengler, Francis Parker Yockey, Wilmot Robertson, Revilo Oliver, and William Gayley Simpson. However, they should not be held accountable for the conclusion arrived at in my manuscript. In that sense the MS is my responsibility alone — as are its failures.

— JvB

FOREWORD

For thou art a Holy people unto the Lord thy God. And the Lord hath chosen thee to be a peculiar people unto Himself above all the nations that are upon the earth.

THE HOLY BIBLE (Torah): Deuteronomy 14:2.

All property of other nations belongs to the Jewish nation which, consequently, is entitled to seize it without scruples... A Jew may act contrary to morality if profitable to himself or to Jews in general.

TALMUD: Schulchan Bruch, Choszen Hamiszpat 348.

We have fooled, bemused and corrupted the youth of the goyim by rearing them in principals and theories known to us to be false although it is by us they have been inculcated.

PROTOCOLS OF THE LEARNED
ELDERS OF ZION: Protocol 9:10.

You have not begun to appreciate the real depth of our guilt. We ARE intruders. We ARE disturbers. We ARE subverters. We have taken your natural world, your ideals, your destiny, and played havoc with them. We have been at the bottom not merely of your last great war but of nearly all your wars; not only of the Russian but of every other revolution in your history. We have brought discord and confusion, and frustration into your public life. We are still doing it. Who knows what great and glorious destiny might have been yours had we left you alone?

MARCUS ELI RAVAGE, JEW *Century Magazine*,
January 1928.

Let me issue and control a nation's money And I care not who makes its laws.

AMSCHEL MEYER ROTHSCHILD, JEW[1] (1743-1812).

---

[1] Throughout this book I have inserted into my own text, and into text quoted from

I

WE ARE WITNESSING today on the world stage a tragedy of enormous proportions: the calculated destruction of the White Race and the incomparable culture it represents. Europe, former fortress of the West, is now over-run by hordes of non-Whites and mongrels. The same is true of Australia and Canada. The once productive White civilizations of Rhodesia and South Africa, extorted by the ILLUMINATI and its enforcement unit, the United States, have been forced into DEMOCRATIC governments, thereby surrendering their White families to the mercy of numerically superior and mentally inferior Negroes whose ancestors were incapable of inventing even the wheel. The most concentrated attacks on the White Race, however, are occurring in the United States of America.

TIME magazine (4-9-90) reports that during the first half of the 21st Century (U. S. Census Bureau statistics), the White population of the United States will become a minority in its own land! "The 'browning of America' will alter everything in society from politics and education, to industry, values and culture... the new world is here. It is now. And it is *irreversibly* the America to come." TIME goes on to say: "The former majority will learn as a normal part of everyday life, the meaning of the Latin slogan engraved

---

others, words to identify individuals as Jews so that the reader will not have to depend upon context or memory to make the proper identification. — JvB

on our coins — *E pluribus unum*, one formed from many."

Ben Wattenberg, JEW, spokesman for American Enterprise Institute, Washington, D. C., commenting on America's static White birthrate, miscegenation and the flood of non-White immigration enthusiastically states: "There is a nice chance that the American myth is going to ratchet another step, in the 1990's and beyond, toward this idea that we are the UNIVERSAL NATION. That rings the bell of manifest destiny! We are a people with a mission and a sense of purpose, and we believe we have something to offer the world!"

The "American myth" (created by JEWS) alleging our Founding Fathers intended that all races, from pygmy to Ainu, be invited to our shores, is based on Thomas Jefferson's words in the Declaration of Independence: "...all men are created equal." The meaning of this much quoted statement has been distorted by the ILLUMINATI which subjectively is re-writing history and wielding the alleged "HOLOCAUST" like a battle-ax at the heads of those proclaiming genetic certainties: Men and races are NOT created equal.

Jefferson's statement can be understood only in context of his Era. Our Founding Fathers were Aryans, men of good breeding who understood, empirically, the great differences existing between strains of horses; strains of live-stock; races of men; and between individuals: knowledge confirmed today by the natural sciences of Genetics, Eugenics, and Anthropology. Hitler, as American boobs are beginning to learn, was not all wrong.

The Framers of our Constitution, representing thirteen slave holding colonies expected to build a bastion of Western Culture in America *for their White progeny*. Jefferson, owner of many slaves, was NOT endorsing racial equality. The thought would never have entered his head (He also said, "...the two races equally free cannot live together under the same government."). Jefferson referred to *equality before the law* — as it pertained to the burning issue of the day: "Taxation without representation."

The Founders also wanted a government in which the supreme power lies in the People. The Founders knew, however, that in this very imperfect world *intelligent and capable people are always outnumbered by the unintelligent and incapable. Ergo*, the majority vote nullifies the intelligent vote. The Founders also knew that the masses are easily controlled by unscrupulous, ambitious men. Therefore, in their wisdom the Founders created a Republic with strong checks and balances — NOT a DEMOCRACY — knowing that Democracy is intended to destroy the freedoms it presumes to protect. *Accordingly, the franchise was held so precious that it was limited* to White men deemed capable of exercising responsible votes. The Framers were influenced by Plato's discourses contemning "rule by the majority," and by the history of that remarkable city-state, Athens, during the Golden Age of Pericles (c. 430 B.C.). Athen's total population of 130,000 consisted of 50,000 citizens (Greeks, closely inbred); 25,000 metics (Aliens in residence); and 55,000 slaves. In that highly acclaimed "Democracy" — which disproportionately produced many of history's greatest men — women, metics, and slaves were denied the vote; and citizens were forbidden to marry slaves.

Alexis de Tocqueville observed: to establish a power base in a DEMOCRACY it requires only that one profess belief in egalitarianism. This is precisely the stratagem initiated by the ILLUMINATI during the last half of 19th Century America. Fat with profits harvested in the Civil War, JEWS were like worms attacking a ripe cornfield. Their strategy, in accordance with the PROTOCOLS was: 1) Convert the American Republic into a DEMOCRACY; 2) Establish a Rothschild central-bank; 3) Capture the mass-media; 4) Enact a personal income tax; 5) Destroy White nationhood; and 6) hitch America's incredible resources, strength and creative energies to JEW aspirations, among which was the destruction of Germany, avowed enemy of LIBERALISM/ MARXISM/JEWRY and Fatherland of the White Race. Emma Lazarus, JEW (1849-1887), signaled her tribe's intentions toward our Republic in a poem, ("The New Colossus") inscribed on the base of the Statue of Liberty, inviting the world's "wretched refuse" to America's golden shores — Yahweh's GARBAGE DUMP. JEWS tend to destroy what they most envy.

LIBERALISM/JEWRY/MARXISM was the formula used by Woodrow Wilson, and Franklin D. Roosevelt, both Democrats, to betray their Nation. The former a naïf, bleeding heart sophist, blackmailed for his "Peck-o-dills" by

U. S. Zionists; the latter a ruthless egotist bearing deep-seated malice toward his own race ("Some of my best friends are communists"). Under Wilson, DEMOCRACY replaced our Republic; America's monetary system was placed in ILLUMINATI hands; and JEWS received the Balfour Declaration (guaranteeing a Jewish "Homeland"), *quid pro quo*, for bringing America into WWI. Under Roosevelt, LIBERALISM/MARXISM/JEWRY triumphed over Western Civilization. JEWS were guaranteed the state of ISRAEL *quid pro quo* for again bringing America into war against Germany (WWII). "The most gallant stag can be brought to its knees with enough dogs at its throat." (William G. Simpson)

The "people with a mission" referred to by Ben Wattenberg, JEW, above, are GOD'S CHOSEN PEOPLE whose messianic mission, as the Old Testament, Talmud and Protocols make abundantly clear, is the destruction of all Gentile nations through miscegenation and wars. The resultant dispirited, "brown proletariat-herd" is to be known euphemistically as the UNIVERSAL NATION.

Since WWII the ZIONIST OCCUPIED GOVERNMENT OF THE UNITED STATES (ZOG) has welcomed huge numbers of fecund non-White immigrants predicated upon the ideology that diversity is better. Paradoxically, the LIBERAL establishment is engaged in a counterculture campaign designed to eliminate diversity through racial miscegenation. These inconsistent concepts share a singular ILLUMINATI goal —

destruction of the Aryan race.

Approval of inter-racial breeding is predicated on idiotic Christian dogma that God's children must love their enemies (a concept JEWS totally reject); and on LIBERAL/MARXIST/JEW propaganda that all men/races are created equal. These genocidal ideologies, preached from the American pulpits, taught in American schools, legislated in the halls of Congress (confirming TALMUDIC conviction that goyim are stupid sheep), are expected to produce a single, superintelligent, beautiful, non-White "American" population. Eliminating forever racism, inequality, bigotry and war. As with ALL LIBERAL ideologies, miscegenation is totally inconsistent with Natural Law: the species are improved through in-breeding, natural selection and mutation. Only the strong survive. Cross-breeding Whites with species lower on the evolutionary scale diminishes the White gene-pool while increasing the number of physiologically, psychologically and behaviorally deprived mongrels. Throughout history improvident Whites have miscegenated. The "brotherhood" concept is not new (as LIBERALS pretend) nor are the results — which are inevitably disastrous for the White Race — evident today, for example, in the botched populations of Cuba, Mexico, Egypt, India, and the inner cities of contemporary America.

How differently TALMUDISTS protect *their* genepool! JEWRY has no intention of becoming part of the UNIVERSAL NATION they are creating for the dumb *goyim.* United Nations representative Count Folke Bernadotte, before the Irgun murdered him, proposed that Palestinians and JEWS live together under a DEMOCRATIC government. Palestinians accepted. JEWS violently refused, demanding a State exclusively for JEWS. DEMOCRATIC DIVERSITY is good only for *goyim!* JEWS — who have made anti-Semitism a profitable business: who bomb their own synagogues; scribble graffiti on their own tombs; mouth "HOLOCAUST" lies — are revealed today as the world's most virulent ANTI-SEMITES: murdering Arabs at every opportunity and screaming for U.S. assistance when the dispossessed "terrorists" fight back.

Survival of the JEW nation depends upon maintaining its status as GOD'S CHOSEN PEOPLE. The TALMUD, therefore, makes it a crime for JEWS to marry non-JEWS. But not always. Male JEWS, seeking to invigorate sickly tribal genes may receive rabbinical dispensation to mate with trophy Gentile women. The mongrel offspring (bastards) of those mixed marriages are considered non-JEWS; however, sons of those marriages can redeem the JEW lineage by marrying JEWESSES, whose issue is always considered JEWISH. Selah, the TRIBE captures healthy Gentile genes! In a patriarchal society, as the JEWS', the above described dispensation indicates a biological necessity. It was common practice for wealthy JEWS, following the wars, to search the ruins of Europe for starving Aryan widows and orphans to take back to the States.

Steven Spielberg, JEW, pusillanimous Hollywood director, paid $22-million to Kate Capshaw, enterprising White hustler, before she would commit to the marriage bed (*Vanity Fair*, Oct. 1997). She then dutifully bore him two future candiates for America's booming nose-job industry. Such is the life of a bird in a gilded cage. It is not clear what remuneration Vice President Al Gore received, *quid pro quo*, for arranging the marriage of his blonde daughter to the scion of the wealthy Schiff tribe (Kuhn Loeb & Co., JEWS), a banking cabal notorious for financing the Bolshevik Revolution in which millions of unarmed Moslems, and Christians were murdered in the same manner that Texas ranchers round-up and slaughter jack-rabbits.

In 1933 Germans in democratic elections opted for a German State exclusively for Germans (Aryans) — offering to help Zionists colonize JEWS in Palestine. WORLD JEWRY went berserk unilaterally declaring war (1933) on Germany. It is inconceivable to JEWS that any race but GOD'S CHOSEN should have its own State. ILLUMINATI ordered ALLIED forces to incinerate Germans in their cities, farms, and hamlets: advising the World that Nation States will not be tolerated — except in Israel, and that WORLD JEWRY may live within whatever foreign nation it wishes.

The phrase *E pluribus unum*, which appears on U.S. coins, referred to White immigrants who, upon reaching the United States, abandoned their ethnicity and assimilated into one White gene-pool (Nation): the same Aryan Nation that populated the great States of Europe. Here, instead of calling themselves English, French, Scots, Germans, Poles, *et al.*, they called themselves Americans. Therefore, until WWII the entire world thought of Americans as White. No longer. We are known today as the "ugly American." This is no longer our country. Shamefully, White America capitulated to the JEWS without firing a shot — whilst the American Indian fought for his land almost to the last man, leaving a legacy of bravery.

The world *homosapiens* population today is 6-Billion, of which 800-Million (13%) are White. Democratizing the world will provide the same result as pouring a container of milk down a New York City sewer. The White population simply will miscegenate into the muck and disappear — *forever* — as befitting a species lacking the Will to survive.

II

From the earliest days of their history JEWS lived among alien nations. Strabo, the great geographer (c. 100 B.C.), wrote that HEBREWS clandestinely controlled almost every prosperous People on earth. That seems a fair statement. Josephus, HEBREW historian of about the same period, boasted there is no nation HEBREWS have not penetrated. 400-years after Cheops' first pyramid a trickle of HEBREW immigrants crossed the Suez isthmus into prosperous Egypt during the reign of Pepi II (2738-2644 B.C.). The trickle became a stream. Bribery, political and moral corruption burgeoned. The Egyptian dynasty verged on collapse. Nefer-rohu writes: "Every mouth is full of 'Love me!' and everything good has disappeared." "The robber is now the possessor of riches... I show thee the owner in need and the outsider satisfied..." HEBREWS were not held in bondage by the Pharaoh. It was the other way around. Eventually the camel was kicked out of the tent and Egypt began a cultural and economic renaissance.

The twelve HEBREW tribes to whom Yahweh promised the World were united for less than 100-years ("Golden Years") under kings Saul, David and the bastard Solomon. Torn by internecine strife and heavily taxed to support the "wise" king's excesses the tribes unwisely split into two parts (922 B.C.): Israel with 10 tribes, to the north; and Judah (containing Jerusalem) with 2 tribes, to the south. Assyrians (Syria, Semites) killed or assimilated the northern tribes — which disappeared forever from history. Then Judah was defeated in battle by Babylonians (Iraqis, Semites). Surviving Judeans were held in Babylonian captivity. Later those held in positions of trust (530 B.C.) betrayed Babylon to the Persians (Iran, Aryans) even as JUDEANS later betrayed the Greek-Roman cities of Asia Minor to the Patricians, as JEWS in the 20th Century betrayed America's military secrets to the Soviet Union, Israel and China. (The O.T. Book of Esther reveals the JEWS' concept of a heroine). Persia allowed the JUDEANS to return to Jerusalem and rebuild their temple. In 330 B.C. Alexander the Great (Macedonians, Greeks, Aryans) conquered Persia. Eventually Hellenism was replaced (27 B.C.) by the great Roman (Aryan) hegemony.

Under Hellenism and later Rome the objective was to bring together as a functioning entity the heterogeneous populations of Asia and the mid-East. Improvements were made in government and civic affairs; roads and aqueducts were constructed, trade routes and businesses established (more HEBREWS lived in Alexandria than in Jerusalem).

The concept of Western Reason was introduced into education, i.e., the objective search for FACTS as opposed to subjective (HEBRAIC) reasoning. All of the conquered areas profited. However, GOD'S CHOSEN had their own agenda. Hebrews split into two substantive camps: the High Priests and business community which cooperated with the satrap governments for political favor and monetary profits; and the traditional looney religious zealots seeking martyrdom, and death to Gentiles. To Greece-Rome, Judeans appeared of little importance — until a treasonous 5th-column spread throughout the region. The air filled with rumors, slander, superstitions and dire omens. Usury, bribery, extortion soared. Morale and business suffered. Government officials and army officers were assassinated. Pushed beyond patience as many nations have been, first Greece, then Rome struck back hard. And they have been demonized for their actions ever since. Antiochus IV Epiphanes, the ruling Ptolemy, attempted to gain Hebrew cooperation through edicts supporting the Torah, the High

Priest, and the business community. However, his patience ran out when he learned of another armed Israeli rebellion (169 B.C.). "Raging like a wild beast," Antiochus marched against Jerusalem where — after his Hebrew supporters treacherously opened the city gates — the Greeks killed 80,000 ISRAELIS in three days, and sold at least that many into slavery.

Rome, too, having experienced 100-years of HEBREW lies and treason (7-Million Hebrews lived within the Roman Empire), and smarting under another rebellion in Palestine, ordered the Temple in Jerusalem destroyed (70 A.D.). In addition, according to Tacitus, 600,000 of the 2.5-Million ISRAELIS living in Palestine were slain in combat (Josephus, the Elie Wiesel of his day, claimed 1,197,000 men, women, and children were murdered).

In 115 A.D., HEBREWS and Gentiles killed one another in Egypt, Mesopotamia, Cyprus and Cyrene. During the Diaspora (i.e., Hebrews banished from Canaan) "God's Chosen" scattered throughout the Mediterranean littoral. Tragically for the West, many of them joined the Hebrew enclave in Rome where as early as 63 B.C. it is recorded Hebrews caused economic problems by exporting gold from Italy. Their corrupt influence was powerful enough to bribe Roman judges and influence foreign policy. The pitiful tale of ISRAELIS forced to live in the Diaspora is another HOAX. Only a small HEBREW population ever lived in Palestine; genetically they are compelled to live among host nations. The ISRAELI administrative capital was not Jerusalem but Babylon. There, a NASI (Chief) administered the far-flung Hebrew nation. Joseph Ben Tobiah, JEW (c. 240 B.C.) is described as "the prototype of the INTERNATIONAL FINANCIER for whom neither frontiers nor restrictive ethical considerations exist... the first great JEW banker." (Peter Green, *Alexander to Actium*).

From the Pharaohs to Hammurabi to modern times JEWS have been the object of dread and disgust:

(CICERO) JEWS belong to a dark and repulsive force. (TACITUS) They are always ready to show compassion to one another while reserving bitter enmity toward all others. (CONSTANTINE) The JEWS are a nefarious and perverse sect. (THE KORAN) Satan has prevailed upon them. JEWS are the party of Satan. (GOETHE) This crafty race has one great principle: as long as order prevails there is nothing to be gained. (VOLTAIRE) All JEWS are born with a raging fanaticism in their hearts, just as Bretons and Germans are born with blond hair. I wouldn't be surprised if these JEWS would not some day become deadly to the human race. (WASHINGTON) The JEWS work more effectively against us than the enemy's armies. (JEFFERSON) Dispersed as JEWS they still form one nation, foreign to the land they live in. (FRANKLIN) I fully agree with General Washington that we must protect this young nation from an insidious influence and penetration. That menace, gentlemen, is the JEWS. (NAPOLEON) The JEWS are the master robbers of the modern age; they are the carrion birds of humanity. (LISZT) The presence of the

JEWS in the midst of the European nations is a cause of many evils and a serious danger. (HEGEL) The state is incompatible with the JEWISH principle. (LORD HARRINGTON) JEWS have ever been the greatest enemies of freedom. (HUME) The JEWS have a peculiar character and are known for their fraud. (U. S. GRANT) The JEWS, as a class, violating every regulation established by the Treasury are hereby expelled from that department. (SOMBART) Wars are JEWS' harvests. (DOSTOYEVSKY) JEWS are draining the soil of Russia. (JUNG) The JEW has never created a cultural form of his own and as far as we can see never will. (R. L. STEVENSON) JEWS lead on the farmer into irretrievable indebtedness and keep him ever after as their bond-slave. (R. WAGNER) On one thing I am very clear: that is the deflection and falsification of our cultural tendencies can be attributed to JEWISH influence. (LINDBERGH) We are disturbed about the effect of the JEWISH influence in our press, radio, and motion pictures. (NESTA WEBSTER) England is no longer controlled by Britons. We are under an invisible JEWISH dictatorship. (KEROUAC) The real enemy is the Communist, the JEW. (J. R. LOWELL) Where would the JEW be among a society of primitive men without pockets? (MALCOM X) You can't even say JEW without him accusing you of antiSemitism. (MENCKEN) It seems to me, save for a few bright spots, the TALMUD is quite indistinguishable from rubbish. (G. B. SHAW) This is the real enemy... the oriental parasite; in a word the JEW. (SOMBART) Turn to the pages of the TALMUD... JEWS were taught early on to look for their chief happiness in money. (MARK TWAIN) I read in the *Encyclopaedia Britannica* that the JEWISH population in the U.S. was 250,000; I wrote the editor that I personally was acquainted with more JEWS than that. I am of the opinion that we have an immense JEWISH population in the United States. (THOMAS WOLFE) JEWS seduce pure young Christian boys (and girls) because they love them and want to destroy them.[2] Behind all Western wars and revolutions lurks the International JEW, forever wailing anti-Semitism, while sucking Gentile blood.

> We are not hyphenated JEWS: we are JEWS with no qualifications or reservations... Your spirit is alien to us... your national ambitions and aspirations are alien to us. We are a foreign people in your midst, and we emphasize we wish to stay that way... we recognize a national unity of Diaspora JEWS no matter in which land we reside. Therefore no boundaries can restrain us from pursuing our own JEWISH policies...
> DR. JAKOB KLATZKIN, JEW, "Krisis und Entsheidung."

In the Modern Era JEWRY was expelled, punished or exposed by many Aryan States including the following:

1215 CATHOLIC 4th LATERAN COUNCIL — restricted JEWRY for slave trade, prostitution, and pimpery.

1253 FRANCE — restrictions for violating Civil Law.

1255 ENGLAND — 18 hanged for ritual murder.

---

[2] quotations are from the book ANTIZION, compiled by William Grimstad, Noontide Press.

1275 ENGLAND — Parliamentary proscription of JEW usury.

1290 ENGLAND — expelled from England for treason, etc.

1300 RUSSIA — ongoing warfare between Aryan Rus and Khazars culminating in Bolshevik Revolution and ILLUMINATI take-over of Russia/Eastern Europe, and America.

1348 SAXONY — expels JEWS to Poland, Turkey; treason.

1360 HUNGARY — expels JEWS for violations of Civil Law.

1370 BELGIUM — expels JEWS for usury, treason.

1380 SLOVAKIA — expels JEWS for usury, treason, pimping.

1420 AUSTRIA — expels JEWS for violation of Civil Law.

1444 NETHERLANDS — expels JEWS for usury, treason, pimping.

1492 SPAIN — expels JEWS for blasphemy, treason.

1495 LITHUANIA — expels JEWS for violation of Civil Law.

1498 PORTUGAL — expels JEWS for blasphemy, treason.

1540 ITALY — expels JEWS for blasphemy, murder, pimpery.

1551 BAVARIA — expels JEWS for treason.

1776 FRANCE/BAVARIA — ILLUMINATI banned.

1913 RUSSIA — expels Bolsheviks for treason, murder.

1935 GERMANY, ROMANIA, HUNGARY, AUSTRIA, CROATIA, VICHY FRANCE, expel JEWS for treasonous activities, usury, murder.

1953 U.S.A. — Congress identifies and convicts JEW spies.

1966 U.S.A. — Senator McCarthy proven correct re JEW spies.

1990 CANADA — Zundel Trials prove "HOLOCAUST" a HOAX.

1999 U.S.A — JEW espionage.

> The JEW has already emancipated himself in the JEWISH way: The JEW who is for example merely tolerated in Vienna determines by his money power the fate of the entire German Empire. The JEW who is without rights in the smallest German state decides the fate of Europe.
> KARL MARX, "A World Without Jews," 1840

III

In Nature all organisms feed on other organisms. In that sense Mankind is parasitical because it feeds on other living things. However, the only human parasite that embeds itself in the sinews of other humans is the JEW. Their genius lies in cunning; in their chameleon-like ability to deceive; and, as Cicero points out, their malevolence in appealing to the baseness that lies deep in the souls of all men. Publicly the JEWS evoke PITY. Presenting themselves as JUDEANS wandering forever in Diaspora: tragic, defenseless victims, persecuted by EVERYONE in a bigoted, anti-Semitic world! Beneath this chimerism international JEWRY is a virulent, organized, powerful, enormously wealthy TETRAD combing NATION/LAW/RELIGION/CULTURE: which alone commands allegiance; traverses all national boundaries; and holds in utter contempt the Gentile nations that their genocidal GOD has commanded them to destroy.

> The indignation of the Lord is upon all nations and his fury upon all armies. He will utterly destroy them... their slain shall also be cast out and their stink shall come from their carcasses... for it is the year of the Lord's vengeance and the year of recompense for the controversy of Zion.
>
> THE HOLY BIBLE: Isaiah 34:2.

Edward Gibbon, in his *The Decline and Fall of the Roman Empire*, describes JEWS as "a race of fanatics... with an irreconcilable hatred of Mankind." Arnold Toynbee calls JUDAISM a "Fossil religion." Winston Churchill denounces JEWS as "A gang of personalities from the underworld CONSPIRING to overthrow Western Civilization." Rabbi Stephen Wise, leader of "American" JEWRY during WWII, and instrumental in creating the "HOLOCAUST" (HOAX) said: "I am not an American citizen of JEWISH faith. I am a JEW. I have been a JEW for a thousand years. Hitler was right — we are a People." Yes, Hitler was right.

In this Foreword we have reviewed briefly the intentions of our Founding Fathers to create a bastion of Western Culture in America for their White progeny. Current U. S. Census Bureau statistics reveal that White Americans are being eradicated. We also explored a brief history of the HEBREWS/JUDEANS/ISRAELIS because, as Spengler so convincingly demonstrates — and as America can now attest — history unfailingly repeats itself. The ancient JEW cancer is now embedded in America's sinews.

The Rules of Navigation tell us that to set a new course we first must know where we are; to know where we are we must know where we have been. Therefore, we intend to briefly examine the history of the CONSPIRACY; followed by a description of the CONSPIRACY in action: LIBERALISM/MARXISM/JEWRY; and finally we will offer a plan to remove the cancer from our Cultural Organism. *If it is not removed we die.*

REMEMBER: White genes cannot be created, they can only be transmitted. We Aryans can always build another State upon the ruins of the old; but once the White genepool is polluted YOU CAN KISS THE BLONDES,

REDHEADS AND FAIR SKINNED BRUNETTES GOODBYE FOREVER!

CHAPTER 1

THE CONSPIRACY

For thou art a holy people unto the lord thy God and the lord hath chosen thee to be a peculiar people unto himself, above all the nations that are upon the earth.

HOLY BIBLE: Deuteronomy 14:2.

The indignation of the Lord is upon all nations, and his fury upon all armies. He will utterly destroy them... their slain shall also be cast out and their stink shall come from their carcasses... for it is the year of the Lord's vengeance and the year of recompense for the controversy of Zion.

HOLY BIBLE: Isaiah 34:2.

Extermination of Christians necessary.

TALMUD: Zohar II 43a.

It is more wicked to question the words of the rabbis than Torah.

TALMUD: Michna Sanhedrin 11:3.

The administrators, whom we shall choose from among the public with strict regard for their servile obedience, will not be persons trained in the art of government, and therefore will easily become pawns in our game, in the hands of men of learning and genius who will be their advisors: specialists bred and reared from early childhood to rule the affairs of the whole world.

PROTOCOLS OF THE LEARNED
ELDERS OF ZION, Protocol 2:2.

All vows, oaths, promises, engagements, and swearings which I make in the future shall be null from this Day of Atonement until the next.

TALMUD: Kol Nidre Oath.

THE TORAH

WHEN HISTORIANS publicly commit to a CONSPIRACY THEORY the media goes berserk, labeling them Nazis, bigots, paranoids, fools. Why such furious denials? Since the beginning of recorded history men have conspired to rule the world, or what they thought to be the world. Why should it be any different today? It isn't. There is a conspiracy, working at this moment, to destroy Western Civilization and the Aryan Nation that created it. This is not a new conspiracy. It began over 3000-years ago as spoken tribal legends, which eventually were collected in the Torah (c. 900 B.C.), a tapestry of myths and tales plagiarized, largely, from Egypt, Mesopotamia, Babylon, and Greece. The Mosaic Law, the Garden of Eden, the Flood, the story of David, all came from non-Hebraic sources. The idea of monotheism was borrowed (c. 1400 B.C) from Pharaoh Iknaton. Into this rich tapestry the Hebrews wove threads of their own history as they believed it to be, or desired it to be — the *modus operandi* of Hollywood scriptwriters today. The fictitious protagonist of these self-serving tales is Yahweh (Adonai, Jehovah, God): a jealous, vengeful, wrathful, genocidal, anthropomorphic tribal god, created in the image and likeness of the Hebrews who created him. Naturally, this BIG HEBREW in the sky LOVES the HEBREWS. All other nations are considered cattle to be used, milked and exterminated.

> For thou art a holy people unto the lord thy God and the lord hath chosen thee to be a peculiar people unto himself, above all the

nations that are upon the earth.

THE HOLY BIBLE, Deuteronomy 14:2.

Ye shall be a treasure unto me above all people: for the earth is mine.

THE HOLY BIBLE, Exodus 19:5.

Remember, these delusions of grandeur were written by HEBREWS about themselves. Megalomaniacs of such magnitude generally are manic-depressives confined to insane asylums.

The treasure of treasures is Abraham whom Yahweh "loves above all others." We are told that Abram (Abraham) and his wife Sari (Sarah), who also is his half-sister, journeyed to prosperous Egypt looking for loot. There, Abraham arranges an assignation between his sister and the Pharaoh. Yahweh, omnipresent, catches them *en flagrante delicto*. The Pharaoh, unaware he has committed adultery, presents Abe and Sari with cattle, servants, silver and gold "and Abraham was very rich." But, JEHOVAH is a jealous god and WRATHFUL (Gen.12); NOT at the pimp Abraham whom he loves above all others; NOT at the hustler Sari. He's furious with the duped gentile, Pharaoh, and visits a plague upon Egypt (Spielbergism). Many years later (Gen. 20) in a repeat scenario Sarah, then 92-years old, hustles Pharaoh Ambimilech. God said to Ambimilech: "behold thou art but a dead man... for she is a man's wife!" Real history records JEWS were expelled from Egypt for treason and for transmitting the plague — as JEWS were carriers of typhus during World War II (See Chapter 6, "HOLOCAUST").

In another example of GOD's hatred for Gentiles we learn that Abraham, patriarch of Israel, had his eyes focused on Canaan, a "land of milk and honey" belonging to a pastoral Semitic tribe — the Philistines (Palestinians). As luck would have it Yahweh fashions a sweetheart arrangement with his pimp pal Abraham:

> And I will give unto thee and thy seed after thee the land wherein thou art a stranger, all the land of Canaan, for an everlasting possession; and I will be their God.
>
> GENESIS 17:8.

JEHOVAH, like Alley Oop, says whatever the scriptwriters print in the blurbs. Those who find it compelling to believe Yahweh created a flat earth, circa 5000 B.C., spoke from a burning bush, bared his buttocks, parted the Red Sea, and loves JEWS above all other nations, share a childish credulity with those who believe millions of JEWS died in German gas-chambers. It also confirms JEWISH conviction that Gentiles are stupid sheep. It makes one want to puke.

The TORAH commands Gentiles to worship JEHOVAH or suffer the torments of Hell. On the other hand JEHOVAH assures JEWS they may rob, cheat, rape, and slay Gentiles with impunity. He promises that JEWS alone shall inherit the Earth.

THE TALMUD

THE HOLY BIBLE informs us that Moses, a Hebrew (or was he Egyptian?), climbed Mt. Sinai (c. 1300 B.C.) to confer with Yahweh, who gave him THE LAW (The Ten Commandments) which Moses wrote down on two stone tablets (there was no Hebraic alphabet in those days so the writing may have been cuneiform, hieroglyphic, Chinese, or whatever). Traditionally, Moses also wrote the TORAH (Pentateuch). Centuries later Pharisees claimed that God orally interpreted THE LAW given Moses. The Pharisees claimed that Yahweh's oral interpretation was identical with their oral interpretation. Thus, the PHARISEES' ORAL LAW and THE TORAH are recognized as THE HOLY WORD. The Pharisees' ORAL LAW, called Pharisaism, which Jesus despised as the "Synagogue of Satan," was eventually written down and became the TALMUD (500 A.D.).

> The TALMUD consists of 63 books of legal, ethical, and historical writings of the ancient rabbis (22 B.C. — 500 A.D.). It was edited 5-centuries after the birth of Jesus. It is a compendium of law and lore: the legal code which forms the basis of JEWISH religious Law and the book used in the training of rabbis; it is the very foundation of JEWISH life. It is taught to JEWISH children as soon as they are able to read.
>
> Rabbi Morris N. Kertzer, President, Jewish Chaplain's Association, Armed Forces, U.S.A.; spokesman for the American Jewish Committee (the "Vatican of Judaism").

There are two TALMUDS: the Palestinian, and the Babylonian. It is the Babylonian TALMUD (Socino Ed.

1935), used by most JEWS that we, largely, will refer to here. It is a huge tome; much of which is dull, the syntax cumbersome; herein the genetic schizophrenia of JEWS is manifest: it is boastful, despondent, vindictive, vulgar, dishonest, hatefilled. The TALMUD is concerned with almost every conceivable aspect of JEWISH existence, little is left to chance, from how to use seeds and herbs, to diet, and sexual relations; when to lie; whom to kill; what goat to sacrifice; Cabalism, numerology, necromancy, thaumaturgy, and obsessions with Hollywood-style perversions, body functions, etc. Nevertheless, throughout, the rabbis wove the thread of JEWISH philosophy, JEWISH Law, and JEWISH "history." Here is the grist underlying the JEWS' goal to rule the world, garner its wealth, and enslave the Gentiles. It is this Luciferian credo, that is changing the United States into an ILLUMINATI controlled, non-White nation, soon to become part of One Mongrel World.

> Gentiles prying into JEW LAWS will receive death.
> > TALMUD: Sanhedrin 59a.

> Do not save Christians in danger of death.
> > TALMUD: Hilkoth Akum X, 1.

> Kill the best Gentiles!
> > TALMUD: Sanhedrin 59.

> A woman who has intercourse with a beast is eligible to marry a priest.
> > TALMUD: Yebamoth 59b.

> A maiden three years and a day may be acquired in marriage by

coition.

TALMUD: Sanhedrin 55b.

Pederasty with a child below nine years of age is not deemed pederasty.

TALMUD: Sanhedrin 54b-55a.

Jesus was illegitimately conceived during menstruation.

TALMUD: Kallah 1b (18b).

When a grown up man has intercourse with a little girl, less than 3-years old, it is as nothing.

TALMUD: Kethuboth 11a-11b.

Sexual intercourse is permitted with a dead relative.

TALMUD: Ya Bhamoth.

Let us all remember that we are a distinct nationality of which every Jew — what ever his country, his station, his shade of belief — is necessarily a member.

LOUIS DEMBITZ BRANDEIS,
JEW, U.S. Supreme Court.

Michael Redkinson, JEW, and Rabbi Isaac Wise, "two of the world's greatest authorities on the TALMUD," collaborating on the celebrated tome, *History of the Talmud*, have this to say:

The source from which Jesus of Nazareth drew the teachings... that enabled him to revolutionize the world... is the TALMUD. It is the written form of that which, in the time of Jesus, was called the traditions of The Elders of Zion, to which he makes frequent allusions.

Redkinson and Wise, of course, are LIARS. The TALMUD resounds with hatred for Jesus:

Jesus was conceived while Mary was menstruating.

TALMUD: Kallah 1b.

Jesus is the bastard son of Pandira, Roman soldier.

TALMUD: Sanhedrin 67a.

Jesus is in Hell, punished by being boiled in hot semen... all Christians are boiled in shit!

TALMUD: Libre David 37.

And the New Testament clearly shows Jesus' disdain for the Pharisees and their oral (TALMUDIC) teaching:

I know the blasphemy of them who say they are the Children of God, but are of the Synagogue of Satan! For ye are of your father the Devil, and the lusts of your father ye will do. He was a murderer from the beginning and abode not in the truth for there was no truth in him... When he speaketh a lie he speaketh of his own for he is a LIAR and the father of it.

JESUS, JOHN 8:1

Under the Pharisees' direction the Temple had become the Federal Reserve System of its day. Christ drove the usurers from the Temple with a snake whip, indirectly attacking the Pharisees' purse. That sealed his fate! The Anti-Defamation League of his day acted quickly. Using standard procedures they defamed Jesus ("L'Infamie") to get the mob on their side — as centuries later they would defame Marie Antoinette, the Romanovs, Hitler, Gen. MacArthur, McCarthy, *et al*). Then, Jesus was framed by the Sanhedrin, who had Him arrested, tried, sentenced, and crucified. (Pope John Paul, 1995 A.D., denied the HOLY WORD, pronouncing that *JEWS had no part in the death of Jesus Christ!*).

His blood be on us (JEWS) and upon our children!

MATTHEW: 27:24-25.

I am innocent of the blood of this just man!

THE SYNOPTICS: Pontius Pilate.

Jesus fornicates with his jackass.

TALMUD: Sanhedrin.

Rodkinson and Wise with goose-grease chutzpah say:

The TALMUD has survived in its entirety, not a single letter of the TALMUD is missing... and now it is flourishing to such a degree as cannot be found in its past history. It dominates the minds of a whole people, who venerate its contents as Divine Truth.

One of those "Divine Truths" from the TALMUD is the holy KOL NIDRE OATH (All Vows Prayer). It is recited thrice by the synagogue congregation as prologue to YOM KIPPUR rites, (The Day of Atonement) "The Highest of Holy Days." It has also been set to music by Felix Mendlessohn, JEW (Marrano). Most Christians, including the clergy, believe the KOL NIDRE OATH is a profound vow to God. In FACT the TALMUD demands that every JEW must break in advance all oaths and sworn declarations a JEW might make to a Gentile during the ensuing year:

"...my promises shall not bind... my vows shall not be reckoned vows... nor my oath oaths... every vow which I make in the future shall be NULL from this Day of Atonement until the next."

TALMUD: Kol Nidre Oath.

Joseph G. Burg, JEW, author of "Zionist Nazi Censorship"; "Guilt and Fate," and several other important books on WWII, testified for the defense at the on-going *Canada v. Ernst Zundel*, "Holocaust" Trials, in Toronto, Ontario, Canada (blacked-out in the U. S. A.). Burg stated that JEW "Holocaust" survivors invented the gas-chamber stories. But, as their testimony was sworn before a Gentile court they could LIE with impunity.

> If those Jews had sworn before a rabbi wearing a skull cap then these false statements, these sick statements, would go down by 99.5%, because the superficial oath was not morally binding on JEWS.
>
> JOSEPH G. BURG, JEW,
> Zundel Hate Crimes Trials, 1988.

> JEWS may lie and perjure to condemn Christians.
> TALMUD: Babha Kama 113b.

> The TALMUD is the very foundation of JEWISH life. It is taught to JEWISH children as soon as they are old enough to read.
> RABBI MORRIS KERTZER,
> American JEWISH Committee.

The TORAH, then, was created to inspire and control a "stiff necked," defeated people; while the TALMUD was a pragmatic interpretation of that MYTH. High-placed Pharisees and priests, profoundly aware of the Jehovah HOAX, also understood that TORAH/TALMUDISM not only supported their life-styles, but was the glue that held together the Hebrew nation.

Beautiful continents rich in natural resources were waiting to be discovered and civilized. But JEWS produced no explorers or conquerors. They might have assimilated within the Semitic nations. Instead, compelled by the genotype of their species, and convinced of their "CHOSEN" status, JEWS implanted themselves like leeches within the Gentile nations they secretly vowed to dispossess and destroy.

Wherever TALMUDISM appeared "anti-Semitism" followed as night follows day. JEW communities — ghettos, with synagogues and rabbis forming the operative nuclei — designed to keep goyim out, invariably became enclosures to keep JEWS in. Gentiles could not tolerate this alien, corrupt, manic-depressive nation in their midst.

Psychologists report that children conditioned to develop exaggerated or unfounded levels of self-esteem — and unnatural feelings of self-love — who are taught to think of themselves unrealistically as better than everyone else invariably suffer deep depression when their achievements fail their expectations. When they are criticized by others, or don't get their way they resort to tantrums and violence. They consistently blame others for their inadequacy. They hate their superiors upon whom they seek vengeance.

JEWS especially envy and hate the Aryan Nation whose remarkable achievements and physical beauty JEWS find humiliating — bitter, bitter vetch to swallow day after day, year after year, generation after generation — especially for those who so fervently believe themselves God's Chosen People. The TORAH/TALMUD CONSPIRACY required a new approach, without sacrificing tradition, to deal with contemporary political problems. It should come as no surprise then, to discover that certain Elders of Zion — after centuries of frustrations and humiliations — took matters into their own hands and formulated a plan to implement and expedite JEHOVAH'S unfulfilled promises. THE PROTOCOLS OF THE LEARNED ELDERS OF ZION.

> We shall have World Government whether or not we like it. The question is only whether World Government will be achieved by consent or by conquest.
>
> JAMES WARBURG, JEW, Banker, 1953,
> U. S. Congressional Hearing.

> The truth is that for the last 147-years the fire of revolution has smoldered steadily beneath the ancient structure of civilization.. it is not local, but universal... its causes must be sought in a deep-laid conspiracy... which constitutes the greatest menace that has ever confronted the human race... the conception of the Jews as the Chosen People ...forms a concerted attempt to achieve world-domination.
>
> NESTA H. WEBSTER, *World Revolution*, Briton Press 1971.

> This movement among the Jews is not new. From the days of Spartacus-Weishaupt to those of Karl Marx and down to Trotsky (Russia), Bela Kuhn (Hungary), Rosa Luxembourg (Germany), and Emma Goldman (United States), this worldwide conspiracy for the overthrow of civilization and the reconstruction of society on the basis of arrested development, envious malevolence, and impossible equality has been steadily growing. It played, as Mrs. Nesta Webster, historian, has so ably shown, a definitely recognizable part in the tragedy of the French Revolution, and the mainspring of every subversive movement during the Nineteenth Century ...the majority of the leading figures are Jews. Moreover, the principal inspiration and driving power comes from Jewish leaders.
>
> WINSTON CHURCHILL, *Illustrated Sunday Herald* (1920).

Amshel Mayer Rothschild, JEW, (1743-1810) patriarch

of the Frankfort, Germany, banking family, was intrigued by ancient scrolls bearing Hebrew Protocols that he had acquired for his library. He commissioned Adam Weishaupt, an apostate Jesuit priest, to up-date them. In the fateful year, 1776 A.D., Weishaupt presented the *Einigen Original Scripten* (Protocols) to Rothschild accompanied by an organizational paradigm, designed to implement the revised Protocols, which he named "THE ILLUMINATI" after Lucifer (Satan), "The Bearer of Light." Its objective: ONE WORLD ILLUMINATI GOVERNMENT.

The Weishaupt/Rothschild documents were revealed to the world (1784) "by an act of God" when a Rothschild courier and his horse were struck dead by lightning in Ratisbon enroute to Paris. Bavarian authorities discovered a copy of the *Einigen Original-Scripten* in the saddlebags. The ILLUMINATI was promptly outlawed, and the Grand Orient Lodges, wherein the conspirators met, were permanently closed. The ILLUMINATI, then, quickly infiltrated Freemasonry Lodges throughout Europe, from which the French (JEW) Revolution was fomented and directed.

Many years later the Protocols, again revised, reappeared in St. Petersburg, Russia, around the time of the Bolshevik, JEW, revolution there. Victor E. Marsden, correspondent for the London *Morning Post* (during an era when integrity of the press was considered sacrosanct) acquired a Russian edition (*Cionski Protocoli*) of Weishaupt's work, in a cloak and dagger caper, from Professor Sergyei Nilus, an Orthodox Catholic priest. Marsden translated it into English, publishing it under the title: *The Protocols of the Learned Elders of Zion.* For his temerity Marsden was murdered. Nilus' original copy of the Protocols, bearing the date August 10, 1906, is now in the British Museum, London.

In the U.S.A., Henry Ford, Sr., founder of the Ford Motor Company, ordered millions of copies of the Protocols printed, in several languages, and distributed throughout the world. World JEWRY vehemently protested the Protocols were "forgeries" (sic). Ford replied, (*New York World*, 2-1721), "The only statement I care to make about the Protocols is that... they have fitted the world situation up to this time. They fit it now." Senator Jacob Javits, JEW, chaired a U.S. Senate Investigating Committee to report on the Protocols. The U. S. Senate, who does what it is told, confirmed the Protocols were "forged" (sic). Forgeries of what? No debate was conducted on the correlation between the Protocols and what has occurred on the World stage!

> 300-men, all acquainted with each other, control the economic destiny of the continent.
> WALTER RATHENAU, JEW, powerful German financier.

> The World is ruled by very different personages that those who are not behind the scenes would imagine.
> BENJAMIN DISRAELI, JEW, Prime Minister, Great Britain.

> You have not begun to appreciate the real depth of our guilt. We

are intruders. We *are* disturbers. We *are* subverters. We have taken your natural world, your ideals, your destiny, and played havoc with them.

MARCUS ELI RAVAGE, JEW, *Century Magazine* (January 1928).

The meaning of the history of our last century is that today 300 Jewish financiers, all masters of Lodges, rule the world.

JEAN IZOULET, Jewish Alliance Israelite Universelle (1931).

THE PROTOCOLS OF THE LEARNED ELDERS OF ZION, containing 24 Protocols, are divided into Articles. Several PROTOCOLS may have been deleted by Professor Nilus because he deemed them harmful to the Church. Herein, because of limited space, the PROTOCOLS will be abridged. (Edward Gibbon reminds us — *The Decline and Fall of the Roman Empire*, Chapters XV, XXVIII, XLVII, XLIX — that the Jewish conspiracy was behind the fall of ALL of civilized antiquity).

THE PROTOCOLS OF THE LEARNED ELDERS OF ZION

Protocol 1: Political freedom is an idea, not a fact. One must know how to apply this idea as bait whenever it appears necessary to attract the masses of the people to one's party for the purpose of crushing whoever is in authority. This task is made easier if the opponent himself has been infected with the idea of freedom, so-called liberalism, and for the sake of an idea is willing to yield some of his power. It is precisely here that the triumph of our theory appears; the slackened reins of government are immediately, by the

Law of Life, caught up and gathered together by a new hand; because the blind might of the nation cannot for a single day exist without guidance, and the new authority merely fits into the place of the old authority weakened by liberalism.

Our right lies in force. The word "right" is an abstract thought proved by nothing. The word means no more than: Give me what I want in order that I may have proof that I am stronger than you.

Our power in the present tottering condition of all forms of power will be more invincible than any other because it will remain invisible until the moment when it has gained such strength that no cunning can undermine it.

Behold the alcoholized animals bemused with drink, the right to an immoderate use of which comes with freedom. It is not for us and ours to walk that road. *Goyim* are bemused with alcohol, and from early immorality into which it has been induced by our special agents.

Protocol 2: The administrators, whom we shall choose from among the public with strict regard for their servility, will not be persons trained in the art of government, and will therefore become pawns in our game: in the hands of men of learning and genius, specialists bred and reared from early childhood to rule the affairs of the whole world.

In the hands of the States there is a great force that creates the movement of thought in the people. That is the Press!

It is in the Press that the triumph of freedom of speech finds its incarnation. But the *goyim* have not known how to make use of this force and it has fallen into our hands.

We shall instigate economic and military wars between the *Goyim* states. When wars are over both sides are devastated and at the mercy of our international finance. This is the "Jewish Harvest." First, we manufacture the huge war machines. Second we destroy the flower of White manhood thereby weakening the racial stamina of the *Goyim*. Third, the White nations are prostrate under huge debts and we profit interest upon interest.

Protocol 3: And thus the people condemn the upright and acquit the guilty, persuaded ever more it can do whatever it wishes. Thanks to this the people are destroying every kind of stability and creating disorders at every step. By encouraging abuses of power by rulers, and by agitating and stirring up the mob the press "will put the final touch in preparing all institutions for their overthrow and everything will fly skyward under the blows of the maddening crowd."

We appear on the scene as alleged saviors of the worker from oppression then propose to him to enter the ranks of our fighting forces — Socialists, Communists, Anarchists — to whom we always support in accordance with an alleged brotherly rule.

Protocol 4: In order to give the *goyim* no time to think

their minds must be diverted toward industry and trade. Thus all the nations will be swallowed up in the hot pursuit of gain. Gentile Masonry blindly serves as a screen for us and our objects, but the plan of action of our force, even its abiding hiding place, remains for the whole people a mystery, and they will not take note of their common foe.

Protocol 5: In order to put public opinion into our hands we must bring it into a state of bewilderment by giving expression to all sides to many contradictory opinions, and for such a length of time as will suffice to make the goyim lose their heads in the labyrinth, and come to see that the best thing is to have no opinion in matters political, which it is not given to the public to understand because they are understood only by him who guides the public. This is the first secret.

By all these means we shall so wear down the goyim that they shall be compelled to offer us international power of a nature that by its position will enable us without violence gradually to absorb all the State forces of the world and to form a SuperGovernment.

Protocol 6: The establishment of huge financial monopolies: finance, publishing, oil, sugar, steel, medicine, railways, liquor, food, clothing — containing reservoirs of colossal wealth upon which *Goyim* must depend in order to exist.

The *Goyim* must be deprived of their farms and ranches

which will be achieved by loading them with debts which must be ruthlessly exploited.

Protocol 7: Our agents are in the governments of all countries of the world advising their leaders. Thus we have an international network while the *Goyim* has none. Through economic treaties and loan obligations, and the hostilities and intrigues they create, we will so entangle the threads of world governments that they will be unable to act without our approval. If one nation dare oppose us we will collectively organize their neighbors and destroy that country through universal war.

Protocol 8: We have infiltrated the *Goyim* courts of law and degraded it into a legal jungle. We are now in a position to tell you with a clear conscience that at the proper time we, the law-givers, shall execute judgment and sentence; we shall slay and we shall spare; we as head of our troops are mounted on the steed of the leader. And the weapons in our hands are limitless ambitions, burning greed, merciless vengeance, hatred and malice!

Protocol 9: From us the all-engulfing terror proceeds. We have in our service persons of all opinions, of all doctrines: monarchists, demagogues, socialists, Communists Christians, utopian dreamers of every kind. All are harnessed to our task: everyone of them is boring away at the last remnants of authority, striving to overthrow all established forms of order. By these acts all States are in torture; they exhort to tranquility, are ready to sacrifice everything for peace. But we will not give them peace until they openly acknowledge our International Super-Government with submissiveness.

Protocol 10: We have drawn up a master-plan to bring all the nations of the earth under one despotic Jewish dictator, by subjecting all the peoples of the earth to such terrible suffering, confusion, and torment that they will in desperation accept whatever we offer to them.

To secure this we must have everybody vote without distinction of classes and qualifications in order to establish an absolute majority, which cannot be got from the educated propertied classes. Democracies and Republics with everybody having a vote down to the last scum and rabble provides us with our great opportunity.

Protocol 11: The *goyim* are a flock of sheep and we are their wolves. And you know what happens when the wolves get hold of the flock? God has granted us, His Chosen People, the gift of dispersion and in this, which appears in all eyes to be our weakness, has come forth all of our strength, which has now brought us to the threshold of sovereignty over all the world.

Protocol 12: Not a single announcement will reach the public without our control. This arises through the total control of the Press, and control of Masonry at the highest levels.

Protocol 13: In order that the stupid *goyim* may not guess what we are all about we further distract them with amusements games, pastimes, sex, people's palaces... Who will ever suspect that all these peoples were stage-managed by us to conform to a political plan which no one has so much as guessed at in the course of many centuries? Liberals and Utopian dreamers, whom we will discard once we take over, will take a great part in wrecking *goy* institutions.

Protocol 14: In countries known as progressive and enlightened we have created a senseless, filthy, abominable literature, which we will use to provide a telling relief by contrast to our government when we attain to power...

Protocol 15: We shall slay without mercy all who take arms to oppose our coming Kingdom.

We shall remake all legislatures, all our laws will be brief, plain, staple, without any kind of interpretations, so that anyone will be in a position to know them perfectly. The main feature will be submission to orders and this principle will be carried to grandiose heights.

Protocol 16: In order to destroy all collective forces save ours we shall emasculate the first stage of collectivism, the universities, by re-educating them in a new direction. Their officials and professors will be appointed with special precaution and dependent upon our government; and they will be inculcated with detailed secret action-programs, in order to perform their profession.

We shall erase from memory of men all facts of previous centuries which are undesirable to us and leave only those which depict all errors committed by *goyim* governments. There will be no such thing as freedom of instruction. All people will be initiated into one faith: Judaism.

Protocol 17: We have long past taken care to discredit the clergy of the *goyim* and thereby to ruin their mission on earth. Day by day their influence on the peoples of the world is failing.

Freedom of conscience has been declared everywhere. Only years separate us from the complete destruction of Christianity.

Protocol 18: When our Jewish King of the World is in power he will be protected by an aura of mystical Deity, that we will create, making the stupid *goyim* think of him as a God.

Protocol 19: No dabbling in political affairs will be allowed the *goyim*. Anyone leading an opposition movement will be put to trial in the same category as thieving or murder, or any other abominable and filthy crime. Citizens will have no more influence or control in the affairs of politics than a herd of livestock or cattle.

Protocol 20: The sum total of our actions is settled by the question of figures. The ruin of the Gentile States has been accomplished by withdrawal of money from circulation. We alone own their banks and control their fiscal policies. They are bound to us irrevocably by long-term debts and the interest we exact on those debts.

So long as loans were internal the *goyim* only shuffled their money from the pockets of the poor to the wealthy. When we bought the necessary persons in order to transfer loans into the external sphere all the wealth of the States flowed into our cash boxes and the *goyim* began to pay us the tribute of subjects.

Protocol 21: We shall replace the money markets by government credit institutions, the object of which will fix the price of industrial values in accordance with our views. These institutions will be able to fling 500-millions of industrial paper in one day, or to buy up, from that amount. Therefore all industrial undertakings will come into dependence upon us. You may imagine what immense power we shall thereby secure for ourselves.

Protocol 22: In our hands is the great power of our day — gold: in our storehouses we can procure any amount we please. True force makes no terms with any 'right,' not even with that of God: none dare come near to it so as to take so much as a span away from it.

Protocol 23: After our agitators have stirred up dissension, revolution, and the fire of anarchy all over the world, when the Chosen One is on the throne, then these agitators will have played their parts. Having served their usefulness then it will be necessary to sweep them away from his path on which must be left no knot, no splinter.

Protocol 24: The coming King of the World will emanate from the ancestral lineage of King David. He will be selected by the Elders of Zion because of his outstanding ability. Only the King and three Elders of Zion will be privy to the mysteries, and secret schemes of the government. None will know what the King wishes to attain by his disposition and therefore none will dare to stand across an unknown path.

> Anyone like the author, who has...seen and heard with ominous dread the aims... of JEWISH economic, political and intellectual life can assert that they (the PROTOCOLS) most unalloyed expression of the JEWISH spirit... that an Aryan mind... could never under any circumstances have devised these methods of action; these underhand expedients and these swindles as a whole.
>
> ARTHUR TRIBITSCH, JEW,
> "Deutscher Geist oder Judentum."

> It is... impossible for any intelligent person... to read... the Protocols... without being astounded by their prophetic insight... In truth, however, we do not need the Protocols... to tell us of these things... What interests me is what I have discerned of the organized use of evil to subvert Western civilization and bring our traditional values crashing to the ground so that a totally different, a blood-chilling and hateful influence may henceforth dominate the world... Statesmen like Churchill, and Lloyd George; writers like Belloc and Wickham Steed, editors like H. A. Gwynne; Jews themselves of the caliber of Disraeli and Oscar Levy, have all contributed their testimony... to a vast accumulation of evidence... Jewish power is real.
>
> A. K. CHESTERTON,
> "The Learned Elders and the BBC."

All Gentiles should read the PROTOCOLS OF THE LEARNED ELDERS OF ZION in its entirety to understand why JEWS so vehemently protest its authenticity. Here is JEW tribal insanity reflected as in a mirror, darkly: frozen in eternity for all Mankind to see, understand, and resist.

CHAPTER 2

THE KHAZARS INVENT JUDAISM

The rats are underneath the piles; The JEW is underneath the lot.
T. S. ELIOT, "Burbank with a Baedeker..."

The fault, dear Brutus, is not in our stars, but in ourselves, that we are underlings.
WILLIAM SHAKESPEARE, "Julius Caesar"

The genetic Khazar-derivation of most Jews — only the Sephardic may be accounted Hebrews by blood — has been long if not widely known. Dunlap at Columbia University, Bury in England, Poliak at Tel Aviv University have researched this "cruelest of jokes" and won research acceptance over the past half-century.
ALFRED M. LILIENTHAL, JEW, *The Zionist Connection.*

The conversion of the Khazars (to Talmudism) had considerable and lasting impact on the Western World.
ENCYCLOPEDIA BRITANNICA (1956)

It strikes me that the Jews are specialized for a parasitical existence upon other nations, and there is need of evidence that they are capable of fulfilling the varied duties of a civilized nature by themselves.
SIR FRANCIS GALTON (1812-1911), founder of Eugenics.

Around 600 A.D. a belligerent tribe of half-Mongolian people, similar to the modern Turks, conquered the territory of what is now Southern Russia. Before long the kingdom (khanate) of the Khazars, as the tribe was known, stretched from the Caspian to the Black Sea. Its capital, Ityl, was at the mouth of the Volga River.
SOLOMON GRAYZEL, JEW, "A History of the JEWS"

S WE HAVE learned, world history is punctuated with accounts of HEBREW deceit, treason, treachery, and deception. One of the most significant, if not thaumaturgical deceptions, was the CONVERSION, by Sephardic rabbis from Constantinople, of about three million pagan KHAZARS — an ASIATIC tribe with Mongol-Turkic affinities — to the Hebrew religion (TORAH/ TALMUDISM) and then convincing Christendom that Khazars are Biblical Judeans in Diaspora! The Khazar's ancient homeland was in the heart of Asia. They were a warlike, predatory nation whose religion was a mixture of phallic worship, idolatry, and lewdness. Disliked and feared for their psychopathic behavior, the Khazars were driven out of Asia by neighboring tribes. The ignominious retreat became an invasion of eastern Europe where, "driven by their own desire for plunder and revenge" (Jewish Encyclopedia) the Khazars conquered and subdued twenty-five pastoral nations which they placed under "protective custody" and from whom they exacted tribute. The Khazars settled in the area between the Black and Caspian Seas, gradually extending their conquests northward along the Don and Volga Rivers until the Khazar Khanate encompassed over 1-million square miles. By 1000 A.D. KHAZARIA was the largest kingdom in eastern Europe and one of the wealthiest (in loot not culture). Yet, today, Khazars have been virtually deleted from world history *because JEWS want the world to forget they are direct descendants of Asiatic Khazars.* JEWS want us to believe they are descendants of Biblical HEBREWS. They are NOT! Therein lies a story.

The Khazars' Hollywood-like sexual excesses were corrupting tribal morale and undermining military discipline. Khagan Bulan wanted and needed a formal religion to instill discipline and create tribal unity. In 730 A.D., Bulan invited representatives of Islam, Christianity, and TALMUDISM to discuss religion with him. After much deliberation the shrewd Khagan selected the Hebrew religion, i.e., TALMUDISM (now called JUDAISM), to become the adopted religion of all Khazars. (Like St. Augustine, HEBREW, Bulan aspired to chastity and continence "but, dear Lord, not yet."). *Khagan Bulan and 4000 feudal Khazar nobles were quickly converted to TORAH/TALMUDISM* (4001 foreskins!). Gradually, millions of Khazars joined the ranks of GOD'S CHOSEN. Bulan, of course, knew TALMUDISM was a scam. It mattered not as long as his subjects believed. Nor did it matter that Khazars weren't Hebrews (Semitics). That was easily handled. Just LIE! Claim to be JUDEANS! Emerging Christian Europe would accept "Asiatic/ Judeans" just as they naively accepted the Hebrew tribal-diety Yahweh as their God. Undoubtedly, most enticing to Bulan was Jehovah's covenant with his Chosen People — and the Protocols designed to make those hallucinations come true. Khazars (see: The Mob, USA) were chiefly extortionists, slave-traders, pimps, assassins, usurers, despised by their Gentile neighbors. After generations of warfare against the Rus, Varangians, Slavs and Arabs the Khazars (JEWS) were totally defeated (1300 A.D.) on the battlefields. Bereft of their land they dispersed throughout Europe, and elsewhere, explaining why 700-years later *so many unwanted*

JEWS reside in Hungary, Poland, Russia, Ukraine, Lithuania, Rumania, Galicia, Austria — and Israel! Culturally the Khazars left very little to posterity. Not even a hint of their language exists. But of the poison they bequeathed there exists much (see, ILLUMINATI). Never before have two such deviant races, ASIATIC KHAZARS and SEMITIC HEBREWS, shared so many repellent characteristics.

To further explain the devastating effect Khazars have had upon Mankind we must briefly visit England.

In 1775, while Adam Weishaupt, Satan worshiper, revised the PROTOCOLS for Rothschild, JEW/KHAZAR; the British dramatist William Sheridan, in his play The Rivals, coined the word "JEW": a derivative of the word "JUDEAN." The word "JEW" had been used throughout history in a slangy context (as "Hebe" was used for Hebrew; or "Yid" for Yiddish). *It was Sheridan, however, who first legitimized the word "JEW", using it in print as a proper noun meaning a JUDEAN of HEBRAIC faith, but applying it to a KHAZAR character.* IT IS IMPORTANT TO KNOW the word "JEW" does not appear in the original Old Testament written in Hebrew; nor does "JEW" appear in the Targums — O.T. translated into Aramaic; nor does "JEW" appear in the Septuagint (TORAH) — translation of the Aramaic into Greek (3 B.C.). The word "JEW" does NOT appear in any early translations of the HOLY BIBLE (The Latin Vulgate, Rheims/Douai, King James, et al). Therefore, because the word "JEW" was not used until 1775, it is WRONG to call Biblical patriarchs

JEWS. They were not. They were HEBREWS. Jesus Christ WAS NOT A JEW. He was a rabbi (teacher) who worshipped the Mosaic Law and despised the Pharisaical Oral Law (Talmud). Jesus (if he did exist) was born in Galilee ("Unclean Land of the Gentiles"). He may have been Semitic but he could just as easily have been Aryan. The New Testament conflicts on his lineage. One thing is certain, he was NOT a JEW (Khazar). *It is also erroneous and deliberately deceptive, to apply the word "JEW" to Hebrews/Israelis (Semitics). Finally, the smear word "antiSemite," as applied to KHAZAR haters is oxymoronic. The right word is "Judeophobe."*

> The study of Judaism is that of the Talmud, as the study of the Talmud is that of Judaism...they are two inseparable things, or better, they are one and the same.
> ARSENE DARMESTETER, JEW, "The Talmud."

After 1776 the Khazars' PR ploy began to pay off: they were accepted by Christendom (the neutered lions) as remnants of the Judean tribe (Hebrews) in Diaspora and were officially designated "JEWS." Penultimately, Pharisaism became Talmudism; and finally Talmudism became JUDAISM: the religion of today's KHAZARS. The words "JEW" and "JUDAISM" began to appear, for the first time, in revised editions of the Talmuds, and began to appear in ALL revised editions of the Holy Bible. Today, Ashkenazim (Asiatic/Khazar); and Sephardim (Biblical Hebrews/ Israelites) — who correctly HATE one another — are lumped together as "JEWS." Thus, Khazars (with a wink of an eye) abandoned their Asiatic affinities and became "Hebrews;" became Yahweh's Chosen People, beneficiaries of the Covenant, and heirs to Palestine and all the minerals and other goodies therein. In addition, Khazars fortified their racial hatred of the Aryan tribes with TALMUDIC HATRED FOR ALL GENTILES. Anthropologists refer to Khazars as Mongol-Armenoid JEWS. Historians refer to them as Ashkenazi (Asiatic/European JEWS). Psychiatrists refer to them as manic-depressives. JEWS deserve their sobriquet: "Masters of deceit." Ergo, today all so-called "JEWS" fanatically believe (or pretend) they are God's Chosen People elected to rule the world. ANY means may be employed to achieve that DELUSION. Such mind-sets are symptomatic of psychopathic personalities, and are associated with dementia praecox, megalomania, infantilism, meshuggenah, manic-depression, delusions of grandeur, sadism, et al. Another conclusion that logically may be drawn from this insane charade, is that any people — say 10-million Watusi, or 50-million Chinese — need only convert to JUDAISM and they then have Khazarlike "rights" to own Palestine, kill Arabs, and destroy Gentiles everywhere!

> The Jews might have had Uganda, Madagascar and other places for the establishment of a Jewish Fatherland, but they want absolutely nothing except Palestine: not because the Dead Sea water can by evaporation produce 5-trillion dollars worth of metalloids, not because the subsoil of Palestine contains twenty times more petroleum than the combined reserves of the two Americas; but because Palestine is the cross-roads of Europe, Asia, and Africa; because Palestine constitutes the veritable center of world political power, the strategic center for world control.

NAHUM GOLDMAN, President, World Jewish Congress.

Chaim Weizmann, JEW, the British War Cabinet, and French Foreign Office were convinced by 1916... that the best and perhaps the only way (which proved so to be) to induce the American President to come into the war (WWI) was to secure the cooperation of Zionist JEWS by promising them Palestine, and thus enlist and mobilize the hitherto unsuspectedly powerful forces of Zionist JEWS in America and elsewhere in favor of the Allies on a quid pro quo contract...

SAMUEL LANDMAN, JEW,
"Great Britain, the Jews & Palestine."

Next, we will briefly examine the ILLUMINATI which today marks the culmination of the CONSPIRACY. The ancient myths and the LIES and the comic-book characters come to life. The HOAX becomes reality.

CHAPTER 3

THE ILLUMINATI

The World is ruled by very different personages than those who are not behind the scenes would imagine.
BENJAMIN DISRAELI, JEW, British Prime Minister, 1868

300 men, all members of Lodges, all acquainted with each other, control the continent.
WALTER RATHENAU, JEW, German Minister of Foreign Affairs (President of 84 major German companies, murdered 1920).

Since I entered politics I have chiefly had men's views confided to me privately. Some of the biggest men in the United States in the field of commerce and manufacture are afraid of somebody, are afraid of something. They know there is a power somewhere so organized, so subtle, so watchful, so interlocked, so complete, so pervasive, that they had better not speak above their breath when they speak in condemnation of it.
WOODROW WILSON, President U.S.A., *The New Freedom*.

One by one JEWS were getting control of the big newspapers ...Jewish banks were supreme. They captured the U.S. treasury. They forced upon Woodrow Wilson the appointment of Paul Warburg, JEW, on the Federal Reserve Board, which he dominates....whose brother Max Warburg (Head of German Intelligence) is a prominent figure in German finance.
SIR CECIL SPRING-RICE, British Ambassador to the United States, Germany, and Russia (1916)

The amount of our National Debt is the measure of our enslavement to Jewish World Finance. We live in a democracy yet loans are contracted that always cost more than the amount of the loan and no one has a word to say about it. We Americans do not know how much interest we pay every year and we don't know to whom we pay it.

HENRY FORD, Sr., The International Jew.

What is important to dwell upon is the increasing evidence of a secret conspiracy throughout the world for the destruction of organized government and the letting loose of evil...prominent politicians, philosophers and soldiers are found at critical moments giving views of an absolutely non-moral description, which are not in accord with their behavior in ordinary life...it is here that the conspiracy of evil against humanity become recognizable.

CHRISTIAN SCIENCE MONITOR,
"The Jewish Peril", 619-20.

The purpose is nothing less than to create a world system of control in private hands able to dominate the political system of each country and the world economy.

CARROLL QUIGLEY, Prof. Georgetown U.,
Tragedy and Hope.

The meaning of the history of the last century is that 300 Jewish Financiers, all Masters of Lodges, rule the World. (1931)

JEAN IZOULET, JEW,
Jewish Alliance Israelite Universelle.

Mr. Speaker, it is a monstrous thing for this great Nation to have its destiny presided over by a traitorous Federal Reserve System acting in secret with International Usurers.

LOUIS T. McFADDEN,
Chr. House Banking Committee, 610-32.

The Trilateralists don't secretly rule the world, the Council on Foreign Relations (CFR) does that.

WINSTON LORD,
former Chairman of the CFR.

The members of the CFR are persons of much more than average influence in their communities. They have used the prestige of their wealth, their social position, their education to lead their country toward bankruptcy and military debacle. They should look at their hands. There is blood on them.

CHICAGO HERALD TRIBUNE.

What the Trilateral Commission truly intends is the creation of a world-wide economic power superior to the political governments of the nation-states involved... as managers and creators of the system they will rule the future... Populations are treated as nothing more than producing economic groups. Freedom (Political, Spiritual, Economic) is denied any importance.

U.S. SEN. BARRY GOLDWATER, JEW, *With No Apologies*.

At Secret Meetings in Switzerland 13 People Shape the World's Economy. The Bank of International Settlements was established in 1930 to assist in the payments of reparations owed by Germany and other losers in WWI to the victors. Today it protects the world financial system. The most powerful voices are U.S representative Alan Greenspan, Federal Reserve chairman and his back-up Alice M. Rivlin. (Both JEWS).

WASHINGTON POST, (excerpted) 6-28-98).

THE MYTH: In the Beginning LUCIFER, "Angel of Light," believed himself greater than Yahweh. Disguised as a serpent in the Garden of Eden, Lucifer seduced Eve (the TALMUD says fornicated with her), breaking God's Laws, introducing sin into the World. For this and other abominations Lucifer and his co-CONSPIRATORS among the Heavenly Host were cast from Heaven. Because he is an archangel Lucifer remains an indestructible malignant spirit created we're told by Yahweh, the "omnipotent"!

O how thou art fallen from Heaven O Lucifer, Son of the

Morning Star! How art thou cut down To the ground which did weaken the Nations!

HOLY BIBLE: Isaiah 14.

Lucifer (Satan, The Devil) established an earthly kingdom where he and his disciples (ILLUMINATI) profited from the tears, toil, sweat and blood of Mankind: garnering men's bodies and souls. Lucifer's enterprise was so successful that Yahweh waxed sorely wroth and in a pique of jealousy (HOLOCAUST numero uno) drowned the entire human race — men, women, and children! — with the exception of Noah, HEBREW, "a lovable drunk," and his family. Albeit, after the mass-drownings everything went to Hell in a basket, again. And again. And again! *The crux of this HEBRAIC myth is: God cannot defeat Satan!*

THE REALITY: the myth explains why Rothschild named the ILLUMINATI for Lucifer, and why he adopted into his cartouche the symbolic Hebraic Snake, representing Lucifer's cunning and deception. Lucifer's apostasy and his modus operandi appeal greatly to Usurers: human snakes with little or nothing to commend them: namely, those of no honor, no courage, no creativity, little skill, ugliness of body and soul. What they possess in abundance is deception, greed, hubris, and malevolence. Why labor, they ask, when one can garner the world's riches through lies, theft, false witness and by appealing to the "baseness that lies within all men's souls"?

A few pages back we met Amschul Mayer Bauer, JEW pawn-broker who discovered he could garner huge profits issuing short-term vouchers in amounts far exceeding his assets. This interestbearing paper, guaranteed by Bauer, was often used as a means of exchange in the market-place. As long as the holders, in concert, didn't demand gold in exchange for their paper Shylock escaped the noose. In short, Bauer issued notes to borrowers, for a fee, representing assets he didn't own (See: Federal Reserve System). He decided to discontinue the pawnshop; changed his sur-name to Rothschild ("Red Shield") and concentrated on his lucrative banking scam. By the end of the 18th Century Rothschild & Sons had become the dominant banking house in Europe, and his scam became the corner-stone of the Rothschild central banking system that now controls the Federal Reserve System). Rothschild had more in mind than money. In him was combined TALMUDIC hatred for Gentiles and the Khazar thirst for revenge against the Aryan race. The name "Red Shield" became the symbol of World Revolution. As you remember, Rothschild commissioned Adam Weishaupt (apostate Jesuit priest kicked out of his post at Ingolstadt University for practicing Satan worship) to update the ancient Protocols. The organization Weishaupt created to implement those plans is the ILLUMINATI.

The ILLUMINATI, is headed by a KHAGAN. The Khagan presides over the KEHILLA (Board of Directors), composed of 13 JEWS, most of whom are International Bankers. Each of these Directors heads a key organizations within the World Revolutionary Movement. Directors rotate as chairman of the ILLUMINATI which seats 300 influential personages, not only JEWS, representing the most important fields of human endeavor: finance, massmedia, government, military, foreign affairs, science, industry, business, education, religion, and so on. However, because it is a SECRET ORGANIZATION it is virtually invisible. Like the wind it is revealed by its influence and damage, to wit:

THE FRENCH REVOLUTION 1778, the first ILLUMINATI coup d'état against Christendom revealed the PROTOCOLS in action.

> When the debt-grip has been firmly established, control of every form of publicity and political activity soon follows, together with a full grip on industrialists (management and labor)... the grip of the right hand establishes paralysis; while the revolutionary left hand holds the dagger and deals the fatal blow.
> SIR WALTER SCOTT, *The Life of Napoleon* (Scott's nine volumes are suppressed because of their Judeophobic position and are never catalogued with his other works).

While M. Basalmo's JEW newspapers slandered Church and State, the ILLUMINATI organized the Reign of Terror. Jacobin Clubs were established throughout France to serve as meeting houses for the canaille.

> There are hints in Restif too of class racialism, of the fears felt by the bourgeois and the artisan for the pale men with dark ill-kempt hair, piercing eyes and shaggy mustaches... his canaille is always dark and glowering... The respectable: the men of property, the virtuous craftsmen are fair and have good complexions.
> BRITISH LITERARY REVIEW,
> Restiff de la Bretonne — accounts of the Terror.

> Continental Freemasonry is, and has been for 200 years, notoriously Jew controlled.
>
> A. K. CHESTERTON, *The New Unhappy Lords* (1974).

L'INFAMIE (lies, slander and false-witness), is one of the JEWS most feared weapons. The victim is unaware of the sly whispers circulated behind his back until he begins to sense stares of condemnation, rejection, and sudden reverses in fortune. *There is virtually no way to refute this anonymous destruction of one's reputation.* For targets of greater magnitude the ILLUMINATI unlimbers its entire character-assassination apparatus, from mass-media campaigns to Congressional investigating committees, IRS intimidation, and SWAT teams.

The gradual change in direction of Western aspirations (c. 1750) proceeding from Culture to Civilization created stress and fractures within the monarchies of Europe, requiring time to diagnose, treat and heal. JEWS sensed in this indisposition an opportunity to attack. What most certainly would have been a peaceful revolution in France was turned into a tragedy. For the first time the West witnessed JEW POWER: The ILLUMINATI fomented the FRENCH REVOLUTION. L'INFAMIE ignited it.

Louis XVI's Queen, Marie Antoinette, was the daughter of Francis I of Austria. Marie's sister, knowing the Bavarian Government had exposed the ILLUMINATI, warned her about the PROTOCOLS and of the impending danger. The Queen wrote:

> I believe that as far as France is concerned you worry too much

about Freemasonry. Here it is far from having the significance it may have elsewhere in Europe.

ILLUMINATI agent Moses Mendelsohn, JEW, commissioned a London jeweler to create a 250,000-livres diamond necklace which was delivered to Marie Antoinette. Leaks of the Queen's "indulgence" appeared in Paris newspapers infuriating government officials, the Church, and the populace. Marie was able to prove she had not ordered the necklace but great damage had been done to the monarchy's reputation. Then Joseph Basalmo, JEW, had 500-thousand pamphlets distributed charging the Queen, "That Austrian whore" (an appellation applied later to the Czarina, by the BOLSHEVIKS), with giving sexual favors to a secret lover in return for the necklace. Spinning the web ever tighter, Basalmo, JEW, forged the Queen's signature on a letter inviting Cardinal Prince de Rohan to meet with her at the royal palace to discuss the necklace matter. An actress was hired to impersonate the Queen. The resultant scenario, with hidden eye-witnesses, implicated the Cardinal in an affair d' amour with the Queen. The scandal engulfed the highest personages of Church and State. The HOAX, for that is all it was, widened the gulf between the monarchy and the populace, lowering their resistance to the ILLUMINATI.

When the *canaille* (JEW agitators in the press and on the streets) had worked France into a frenzy of despair, prison and asylum gates suddenly were thrown open. THE TERROR was unleashed. While criminals and lunatics ran wild, burning, raping killing — screaming "Liberty,

Equality, Fraternity" and waving Rothschild's Red Flag — Jacobin Clubs rounded-up and jailed without trial bourgeoisie and aristocrats: men, women and children listed for extermination by the ILLUMINATI.

Marquis de Mirabeau, and Robespierre, goy leaders of the revolution against their own race, realized too late that men more powerful than they had created THE TERROR. Mirabeau in a final act of redemption, attempted to save the doomed Royal Family. He was thwarted and beheaded. Robespierre, before he was shot in the jaw to silence him, said before the Convention:

> I cannot bring myself to tear asunder the veil that covers this profound mystery of iniquity. But I can affirm most positively that among the authors of this plot are the agents of that system of corruption and extravagance — the most powerful of all the means invented by the foreigners — for the undoing of the Republic: I mean the impure apostles of Atheism; and the immorality that is its base.
> ROBESPIERRE, from *Life of Robespierre*, by George Renier.

Robespierre's discretion in not revealing the CONSPIRATORS availed him not. He knew too much and was beheaded as were almost all goy revolutionary leaders. Now we know he was concealing the identity of: Daniel Itg, (Berlin); Herz Gergsbeer, (Alsace); The Rothschilds, and Sir Moses Montifiore (England), all JEW financiers who sought to institute constitutional monarchy in France as they had in England. Absolute monarchy, combined with nationalism, absolutely rejects usury. The JEWS, then, launched a continental war against France. This required huge foreign purchases by ALL participants:

France, England, Spain, et al, but the ILLUMNATI bushwacked France by refusing to accept payments in assignats. This led to THE TERROR.

"Popular" history depicts Marie Antoinette as a giddy, wanton, compassionless woman who, upon learning the populace had no bread, said: "Let them eat cake." Serious historians have proved the Queen's detractors were JEW LIARS. The Queen bore the suffering inflicted upon her and her family with dignity, and met her death on the Guillotine with great courage.

Napoleon I (1769-1821), also, struggled against the snares and LIES of the ILLUMINATI. Bonaparte's tarnished reputation rests on the fact that he, a hero of the people, opposed interest-bearing money. The chief concern of the Usurer was to continue the wars and finance them.

> It cannot be too strongly insisted that finance and not territory aggrandizement is the key to Napoleon's reign. Had the French Emperor consented to abandon his financial system in favor of the System of London (Central Banking) — that is in favor of loans by the money-market — he could have had peace at any time.
>
> R. MICHAEL WILSON, Napoleon's Love.

During the PENINSULAR WAR (1809) Wellington confronted French troops in Spain. The Iberian coastline was blockaded by the French fleet which interdicted supplies meant for the British forces. The problem was solved by the British House of Rothschild which notified the French House of Rothschild which then smuggled gold to Wellington by mule train through the Pyrenees. Gelt in

JAMES W. VON BRUNN

hand, Wellington purchased supplies and forage from the Spaniards. And what about the troops dying for Ideals, God, and Country? The JEWS smile.

As the battle of WATERLOO developed upon which the fate of England and France rested, the ILLUMINATI hatched a plot that allowed it to learn of the battle's results before the two governments did. A system was devised in which carrier pigeons flew across the Channel (giving rise to the expression: "A little bird told me."). Upon confirmation of Wellington's victory (1815) Rothschild agenteurs in London reported the battle was lost! The British money-market, panicked — investors unloaded valuable stocks and government securities at rock-bottom prices. Behind the scenes Rothschild bought everything he could lay hands on. In France a similar scam was carried out. The dead got buried. The heroes got medals, and the BANKERS smiled.

> The name of Rothschild thus became ubiquitous and it was well remarked that the House was spread like a network over the nations; and it is no wonder that its operations upon the money-market should at length be felt by every cabinet in Europe.
> RABBI MOSE MARGOLUTH (1851).

The AGE OF REASON was the soil from whence sprang the idea of Capitalism: free-enterprise, competition, individualism ("every man for himself"); the monetary system was part of capitalism. The entire thrust of this stage in the organic development of Western Culture has been misdirected by the ILLUMINATI moneymonopoly. Capitalism has come to mean USURY and as you know

76 | P a g e

usury means debt — which is slavery.

The Satanical character of the INDUSTRIAL REVOLUTION, begun in England (c. 1760), bore the cloven imprint of the Rothschilds. It was they who established the building codes, and ordinances, and set standards and values. JEWS hold NO patriotism for their host country: NO love of the landscape, the State, its history, and its people. They view THEIRTALMUDIC WORLD as one without boundaries; upon goyim as THEIR sheep to be fleeced. Had Aryan Man controlled his own MONEY he would NOT have created hellish factory towns, using his own children as slave labor. He would have shaped the Industrial Revolution with the same artistry and love he used in creating his great music, literature, art, sciences and cathedrals. USURY degrades. USURY enslaves.

In COLONIAL AMERICA, after the Bank of England (dominated by JEWS) refused to accept the American colonies' debt-free script, Benjamin Franklin bitterly remarked, "prosperity ended and depression and unemployment set in." To survive, colonists had to mortgage assets and securities to the Bank of England. The War of Independence (1776) was not against George III, as history books would have you believe, but against JEW USURERS.

> The Bank of England refused to give more than 50% of the face value of our Script when turned over as required by law. The circulating medium of exchange was thus reduced by half... The

colonies would gladly have borne the little tax on tea, and other matters, had it not been that England took away from the Colonies their money, which created unemployment...

BENJAMIN FRANKLIN, U.S. Senate Document No.23.

During the ensuing years, before establishing the FED, the ILLUMINATI created financial panics, money shortages and spread L'Infamie, in order to create public dissatisfaction with America's monetary system and replace it with their own.

You are a den of thieves — vipers! I intend to rout you out, and by the Eternal God I will rout you out!

ANDREW JACKSON, President U.S.A., c. 1835

THE CIVIL WAR

A strategic opportunity presented itself when deep social antagonisms began to threaten America's stability. The ILLUMINATI fanned the sparks knowing that they would reap a golden harvest if they could divide the North and the South ideologically and then prod both sides into a protracted, and bloody civil war.

It is not to be doubted, I know with absolute certainty, that the separation of the United States into two federations of equal powers had been decided upon well in advance of the Civil War by the top financial power of Europe.

OTTO VON BISMARCK, Chancellor, Germany.

The American Civil War, in a very real sense, was the continuation of the Revolutionary war fought by our Founders against the Bank of Englana. The Civil War was planned in

London by Rothschild who wanted two American democracies, each burdened with debt. Four years before the war (1857) Rothschild decided his Paris bank would support the South, represented by Sen. John Slidell, JEW, from Louisiana; while the British branch would support the North, represented by August Belmont (Schoenberg) JEW, from New York. The plan was to bankroll, at usurious interest rates, the huge war debts that were anticipated, using that debt to extort both sides into accepting a Rothschild central-banking system similar to the one that had bled (and is bleeding) the nations of Europe, keeping them in conditions of perpetual war, insolvency and at the mercy of JEW speculators.

As in pre-Revolution France ILLUMINATI agitators, like maggots attacking a raw wound, were set to work in the North and the South at all levels of government and throughout society to exploit the divisive issues threatening the nation. The International Bankers were successful. All efforts for North-South peace failed.

> Propaganda pushed the issue of slavery to the fore but the actual purpose behind the war...was to drive both sides to accept the same money system Rothschild had fastened on England and the Continent...to bleed the vast productivity of the whole American People.
> WILLIAM G. SIMPSON, *Which Way Western Man.*

> The government should create, issue and circulate all currency and credit needed to satisfy the spending powers of the government and the buying power of the consumers.
> PRESIDENT ABRAHAM LINCOLN.

Lincoln said he feared the International Bankers more than the Confederacy. He clearly saw the conspiracy developing around him, reaching into his very cabinet. In an effort to defang Rothschild he prevailed upon Congress to issue $150-million "Greenbacks" — interestfree currency backed by the U.S. Government (they have been circulating in the United States debt free ever since). However, International JEWRY refused to accept them. Both sides in the conflict desperately needed large amounts of money to carry on the war. Only Rothschild could provide that money — at usurious rates. BLOODMONEY.

> The United States were sold to the Rothschilds in 1863.
> EZRA POUND, "Impact."

> As a result of the war...the money power of this country will endeavor to prolong its reign by working on the prejudices of the people until the wealth is aggregated into the hands of a few and the Republic is destroyed. I feel more anxiety for the safety of my country than ever before, even in the midst of the war.
> PRESIDENT ABRAHAM LINCOLN.

624,511 soldiers died in the Civil War (1861-1865) 475,881 soldiers were wounded. The figures remain incomplete because some records were not kept, and others were lost, especially during the early stages of the war. After the war, realizing the Union's real enemy was Rothschild, the President, emphasizing the Constitution, made it crystal clear to Congress that:

> The privilege of creating and issuing money is... the supreme prerogative of government!
> ABRAHAM LINCOLN.

The U.S. Constitution gives only Congress the power to coin money and regulate the value thereof; the Supreme Court ruled that Congress may not abdicate that function.

President Lincoln had thrown down the gauntlet. Under his administration a Rothschild central-banking system would not be tolerated.

Lincoln further infuriated JEWRY when he announced his intentions to colonize America's recently manumitted Negroes. JEWS wanted Negroes to remain in the United States as cheap labor (now that they didn't have to be cared for and supported), and also as a divisive racial element available for future revolutionary exploitation.

Lincoln's intransigence sealed his fate. The impediment had to be removed. *Persuasive evidence suggests that Lincoln's assassin, John Wilkes Booth (Botha), JEW, was hired for the hit by Judah Benjamin, JEW, Treasurer of the Confederacy.* Benjamin was a close associate of Benjamin Disraeli, JEW (1804-1881), British Prime Minister. Disraeli, Benjamin and Booth had, together, conferred with the Rothschilds. When Booth escaped from Ford's Theater he fled "quite by chance" over the only road exiting Washington, D.C. not blocked by troops. Found among his possessions was a code book identical to one found in the possession of Benjamin; and another, its pages ripped out, among the possessions of U.S. Secretary of War, Stanton. After the murder Benjamin fled to London, welcomed by his tribe. Recently, Booth's relatives asked that his grave in Maryland be exhumed. They don't believe Booth is in it. But permission was denied

JAMES W. VON BRUNN

by unnamed authorities.

Should you perchance visit the long lines of Yankee and Rebel dead at Pea Ridge, Gettysburg, Shiloh, Chickamaugua, Cold Harbor, Chancellorsville, Antietam *et al* — remember that each Cross represents BLOOD-MONEY and tears and pain exacted by TALMUDIC KHAZAR JEWS.

Thirty-five years after Appomatox, AT THE DAWN OF THE BLOOD IEST CENTURY IN WORLD HISTORY, the ILLUMINATI set the stage for WORLD WAR I. MONEY was manipulated, unemployment soared. Whatever their country of residence JEWS spread L'INFAMIE, as they have in all of their wars and revolutions, demonizing their enemy. Drums began to beat. In America JEWS used flattery and coercion to penetrate the White House. They handled President Wilson — as later they handled FDR — "like a monkey on a string." To the dismay of patriots the U.S. Congress enacted the unconstitutional FEDERAL RESERVE ACT (1913), giving Rothschild total control of America's monetary system. From that moment on the ILLUMINATI has controlled the machinery of the United States Government. (Today, JEWS walk in and out of the Oval Office, and the Treasury, in the manner they walk in and out of the Hillcrest Club, L.A). Immediately JEWS prepared the United States for WWI which, at that time, the American people had no suspicion was being planned. To assure the BANKERS would be reimbursed principal plus interest

82 | P a g e

Congress enacted the 16th Amendment to the Constitution establishing the first personal-income tax in American history. Not only were Americans expected to die in a war against their German kin they were to pay JEWS for the privilege.

That same fateful year, 1913, JEWS established the Anti-Defamation League of B'nai B'rith — whose m.o. *is* Defamation. Its stated purpose is to identify, expose and eradicate "Anti-Semitism" (sic) which is equated with any criticisms of JEWS. Congress cringes before its baleful eyes. The ADL, headquartered in New York City, employs a permanent staff of 225 lawyers, lobbyists, social engineers, educators, and PR specialists. It has regional offices throughout the civilized World.

The B'NAI B'RITH (Sons of the Covenant), a secret cabal, claims tax-deductible status as a religious and charitable organization. Its network penetrates every level of the JEWISH community, here and abroad. Its purpose is to unite all JEWS behind implementation of the Protocols.

As early as 1913 the outcome of the forthcoming war was well known to inside players. The advance-strategy, after the European combatants were exhausted and swamped in debt, was to bring America's unequaled resources and might into the conflict. Brain-washed Americans, in a killing frenzy, rushed "over there" to "save the world for Democracy" — a word that appears nowhere in the U.S. Constitution. *The real objectives were*:

1.   Annihilate Christian Russia, Aryan enemy of MARXISM/LIBERALISM/JEWRY.

2.   Replace Europe's Absolute Monarchies with Democratic governments. Thus, exposing Aryan Christian Europe to the virus of LIBERALISM/MARXISM/JEWRY.

3.   Inundate Europe under mountainous debts to be repaid at usurious interest rates to the ILLUMINATI.

4.   Establish a ZIONIST Homeland in Palestine (Britain's tribute to "American" JEWS for bringing America into the war).

5.   Destruction of Germany. JEWRY had invested heavily in the British Empire, owned by the Bank of England. Germany's merchant marine, inter-continental railway, foreign trade and colonies posed a serious economic threat.

6.   Kill the cream of Aryan manhood, exposing the White gene-pool to miscegenation and White slavery.

In Europe and America the ILLUMINATI placed their goy chess-pieces in high offices. JEWS holding positions of trust within the various European governments, used confidences gained at the highest level to betray their host States and use that knowledge to advance ILLUMINATI objectives. For example: Max Warburg, JEW, head of German Intelligence, financed Lenin's Bolsheviks. Max's brother, Paul Warburg, architect of the Federal Reserve System, bought the presidency for Woodrow Wilson and, with Jacob Schiff, Kuhn-Loeb & Co., financed Leon Trotsky's Bolshevik cut-throats.

Soon thereafter, financial crises began erupting throughout the West creating confusion and despair. Ethnic differences between the European states were exacerbated by L'INFAMIE. The Balkans were turned into a tinder-box of political and racial animosities. Archduke Ferdinand of Austria traveled to Serbia seeking to ameliorate the differences there. He and his lovely wife were murdered in Sarajevo (628-1914), by Gavrilo Princip, Freemason. The dominoes began to fall — one by one.

> The Archduke knew quite well that the risk of an attempt on his life was imminent. A year before the war he had informed me that the Freemasons had resolved his death.
> COUNT CZERNIN, *In the World War.*

> He is a remarkable man; it is a pity that he is condemned, he will die on the steps of his throne.
> LEON PONCINS, Secret Power Behind Revolution.

> The murder of the Archduke ignited material which otherwise would not have taken fire as it did, or perhaps at all. It is therefore important to trace the origins of the plot in which he fell a victim....
> SIDNEY B. FAY, Origins of the World War.

> The Party Line was to unite all revolutionary bodies for the purposes of bringing all the big capitalistic countries into war with each other so that all the terrific losses suffered, the high taxes imposed and the hardships endured by the masses of the population, would make the majority of the working classes react favorably to ...a revolution to end all wars. When all the countries had been Sovietized then the ILLUMINATI would form a totalitarian dictatorship ...It is possible that only Lenin knew the secret aims and ambitions of the ILLUMINATI, who molded the revolutionary action to suit their purpose. The revolutionary leaders were to organize their underground in all countries so as to be able to take over the nation's political system and economy; the International Bankers were to

extend the ramifications of their agencies around the world...
WILLIAM GUY CARR, R.D., *Pawns in the Game*.

A series of assassinations were committed (1881-1914) to advance ILLUMINATI war objectives, the most critical were: Czar Alexander II ("Little Father") Russia, in 1881; the Empress of Austria, in 1893; King Humbert of Italy in 1900; U.S. President McKinley in 1901; Grand Duke Sergius of Russia in 1905; Premier, V. von Plehve, Russia, in 1905; Premier, Peter A. Stolypin, Russia, in 1911; King Carlos and the Crown Prince of Portugal in 1908; Archduke Ferdinand and Duchess, Austria in 1914. All of these murders, and many more, are traceable to Bolshevism, Freemasonry (Masons of the Grand Orient) and other ILLUMINATI sponsored terror groups. At the Austrian Military Trial (10-12-14), investigating the murder of the Archduke, the prosecutor questioned Cabrinovic — the assassin who threw the first bomb — he replied:

> Freemasonry had to do with it because it strengthened my intentions. In Freemasonry it is permitted to kill... Freemasonry had condemned the Archduke to death more than a year before.
> I. CABRINOVIC, Freemason, Serb.

Let me take you back to 1913. If I had stood here in 1913 and told you, "Come to a conference to discuss the reconstruction of a national home in Palestine," you would have looked at me as a dreamer; even if I out of all that followed came a chance, the opportunity, the occasion for establishing a national home for Jews in Palestine. Has it ever occurred to you how out of the welter of world blood there has arisen this opportunity? Do you really believe this has been an accident? Do you really in your hearts believe that we have been led back to Israel by nothing but a fluke? Do you believe there is no greater meaning in the opportunity we have been given?

After two thousand years of wandering in the Wilderness we have a chance and an opportunity bestowed on us, and many sit back and say it is of no interest to us. I wonder if they have thought of the chain of circumstances.

LORD MELCHETT, JEW, Pres., English Zionist Federation.

WORLD WAR ONE (1914) exploded as planned. It was Germany, one of Europe's most cultured and civilized states — who had given to an admiring world her magnificent music, and her scientific genius — who had been specifically targeted for reasons mentioned above and, also, because Germany represented the HEART OF CHRISTENDOM. The JEW controlled media inevitably demonizes its enemies as depraved monsters: German soldiers were accused of amputating the hands of Belgian children; of bayoneting pregnant women then butchering the fetuses; of sinking passenger ships at random, then "obscenely" machine-gunning survivors in life-boats. "Huns" were accused of making lamp-shades and rendering bars of soap from enemy corpses. German-Americans were put out of business. Bricks were thrown through their living-room windows. Total responsibility for the war was laid upon Germany.

Although Russia was an ALLY of Britain and France JEWRY financed the Bolshevik Revolution against the Russian state. L'INFAMIE engulfed the Czar and German born Czarina, creating distrust of the monarchy, and fomenting mutiny in the military. This allowed crack German troops to transfer from the Eastern front to the Western front, where the bloody engagements in no-man's land soon shifted in Germany's favor.

At this critical moment, ILLUMINATIST Baron Edmund de Rothschild, JEW (Bank of England), arranged an audience between Lord Arthur Balfour, British Minister of Foreign Affairs, and Chaim Weizmann, JEW, co-founder of ZIONISM. Weizmann proposed that JEWS would bring America into the war against Germany if Britain, quid pro quo, would guaranty a Jewish Homeland in Palestine. Britain agreed, double-crossing the Arabs (Sykes-Picot Treaty) who had been fighting for Britain against the Turks. The first secret draft of the Balfour Declaration was cabled to President Wilson, whose advisors, Rabbi Wise, Louis Denmitz Brandeis, JEW; Bernard Baruch, JEW, Felix Frankfurter, JEW, Edward Mandel House, JEW, made additions and corrections. Ultimately, Baron Edmund de Rothschild wrote the final draft, changing the line "a homeland for the Jewish Race" to "a homeland for the Jewish People." The text was then typed on British Foreign Office letterhead and signed by Lord Balfour. The last paragraph reads: "I would be grateful if you would bring this declaration to the attention of the Zionist Federation." It was addressed to Baron Edmund de Rothschild who had written the final text and was a member of the ILLUMINATI KEHILLA that had planned America's entry into the war! (Britain earned the sobriquet "Treacherous Albion" after Cromwell gave the Bank of England to the JEWS, 1653).

A "little bird" told Winston Churchill that WWI would

occur September 1914; accordingly, February 1913, he had the British liner *Lusitania* converted into an auxiliary cruiser armed with twelve six-inch naval cannon: a fact published in Jane's Fighting Ships (1914), the standard international naval reference. In America, however, the *Lusitania* was advertised as a passenger ship. The German Admiralty warned, in display ads in the New York Times, that the *Lusitania* was carrying war materiel — therefore, was considered a *prix de guerre*. The U.S. State Department denied German claims. The *Lusitania*, which Churchill had described earlier as "45,000-tons of live-bait" set sail and was torpedoed in deep water off the Irish Coast by a German U-Boat (1915). The *Lusitania* sank, as planned, with great loss of life. (see: WTC, 9-11-01) L'INFAMIE against Germany filled the airwaves, print and pulpit. Within three years, bombarded by incessant lies, *Boobus Americanus* reached a feeding frenzy, swallowed the "bait," and rushed off to Europe to "save the World for Democracy"! (a word not mentioned in the U.S. Constitution) and to kill their own blood-relations — the "Despicable Hun"!

> Chaim Weizmann, the British War Cabinet, and French Foreign Office were convinced by 1916 ...that the best and perhaps the only way (which proved so to be) to induce the American President to come into the war (WWI) was to secure the cooperation of Zionist Jews by promising them Palestine, and thus enlist and mobilize the hitherto unsuspectedly powerful forces of Zionist Jews in America and elsewhere in favor of the Allies on a quid pro quo contract...
>
> SAMUEL LANDMAN, JEW,
> Great Britain, the Jews & Palestine.

In Russia, Lenin's and Trotsky's anarchists converged. Three million unarmed middle-class (Bourgeois), Christians and Muslims, were slaughtered in the initial thrust of the BOLSHEVIK REVOLUTION, and 31-million Europeans died in its aftermath. Millions simply disappeared into the Gulag — forever. Almost the entire White (Petrine) cultural stratum, was wiped out (the "final solution"). Russia, there-after, was lost to the West: its post-revolution population being predominantly Asiatic.

> Nationalism is a danger for the Jewish people. Today, as in all epochs of history, it is proved that Jews cannot live in powerful states where a high national culture has developed.
> THE JEWISH SENTINEL, Chicago 9-24-36.

> I believe national pride (patriotism) is nonsense.
> BERNARD BARUCH, JEW, *Chicago Tribune* 9-25-35.
> (Advisor to Wilson, Roosevelt, Eisenhower).

Colin Simpson, British journalist, acting under the Freedom of Information Act, discovered the missing *Lusitania* Bill of Lading among Franklin Roosevelt's effects at Hyde Park, N.Y. (1973). Roosevelt, a Harvard fop, and Under-Secretary U.S. Navy during WWI, had treasonously concealed from the U.S. Congress the missing Bill of Lading (later he concealed the "bait" at Pearl Harbor, "a date that will live in infamy"). The *Lusitania* was, indeed, loaded with war materiel bound for England (belligerent), and departing from the United States (neutral), thus breaking International Maritime Law. A private salvage company (November 1982), exploring the ill fated ship lying deep off the Irish coast, used underwater camera equipment that revealed a torpedo had struck a compartment holding munitions. The explosion forced the Lusitania's mangled hull *outwards*.

Following the 1918 Armistice, Britain blockaded German ports causing the starvation deaths of over a million Germans, who were reduced to eating garbage and rats. Germany's famous schools and universities were filled with JEWS, while German youth, unable to afford even food, went from the trenches to bread-lines. White slavery flourished as JEWS ostensibly made legitimate job offers to penniless young women who were then shipped to foreign prostitution rings. Today, using the identical scam, JEWS are tricking starving White Russian girls into lives of prostitution in Israel, and elsewhere. They are being used also as breeding stock. ("60-Minutes" CBS, 1998).

The Treaty of Versailles ("Kosher Conference") was designed by the ILLUMINATI to crush Germany, weaken her resistance to Marxism and lay the foundations for World War II — twenty years later.

President Wilson brought to Paris 117 Jews and 39 Gentiles (mostly valets).
COUNT CHEREP-SPIRIDOVICH, *Russia Under the Jews*.

The Jews formed a solid ring around Woodrow Wilson. There was a time when he communicated to the country through no one but a Jew.
HENRY FORD, Sr., Volume II, *The International Jew*.

The heavily populated German Nation was deprived of much of its territory including vital mineral areas and the "Polish Corridor" which... separated the original Duchy of Prussia from the rest of the country.

Germany was deprived of its merchant fleet... and was saddled with an impossible load of reparations. As a result the defeated country was left in a precarious position which soon produced economic collapse. The Austro-Hungarian Empire, ancient outpost of Teutonic peoples and Western Civilization was destroyed ...the new state of Czechoslovakia was given 3.5-million persons of German blood and speech....

Berlin in 1923 was a city in despair. People waited in the alley behind the Hotel Adlon ready to pounce on garbage cans... a cup of coffee cost one-million marks one day, a million and half the next, two million the day following... the German attitude (suspicion and fear) was intensified by the new power German Jews had acquired... from using funds derived from rich raceconscious Jews in other countries and by an inrush of Jews from the destroyed Austro-Hungarian Empire.

DR. JOHN O. BEATY (OSS), *Iron Curtain Over America.*

The devalued German mark enabled JEWS sporting pounds, francs, and dollars to "purchase" German businesses, real-estate and art treasures at a fraction of their intrinsic value (as they did in the South after the U.S. Civil War). Fifteen years later Nazis repossessed those stolen treasures from JEWRY. Today, 1998, JEWS (with U.S. support) are successfully suing nations and individuals to recover "Nazi loot stolen from JEWS." The same loot JEWS initially extorted from a prostrate German nation.

Following WWI, the Allies *extended formal apologies to Germany* for the false atrocity stories. L'Infamie! The Germans, it was acknowledged, had behaved as well or better than their counterparts! The United States *Congressional Record* (Senate, 6-15-33) places the blame for WWI directly where it belongs — the International Bankers caused the war and were its ultimate victors.

WWII (see Chapter 6: The "Holocaust") was formulated at the Treaty of Versailles and was a continuation of the ILLUMINATI program to enslave the nations of the world by placing them under mountains of usurious debt.

Direct intervention with the total military potential of America was essential if the war (WWII) was not to terminate in a Western victory (Germany) over Asiatic Marxist Russia... and result in the creation of a Culture-Nation-State-People-Race unity of the West.

FRANCIS PARKER YOCKEY, *Imperium*.

To one who knows something of the facts of the world and knows also the main details of the American surrender of security and principles at Teheran, Yalta, and Potsdam ...three ghastly purposes come into clear focus:

1) As early as 1937 (Roosevelt's cabal) determined upon war against Germany for no formulated purpose beyond pleasing the dominant Eastern European element... in the National Democratic Party and "holding those votes," as Elliot Roosevelt put it ...to gratify the President's vanity of a third term in office.

2) The powerful Eastern European element, dominant in the inner circles of the Democratic Party, regarded with complete equanimity ...even with enthusiasm, the killing of as many as possible of the Khazar-hated race of Aryans.

3) Our alien dominated government fought the war for the annihilation of Germany, the historic bulwark of Christian Europe... In 1937-1938 the German government made a "sincere effort to improve relations with the United States only to be rebuffed." Germany's appeals for negotiation ...were witheld from the public until ferreted out by the House Committee on Un-American Activities... more than 10-years after the facts were so criminally suppressed.

DR. JOHN O. BEATY, *Iron Curtain Over America*.

Our brief review of these historic DEFEATS reveals they were directed by a force more powerful by far than the

Aryan states actually engaged in fighting. President Wilson said, "there is a power somewhere so organized, so subtle, so watchful, so interlocked, so complete, so pervasive..." that one can detect that Satanic power only through the similarity of its methods, the cohesiveness of its actions, its horrifying RESULTS. JEWRY infiltrated the most sensitive areas of power and trust in ALL Western Nations, while secretly swearing loyalty only to JEWRY. Aryans call this treason. But JEWS regard such accusations as "anti-Semitic," viewing Aryans as cattle trespassing on their World. President Wilson, the United States of America, and Mankind learned these facts too late. Following WWI the ILLUMINATI failed in its bid to establish a League of Nations because the United States Congress refused to surrender sovereignty. Ruffled but determined U.S. members of the ILLUMINATI met in Paris to discuss again means of advancing One World Government. Participants were: Jacob Schiff, JEW (KuhnLoeb & Co., Rothschild agentur); Bernard Baruch, JEW, "Prince of the Kahilla" (who had garnered millions speculating in copper — from which shell-casings are made); Walter Lippman, JEW, (savant/writer); Col. E. Mandel House, JEW (White House-Treasury-Wall Street agent); John D. Rockefeller, JEW; and goy collaborators: Averell Harriman, Christian Herter, and John Foster Dulles. Present in spirit was the gunrunner J.P Morgan, Rothschild agentur. All had profited monetarily from WWI and all, for the same golden reasons, were instrumental in the creation of WWII. None of them ever served active duty in the military. The military served them.

They expected to further advance ILLUMINATI control over the United States. Out of that Paris meeting the Council on Foreign Relations (CFR) was born. At the same time, in England, The Royal Institute of International Affairs was organized by a similar cabal. Both organization reported to the KEHILLA: the board of directors of the ILLUMINATI. The Rockefeller Institute is a subsidiary of the CFR. The Rockefellers, of JEW descent, merged their Chase bank with Warburg's (JEW) Manhattan Bank, and placed a subsidiary of Chase-Manhattan on Karl Marx Square in Moscow to finance the so-called "Cold War," even as we fought no-win wars in Korea and Viet Nam.

> My ancestors may have been Jewish. We're really not sure.
>   NELSON ROCKEFELLER, Vice President, USA, TIME, 10-19-70,
> (Nelson, married to Aryan "Happy" Rockefeller, died of apoplexy while cavorting in bed with his Jewish secretary).

Steven Birmingham's book, *The Grandees: America's Sephardic Elite* (Harper & Row) confirms Rockefeller's Jewish heritage.

In 1973 David Rockefeller formed the Trilateral Commission (TRI), he appointed Zbigniew Brzezinski, security advisor to President Jimmy Carter, to direct it. For many years David Rockefeller chaired both groups (CFR/TRI).

The Bilderbergers, "The Fourth Reich of the Rich," is the European equivalent of the CFR; although its membership is more restricted, more powerful, and maintains a more exclusive social tone. Its meetings, usually held at isolated estates, are ultra-secret and protected by heavily armed ground and air forces. Elite members of the CFR/TRI/ BILDERBERGERS share inter-linking memberships. Recently, Bilderbergers achieved the "unification of Europe." *Not a united Aryan nation* as Charlemagne, Frederick, Napoleon, and Hitler wanted it — but unification through a single currency. Now Europe is totally enslaved to USURY and unable to rebel and challenge INTERNATIONAL JEWRY as Germany did in 1933.

The United Nations was concocted by the ILLUMINATI following WWII. Forty members of the U.S. delegation to the United Nations Conference, held in San Francisco, were members of the CFR, they included: Alger Hiss, chief author of the U.N. Charter which guaranteed that the Security Council (the UN's most important body) would have a Marxist majority; Dean Acheson (Yale, Democrat), later U.S. Secretary of State vowed, after Hiss was convicted of perjury, "I will never turn my back on Alger Hiss!" (Soviet files confirm Hiss was a Soviet agent); Owen Lattimore, and Philip Jessup, branded by the U.S. Senate as "tools of the Soviet"; Harry Dexter White (Weiss), JEW, the driving force behind the Bretton Woods Agreements, which created the International Monetary Fund (IMF), and the World Bank, whose investments are insured by U.S. tax-dollars. White was exposed later as a Soviet spy.

DIRECT QUOTES FROM THE CFR ANNUAL REPORT 1980:

The Purpose of the Council on Foreign Relations is:

1)   Break new ground in the consideration of International issues.

2)   Help shape American foreign policy in a constructive nonpartisan manner.

3)   Provide continuing leadership for the conduct of foreign affairs.

4)   The Council is an educational institution and a unique forum bringing together leaders from the academic, public, and private worlds.

It is the Council's tradition that statements of the speakers will not be attributed to them in public media or forums.

> Council meetings shall generally be NOT OPEN to the public or media... (however it) would be legitimate for government officials to report to his colleagues what he learned at the meeting... or a lawyer may give a memo to his partner, or a corporate officer to another corporate officer. It would not be in compliance however for any meeting participant to publish a speaker's statements in the newspaper, repeat it on TV or radio... a meeting participant is forbidden to transmit any Council statement to a newspaper reporter or other person who is likely to publish it in a public medium.
>
> The Council has no affiliation with the U.S. Government.

Paradoxically, the CFR Report acknowledges that 12% of its 2,164 members ARE U.S. government officials! That means a minimum 260 members, according to this secret organization, hold important positions within the U.S. government! 70% of the membership are from the Washington, D.C./New York City/Boston axis. Most are Marxist indoctrinated: Ivy League, London School of Economics, Georgetown University, Southern Illinois U., etc.

Since WWII almost every Secretary of State has been a CFR/TRI member. The majority were JEWS — including Clinton appointee Madeleine Albright. Recent Secretary of Defense appointments include Harold Brown; James Schlesinger; Cap Weinberger; Henry Kissinger; William Cohen, all JEWS, all CFR/TRI members. None ever wore a U.S. military uniform. All, after their government stints, found employment with the ILLUMINATI, usually on Wall Street. Remember, practicing JEWS make cabalistic KOL NIDRE VOWS to support the TORAH; Marrano JEWS swear to protect the KHAZAR PEOPLE. This explains the breach in U.S. security.

Former CFR president Winston Lord, an advisor to the Clinton White House, married to a Chinese, remarked: "The Trilateralists don't rule the World — the CFR does that."

CFR Case Study #76 (1959) states:

> The United States must strive to build a new International Order... including states labeling themselves Socialist. The social experiment in China under Chairman Mao's leadership is one of the most important and successful in human history.
> DAVID ROCKEFELLER, JEW, Chairman CFR/TRI.

The U.S Senate estimates that about 65-million Chinese were slaughtered under Chairman Mao's leadership in what has proven to be a hideously failed social experiment rejected even by Mao's closest admirers.

CFR members, holding many of the highest positions in the United States government, are appointed — not elected — to their positions of trust by the President. The "invisible government" from which they emerge, the CFR seeks to abandon American sovereignty. The loyalty of the CFR, whose Chairman today is David Gelb, JEW, is not to the U.S. Constitution but to the TALMUD.

> It is in the American interest to put an end to Nationhood.
> WALT ROSTOW, JEW, CFR/TRI, advisor to Pres. Kennedy, and Johnson, helped mastermind Viet Nam "police action."

> Our national purpose should be to abandon our nationality.
> KINGMAN BREWSTER, CFR, former President, Yale University, in CFR Quarterly *Foreign Affairs.*

> De Gaulle could not understand America's conviction of the obsolescence of the nation-state.
> HENRY KISSINGER, JEW, CFR/TRI, *The White House Years.*

While the CFR/TRI goals are ILLUMINATI objectives — and there is at the highest level interlinkage of membership — they have differing, sometimes overlapping, strategies. The CFR appears to be primarily concerned with infiltrating the U.S. government. There they influence the policies of the various departments and agencies coordinating them with ILLUMINATI Expectations. The TRI appears directed toward Internationalizing (Sovietizing) the businesses and industries of the Americas, Europe, and the Pacific Rim (hence the name "Trilateral").

The TRI has about 300 members, 87 from the United

States: the largest segment represents the banking community.

QUESTION/ANSWER BOOKLET

Published by the Trilateral Commission

The TRI is a non-governmental policy-oriented discussion group... not only on issues among these (three) regions but in a global framework as well.

Zbigniew Brzezinski was very important to the formation of the Commission... and is its major intellectual dynamo. Jimmy Carter was a member from 1973 until his election to the

U.S. Presidency when he left in accordance with Commission rules barring members from the National Administration.

The TRI is an independent organization. It is not part of the U.S Government (Please see CFR/TRI Chart, index) or of the United Nations. It has no formal ties with the CFR or Brookings Institute, though a considerable number of TRI members are also involved with one or more organizations of this sort. [See ILLUMINATI graph page 105 — JvB]

The TRI is absolutely not secret. The only off-the-record aspect of the TRI is its meetings.

The TRI welcomes coverage of its activities.

Allegations that the TRI is trying to establish One World Government are totally false... there have been no Commission reports or even a single instance in Commission discussions where any member or task force author proposed that our National Government be dissolved and a World Government created.

The TRI does not lobby for particular legislation or candidates.

Much of the notion that the TRI is a conspiracy rests on the fact that so many members of the Carter Administration, including the President, were former members of the Commission. At first glance this does seem a strange coincidence, but... these facts do not indicate control of the U.S. Government by the Commission.

In complete contradiction to the TRI Question/Answer Booklet are some statements by the "intellectual dynamo" now teaching at Georgetown U., Zibby Brzezinsky, to wit:

The fiction of national sovereignty... is no longer compatible with reality.

Yet, though Stalinism may have been a needless tragedy for both the Russian people and Communism as an ideal... for the world at large Stalinism was a blessing in disguise.

Marxism is simultaneously a victory of the external active man over the inner passive man, and a victory of Reason over Belief.

Marxism theory is this century's most influential system of thought.

America is undergoing a new revolution ...that unmasks its obsolescence.

Deliberate management of America's future will become widespread with the planner eventually displacing the lawyer as the key social legislator and manipulator.

By the year 2000 (in the U.S.A.) it will be accepted that Robespierre and Lenin were mild reformers.

ZBIGNIEW BRZEZINSKI, CFR/TRI,
U.S. Security Advisor, from his book *Between Two Ages*.

The brochures issued for public consumption by the CFR/TRI quite obviously are prevarications that don't reflect the opinions expressed elsewhere by its leadership.

What the Trilateralists truly intend is the creation of a World-wide economic power superior to the political governments of the nation-states involved.... As managers and creators of the system they will rule the future. Most of our foreign aid... is being used to create an International Economy managed and controlled through the mechanism of International conglomerate manufacturing and business enterprise. Populations are treated as nothing more than producing economic groups. Freedom (Political, Spiritual, Economic) is denied any importance in the Trilateralist construction of the next century.

BARRY GOLDWATER, JEW, U.S. Senator, *With No Apologies*.

I am convinced that the CFR together with... associated tax-exempt organizations is the invisible government which sets the major policies of the federal government... I am convinced that the objective of this invisible government is to convert America into a socialist state and then make it a unit in a one-world socialist system.

DAN SMOOT, Prof. Harvard, FBI, *The Invisible Government*.

International Money Power is the most dangerous conspiracy against the freedom of men the world has ever known.

FREDERICK SODDY, Professor, Oxford, Nobel Laureate, F.R.S.

The distinguished Dr. Medford Evans said, "Anthony Sutton's *Western Technology and Soviet Economic Development* is possibly the most important book since the Bible." The author adds that Sutton's, *Trilateralists Over Washington*, and all his books, are required reading for those who understand the evil influences at work destroying Western Culture. These books relate to the Cold War period of U.S./USSR history but they are extremely cogent today. Incredibly, many of those who implemented ILLUMINATI policy during that period enjoy distinguished positions, Citations of Merit, honorable retirement, or burial in Arlington Cemetery. Following are a FEW of Dr. Sutton's research observations (*Western Technology and Soviet Economic Development*):

The Soviets have the largest iron and steel plant in the world. It was built by McKee Corp., it is a copy of the U.S. Steel plant in Gary, Indiana. All Soviet iron and steel technology comes from the U.S., and its allies.

The Soviets have the largest tube and pipe mill in Europe — one million tons a year. The equipment is Salem, Aetna, Standard... If you know anyone in the space business ask them how many miles of tubing goes into a missile.

The standard Soviet truck used in Viet Nam and the MidEast is manufactured at ZIL-130 Plant, which was built by A. J. Brandt Co., Detroit, MI. The Soviet military has over 300,000 trucks all manufactured in plants built by the USA. ("Hanoi" Jane Fonda was photographed waving a Cong flag in one of those vehicles).

The USSR has the largest merchant marine in the world, about 6,000 ships: two-thirds were built outside the USSR. 80% of the engines for these ships were built outside the USSR. None are of Soviet design. Those built inside the Soviet are built with USA technological assistance.

About 100 ships were used on the Hanoi Run to carry Soviet weapons and supplies to the North Vietnamese. NONE of the main engines in these ships was manufactured by the Soviets. All ship building tech comes from the USA or our allies.

During the Viet Nam War ("police action") the Johnson Administration sent equipment and technological assistance to the Soviets that more than doubled their automobile output.

(From 1917 onwards) there was a pervasive, powerful, and not clearly identifiable force in the West making for the continuance of transfers. Surely the political power and influence of the Soviets was not sufficient alone to bring about such favorable (to the USSR) Western policies.... indeed such policies seem incomprehensible IF the West's objective is to survive as an alliance of independent non-Communist nations.

DR. ANTHONY C. SUTTON, Hoover Inst., Stanford , Univ.

U.S.A. ABETS COMMUNISM:

Following WWII, the USA (CFR) double-crossed America's long-time ally Chiang Kai-shek, ABETTING Mao Tse-tung's Communist take-over of mainland China (1950) while vowing to defend Formosa against Mao. Within a year Americans were fighting and dying in Korea, and later in Viet Nam, allegedly to PREVENT Communist expansion in Asia! Meanwhile, the FEDERAL RESERVE SYSTEM financed the Soviet war machine and the CFR/ TRI modernized and expanded it. TREASON!

The ILLUMINATI got us into "no-win" wars in Korea and Viet Nam for two reasons: MONEY, and expectations that the U.S. military would suffer great loss of life — fomenting despair and revolution on Main Street USA. When the U.S. military began to WIN those wars the MASS-MEDIA screamed L'INFAMIE. JEW led cannaille, emerging like rats from the piles and alleyways, condemned alleged U.S. military "atrocities," slandered our officers and men, literally spit on veterans, and succeeded in brainwashing *Boobus Americanus* and a gutless Congress into accepting defeat. (General Douglas MacArthur complained that North Korean generals received his directives, from a spy-ridden Pentagon, before he did). TREASON!

> Treason doth never prosper. What's the reason? For when it doth prosper none dare call it TREASON.
>
> LORD HARRINGTON.

> Tob shebbe goyim harog!
>
> TALMUD: Sanhedrin.

> Give me the power to issue and control the money of a nation and I care not who makes its laws.
>
> ANSELM MAYER ROTHSCHILD.

The foregoing account reveals the merest thread in a tapestry of evil. Reoccurring aspects of ILLUMINATI history is MONEY MANIPULATION; reliance on l'INFAMIE — slander and false witness; and SILENCING those who could testify against them:

In 1780 France, the Royal Family, government leaders, and goy leaders of the Revolution were murdered TO SILENCE THEM.

Napoleon, incarcerated incommunicado on St. Helena Isle, was poisoned TO SILENCE HIM.

In 1918 Russia, the Royal Family members of the court, and government, were slandered and murdered TO SILENCE THEM. (Because JEWS slaughtered, or drove out, the entire Aryan cultural stratum which included scientists, engineers, and other professionals, the Soviet was never more than a paper-tiger until they captured Nazis scientists; and obtained A-Bomb secrets, and technology, equipment and money from the ILLUMINATI).

President Woodrow Wilson, Democrat, died broken in mind and spirit, effectively SILENCED by Sam Untermeyer (JEW) who had confiscated, early in Wilson's administration, the President's indiscreet love letters to Mrs. Peck.

Nazi leadership was slandered, falsely accused; prosecuted by JEWS in American uniforms; condemned by kangaroo courts for ex post facto crimes, then (on the HIGH JEWISH HOLY DAYS) hanged, TO SILENCE THEM.

Other German officers were imprisoned from 15-years to life; upon release many were murdered. 10 May 1941, six months before Pearl Harbor, Rudolph Hess, Anglophile, second in command to Hitler, parachuted from his Messerschmitt 109 over Scotland (his first jump), in a last minute effort to arrange peace between the warring states. Hess was clapped into Spandau prison without trial and held incommunicado for 46-years (21-years in solitary confinement). 17 August 1987, age 93, shortly before his announced release, Hess was murdered. Officially, he committed suicide! (Menachim Begin, ISRAELI terrorist, warned U.S. Pres. Jimmy "Rabbit" Carter, Democrat, CFR/TRI, that Hess must not leave Spandau alive). The Top Secret Hess Files will not be released totally until 2027 A.D.

Franklin Delano Roosevelt, Democrat, suddenly broken in health, died at age 63 before his war to save the world for Communism ended. He fell (or was pushed) headfirst into the embers of a fireplace in Warm Springs, Ga., conveniently SILENCING HIM, and providing him, on his trip to Hell, a taste of Hamburg and Dresden. The ILLUMINATI could not afford to have Congress question FDR (dead or alive). He is buried beneath a four inch thick bronze plate at Hyde Park, N.Y. His autopsy report never released.

Lee Harvey Oswald, John F. Kennedy's alleged assassin, predictably was murdered by a JEW (Jack Ruby), thus SILENCING crucial testimony that would have exposed the real murderer(s) whom Ruby (Rubinstein) had been hired to protect.

Oswald, McFadden, Long, Patton, Forrestal, Isador

Fisch, JEW ("friend" of Bruno Hauptmann), and many other participants in the momentous events of an EVIL ERA were SILENCED — permanently. Leaving ciphers in Western History; to be filled in by subjectively motivated "historians". SILENCE IS GOLDEN!

From the foregoing historical record we can now deduce:

THE ILLUMINATI INTENDS TO REPLACE WESTERN CIVILIZATION WITH ONE WORLD ILLUMINATI GOVERNMENT

This will be achieved through *the power of MONEY which is solely in JEW hands*. The Order of Battle is as follows:

Objectives

1) Destroy Monarchy, Nationalism, Patriotism.
2) Create Democracies (Marxist Governments).
3) Miscegenate the races.
4) Create One World Religion: Judaism.
5) Abandon national boundaries
6) Destroy the nations' military.
7) Destroy the culture-bearing stratum.
8) Control the machinery of government.

Strategies

1) Capture the monetary system.
2) Capture the mass-media.

3) Create wars, debt, bankruptcies, high taxes.
4) Distort language, moral code, ethics, mores.
5) Confiscate private weapons.
6) Control Education, re-write history.
7) Open Mexican border.
8) Infiltrate government, unions, industry.

Tactics

1) Promote interracial integration.
2) Promote Marxism, Freudianism, Boasism.
3) Promote Democracy, anarchy, racial unrest.
4) Slander: national heroes, racial pride, tradition.
5) Employ blackmail, slander, extortion, bribes, murder.
6) Support all dissident factions. Honor the dishonorable.
7) Use ADL, IRS, ACLU, CIA, ATF to punish Aryan patriots.
8) LIE, spread misinformation, disinformation.

> Burn ye all that is in the city and slay with the edge of the sword both man and woman, young and old, and ox and sheep, and burn the city with fire and all that is therein.
>
> JOSHUA 7:21.

Marxism is the modern form of JEWISH Prophecy.
REINHOLD NIEBUHR, in a warmly received speech before
the Jewish Institute of Religion, Waldorf Astoria, NYC.

I do solemnly swear that I will faithfully execute the Office of the President of the United States and will do to the best of my ability to preserve, protect and defend the Constitution of the United States of America.
U.S. CONSTITUTION, Article II, Section 1., Clause 7.

President Bill Clinton, with an Ivy League-Rhodes Scholar-Marxist indoctrinated mind, and subject to both blackmail and extortion, appointed many JEWS/CFR/TRI to sensitive positions in the UNITED STATES

GOVERNMENT, including: SUPREME COURT JUSTICES Ruth Bader Ginsberg, and Stephen Breyer, JEWS; SECRETARY OF STATE, Madeleine K. Albright, JEW; UNDER-SECY STATE, Stuart Eizenstat, JEW; ASST. SECY. STATE, Stanley Roth, JEW; SECRETARY OF DEFENSE, William Cohen, JEW; SENIOR ADVISOR TO THE PRESIDENT, Rahm Emanuel, JEW; WHITE HOUSE ATTORNEY, Bernie Nussbaum, JEW; CEO CENTRAL INTELLIGENCE AGENCY (CIA), John Deutch, JEW (now under investigation for treason); NATIONAL SECURITY ADVISOR, Sandy Berger, JEW; SECRETARY OF THE TREASURY, Robert Rubin, JEW; HEAD OF THE NATIONAL AERONAUTICAL AND SPACE ADMINISTRATION (NASA), Daniel E. Golden, JEW; SOCIAL SECURITY ADMINISTRATOR, Kenneth Apfel, JEW; HEAD OF DEPARTMENT OF AGRICULTURE, D. Glickman, JEW; and several Cabinet posts, including, Robert Reich, Donna Shalala, Alice Rivlin (FED), Robert Morris ("the toe sucker"), et al — all are JEWS whose sole allegiance, bound by the KOL NIDRE OATH, is to the Khazar tribe, and to the TALMUD, which vows the destruction of Western Civilization.

> An analysis of the 4,984 of the more militant members of the Communist Party in the United States showed that 91.4% of the total were of foreign stock or were married to persons of foreign stock.
> U.S. SENATE JUDICIARY COMMITTEE, 1950

> I wouldn't be surprised if someday these Jews would not become deadly to the human race.
> VOLTAIRE

CHAPTER 4

MONEY

And there was a cry of the people...against their brethren the Jews...we have mortgaged our lands, vineyards, and houses that we might buy corn because of the dearth...and lo, we bring into bondage our sons and our daughters to be servants...some of our daughters are brought into bondage already; neither is it in our power to redeem them for other men have our lands and our vineyards...

HOLY BIBLE: NE: 5:1,7.

Our money system is nothing better than a confidence trick... The "money power" which has been able to overshadow ostensibly responsible government is not the power of the merely ultra-rich but is nothing more or less than a new technique to destroy money by adding and withdrawing figures in bank ledgers, without the slightest concern for the interests of the community or the real role money ought to perform therein...to allow it to become a source of revenue to private issuer's is to create, first, a secret and illicit arm of government and, last, a rival power strong enough to ultimately overthrow all other forms of government.

Dr. FRED SODDY, Nobelist, Wealth, Virtual Wealth & Debt.

A great industrial nation is controlled by its system of credit. Our system of credit is concentrated. The growth of the nation, therefore, and all of our activities are in the hands of a few men. We have become one of the worst ruled, one of the most completely controlled and dominated governments in the civilized world...no longer a government of free opinion...but a government by the opinion and duress of small groups of domineering men.

PRESIDENT WOODROW WILSON, 1916.

T HE WEST viewed the JEW as an alien living within its midst. JEWS had no State of their own, no territory. Whatever the landscape they spoke the common language. Publicly they denied a racial identity assuming the outer garments, no matter how preposterous, of whatever nation in which they appeared. Adoption of Christian names, conversions, "nose jobs", and platform shoes were part of the camouflage. JEWRY seemed to be merely a religion. Therefore, JEWRY was politically invisible to the West, and its war against the West was always subterranean, cunning and deceptive. JEWISH strategy was to infiltrate the institutions of Western Culture and destroy them. JEWRY'S primary weapon was money manipulation and USURY.

Early Popes, and Christian monarchs invoked Biblical proscriptions against the "evil and pernicious practice of usury." Money was used strictly as a means of exchange and a storage of value backed by the honor of the State and the productive capabilities of its citizens. Nonetheless, the end result of Christian proscriptions against usury was to make JEWS the masters of European banking.

JEWS have no religious scruples regarding money where goyim are concerned. They now have the means to carry out their war of annihilation of the West. They would not surface as a fighting unit and openly attack their hated enemy. They remained invisible. Their strategy was to *organize the entire JEWISH People into a Fifth Column* whose purpose is to penetrate the West and *destroy everything*. This is being accomplished by exacerbating natural disputes between the Western States and influencing the results in favor of Liberalism as opposed to Authority; that is, materialism, free trade and usury, as opposed to Western Socialism; Internationalism as opposed to Western unity. MONEY was their sword and buckler. Hate and revenge their motif.

> The tactics of this Jewish warfare was employment of money. His dispersion, his materialism, his finished cosmopolitanism, all precluded him taking part in the heroic form of combat in the field, and he was thus confined to the war of lending, or refusing to lend, of bribing, of gaining legally enforceable power over important individuals... The story of Shylock shows the dual picture of the JEW — socially cringing on the Rialto, but emerging as a lion in the courtroom.
>
> FRANCIS PARKER YOCKEY, *Imperium*.

The dawn of the 20th Century found the ILLUMINATI preparing to launch a massive attack upon the West. Not in the light of open discourse, or on the battlefield, but in their usual manner: conspiratorially, from the underworld. Their strategy was to hitch America's resources, wealth and manpower to JEWISH aspirations which included destroying the monarchies of Europe and creating a bogus KHAZAR/ZIONIST state in Palestine. They found their Judas Goat in Woodrow Wilson, Chancellor of Princeton University, an innocent with a vast ego, and a chink in his armor. Unwittingly He became the indispensable, unwitting pawn in the International money game.

Paul Moritz Warburg, JEW, was dispatched to the

United States in 1903 to promote the establishment of a Rothschild central-bank in preparation for WWI which was then on the drawing-board. Warburg, made the Kuhn-Loeb Co., Wall Street Bankers, his base of operations. After meeting Wilson at a University seminar Warburg recommended Wilson to the International banking cabal. Upon further investigation, Rabbi Steven Wise; Jacob Schiff, JEW; Sam Untermyer, JEW, and other Khazar power-players agreed that Wilson would be the ILLUMINATI'S patsy in the White House.

Soon after, Wilson's democratic presidential campaign was announced, promoted and financed by ILLUMINATISTS: Warburg, JEW, and his brothers, Felix, and Max (head of German intelligence and the M.M. Warburg Bank, Hamburg); Adolph Ochs, JEW (publisher, *New York Times*); Henry Morganthau, JEW (tycoon of Negro slum dwellings in Harlem, Manhattan); Jacob Schiff, JEW, (Pres., Kuhn-Loeb Co.); Samuel Untermyer, JEW (powerful corporate lawyer); and Eugene Meyer, JEW, (banker, and owner of the *Washington Post*, the newspaper your Senator reads over morning coffee); and Rothschild agenteur; and internationalist bankers Lazard Freres; J&W Seligman; Speyer Brothers; and the Rothschilds. A few select goyim, including J.P. Morgan, gunrunner, were in on the deal.

To split the Republican vote, the ILLUMINATISTS financed both Teddy Roosevelt and the incumbent Howard Taft in their bids for the presidency. After Wilson won the rigged election (1912), which he attributed to his own charm and ingenuity, Warburg and his cabal put in motion their plan to establish control of America's finances and credit. Warburg introduced Col. Edward Mandell House, JEW, to the President. House became Wilson's alter-ego, confidant and messenger between the Oval Office and Wall Street. In his novel *Philip Dru*, House makes it perfectly clear that his idea of good government is One World Usurocracy. Legislators who didn't share his views were kept from meeting with the President. By manipulating Wilson, bribing members of Congress, and engaging in the most deceitful lobbying campaign in U.S. history, Warburg got what he wanted. During the Christmas Holidays (23 December 1913), when much of the opposition was absent, the U.S. Congress enacted the Federal Reserve Act SELLING AMERICA'S MONETARY SYSTEM to the International Bankers, and dooming Christendom to WWI and WWII; the "Cold War" and all of our "no win" wars.

> This Act establishes the most gigantic trust on earth. When the President signs this bill the invisible government by the Monetary Power will be legalized...the worst legislative crime of the ages is perpetrated by this banking and currency bill. The caucus and party bosses have again operated and prevented the people from getting the benefit of their own government.
> CHARLES LINDBERGH, Sr., U.S. Congress.

Soon thereafter, Sam Untermeyer, JEW, came into possession of Wilson's indiscreet love letters to Mrs. Peck, his mistress, and wife of a friend. The inner circle referred to the President as "Peck's bad boy." Wilson did what he was told to do when he was told to do it, leading to the appointment of Louis Denmitz Brandies, JEW, Zionist, to the U.S. Supreme Court; and pushing America into World War I.

> "Money is the worst of all contraband" said William Jennings Bryan, U.S. Secy. State. And our loans to the Allies during the two and a half years before our entry into the WWI were more accurately acts of aggression than our belated shipments of troops in 1917, after Wilson's declaration of war had given an air of legality to the farce.
> EUSTACE MULLINS, "The Federal Reserve Conspiracy."

> All wars are economic in their origin.
> BERNARD BARUCH, JEW, before Nye Committee, 9-13-37.

Constitutionality of the FEDERAL RESERVE ACT has never been adjudicated although it clearly is unconstitutional.

> ARTICLE I, SEC. 8, CLAUSE 5 U.S. CONSTITUTION: The Congress shall have the power to coin money, regulate the value thereof and of foreign coin, and to fix the standards of weights and measures.

The Clause has never been amended. One may then logically ask: Can Congress legally delegate its Constitutional authority?

> SHECHTER POULTRY v. U.S.A. (29 US 495) (55 US 837.842 (1935):

> 2)   Congress can not abdicate or transfer to others its legislative functions...
> 3)   Congress cannot constitutionally delegate its legislative authority to trade or industrial associations or groups so as to empower them to enact laws...
> 4)   Congress cannot delegate legislative powers to the President...

The Chief Justice stated: The Constitution established a national government with powers deemed to be adequate, as they have proven to be, both in war and in peace, but these powers of national government are limited by the constitutional grants. Those who act under these grants are not at liberty to transcend the imposed limits because they believe that more or different power is necessary. Such assertions of extraconstitutional authority were anticipated and precluded by the explicit terms of the Tenth Amendment: The powers not delegated to the United States by the Constitution, nor prohibited by it to the States, are reserved to the States and to the People.

ALGONQUIN SNC, Inc. v. FEDERAL ENERGY ADMINISTRATION 518 Fed 2nd 1051 (1975):

Conclusion: Neither the term "national security" nor "emergency" is a talisman, the thaumaturgic invocation of which should ipso facto suspend the normal checks and balances on each branch of government...If our system is to survive we must respond to the most difficult of problems in a manner consistent with the limitations placed upon Congress, the President, and the Courts, by our Constitution and our Laws. CONGRESS MAY NOT ABDICATE OR TRANSFER TO OTHERS ITS ESSENTIAL LEGISLATIVE FUNCTIONS.

ART. I, SEC. 10, CLAUSE 1, U.S. CONSTITUTION:

No State...shall make any Thing but gold and silver Coin a Tender in Payment of Debts...

THE U.S. CONSTITUTIONAL INTERPRETER:

If a Law is passed counter to the Constitution it is as though that Law had not been passed.

If Congress may not transfer to others its legislative functions, one might logically ask: Is the FED a Congressional agency? The answer is emphatically stated below!

LEWIS v. U.S. (680 F2d 1239 — July 1982):

> Federal Reserve Banks under the Federal Government Tort Claims Act are NOT Federal Government instrumentalities, but are independent, privately owned, locally controlled organizations.

The critical factor for determining whether an agency is a Federal agency is the existence of Federal Government control over the "detailed physical performance" and "day by day" operations of that entity.

The Supreme Court ruled (above) that Congress may NOT delegate its legislative functions. Does the FED legislate?

Legislate — to make or enact laws.

Laws — rules of action established by custom or laid down and enforced by sovereign authority.

Rule — to regulate, bring under force of Law.

FEDERAL RESERVE SYSTEM REGULATION "Q": does indeed legislate in that it *enacts maximum interest rates that may be paid to depositors by member banks on time and demand deposits.*

The U.S. Constitution gives only Congress this power (above). Regulation "Q" is also a violation of U.S. Anti-Trust Laws, prohibiting the conspiratorial *fixing* of fees, rates and commissions — punishable by fines and imprisonment. Unless you're an International Banker.

One must conjecture why Congress does not repeal the

Federal Reserve Act. It has that right — indeed the DUTY. Why does the Judiciary not rule on the Act's clear-cut unconstitutionality? The answer is obvious. Under a democratic form of government, rather than the Republic our Fore Fathers designed, second-rate Congressmen are elected by mob and media. Federal judges, appointed for life, are selfserving, venal, subject to special interest groups and bribery. They adore living in Hollywood-on-the-Potomac, their fatcat salaries, the perks, the pomp and splendor, the easy pickings. They fear the power of the ILLUMINATI purse. They fear the FED, the ADL, the IRS and what happens to patriots. They fear MARXISM/LIBERALISM/JEWRY. They fear the MEDIA. They love their jobs and don't want to lose them. Where else can sycophants and cowards make so much loot and enjoy so much prestige? Above all else Congressmen love to spend your money ("tax, tax, tax; spend, spend, spend; elect, elect, elect!" Harry Hopkins' advice to FDR's New Dealers). The FED, of course, grows irritable when Congress doesn't borrow and spend. Ergo, Congress' ploy is to profit by the scam while keeping constituents ignorant in La-La-Land.

> Misunderstandings about money have been and continue to be intentional. They derive neither from the nature of money nor from any stupidity of the public... the International Usurocracy aims at preserving intact the public's ignorance of the Usurocratic System and its workings...
>
> EZRA POUND (placed naked in a cage by JEWS who called HIM insane).

Let's take a closer look at the Federal Reserve System your

elected representatives are too ignorant, or too frightened to do anything about.

> Let me issue and control a nation's money and I care not who makes its Laws.
>
> ANSELM MEYER ROTHSCHILD.

Salient Facts About the Federal Reserve System (FED): The FED is not a United States Government agency. It is a private stock company (corporation) patterned after the Bank of England, and other Rothschild central banks. The FED, established by Congress, is privately controlled; its notes are legal tender but are debts of the U.S. government, owed to the Bankers. Commercial paper and government securities are used as fractional reserves to create debt credit. The currency in your wallet represents government debtcredit which is satisfied by your income taxes; you also pay income taxes on the interest your debt-money earns if invested. In sum:

1.   The FED is a privately owned corporation. The word "Federal" is as meaningless, as 'Federal' Tire Company.

2.   The FED operates independently of the Legislative, Executive and Judicial Branches of the U.S. government.

3.   The FED's books have never been independently audited. It refuses U.S. government audit (GAO).

4.   The FED is NOT an agency of the U.S. government, although it was created by Congress, and theoretically can be abolished by Congress. It owns personal property and real estate. Its employees do not draw U.S.

Government paychecks.

5.   The U.S. President, with approval of the Senate, appoints the FED Board of Governors. The majority of them are Wall Street denizens with ILLUMINATI connections. Many are CFR/TRI members. After all, the FED was designed by bankers for bankers.

6.   After deducting operating expenses (?) the FED returns what it considers surplus earnings (?) to the U.S. Treasury.

7.   FED member banks (Chase-Manhattan for example) hold billions of dollars in U.S. Securities (for which they paid nothing), as reserves for loans on which they charge full interest. They return NO profits to the U.S. Treasury.

8.   Member banks use these fractional reserves to extend credit, from 10 to 30 times the amount of the reserves.

9.   Owners of FED Class-A stock have never been revealed. Educated guesses indicate that the following are the largest stockholders: The House of Rothschild, JEWS; Lazar Freres Bank of Paris, JEWS; The Schiff family, Kuhn-Loeb Co., JEWS (U.S. Vice President Al Gore's blonde daughter recently married a Schiff. They "sell" more than the Lincoln bedroom at White House fund raisers); The Lehmann family, JEWS; The Rockefellers; Israel Seif, London, JEWS; The Bank of England, JEWS, etc.

10.   The Federal Open Market Committee (FOMC) is the System's most important policy making body. Composed of the seven members of the Board of Governors, and four member bank presidents, plus the

President of the New York FED Bank, FOMC buys and sells government securities, and oversees the System's foreign exchange. FOMC determines the discount rate charged member banks thereby determining interest rates you pay your lender.

11.   Because changes in interest rates, and the amount of money placed in circulation, have profound affects upon the economy, advance notice (leaks) of forthcoming changes in FED policy would be of tremendous advantage to investors. FED advance policies are, therefore, a closely guarded secret. But is absolute security maintained? Do you believe in the Tooth Fairy? Or do members of the Board of Governors, who serve at the ILLUMINATI'S pleasure, perform as conduits of highly sensitive information? No wonder the skyline of every major city is dominated by banking houses. Since Greed has replaced Honor, Money buys anything — Presidents and Prime Ministers, Popes and prelates, Congressmen and Judges.

12.   The FED is one of many ILLUMINATI central banking systems embedded like fat leeches in World population streams.

13.   At this writing the United States (We the People) are over Six Trillion Dollars in debt. Men in debt labor for others.

> Henry Ford thinks it's stupid and so do I, that for the loan of (its) own money... the United States should be compelled to pay...interest. People who will not turn a shovel of dirt nor contribute a pound of material will collect more money from the United States than all the people who supply all the material and do all the work...why must we pay interest to money-brokers for the use of our own money!
> THOMAS A. EDISON, re Congress borrowing from FED.

There is no dispute about the fact that our economy is built by bankers lending money that they do not possess, never have possessed, and never will possess, on the calculation that they will not be asked for that money in notes, coin or gold...

CHRISTOPHER HOLLIS, "The Breakdown of Money."

We now see that while the basic purpose of money is a means of exchange and a storage of value, the ILLUMINATI distorted that original purpose. Money has become a private MONOPOLY, a COMMODITY, and a means of COERCION. Through the FED's ability to issue our nation's currency as DEBT; to expand or contract the amount of money in circulation (M-1) at will; and to raise or lower interest rates at will, it creates so-called business cycles (boom-bust periods) allowing its masters, ILLUMINATI, to control the vitality of World nation-states and, when necessary, punish them for insubordination (Germany, Rhodesia (Zimbabwe), Austria, Iraq, Libya, and South Africa for example).

THE FED: UNLAWFUL AND TREASONOUS ACTIVITY — AMERICA'S MONEY BORROWED INTO EXISTENCE

When Congress needs money it borrows from the FED. The loans must be paid back — principal plus interest — by the tax-payers. However, no debt-free money is created with which to pay the interest which must be paid out of the money-supply (M-1) which is debt-money! This is similar to paying off interest on your Visa Credit Card account, by using your

Master Card. It's the Old Testament trick of robbing Peter to pay Paul. Payment of principal and interest withdraws money from circulation creating a money shortage. Additional money must be borrowed into circulation with which to pay the interest, creating additional debt.

FEDERAL RESERVE SYSTEM SCAM

Borrowing to Pay 6% Simple Interest on Original $100 Debt[3]

Year Borrowed	Original Debt at Year's	Interest Due Year's	Money In Circulation (M-1)
1	$100.00 $100.00	$6.00	$100.00
2	" 106.00	6.36	"
3	" 112.36	6.74	"
4	" 119.10	7.15	"
5	" 126.25	7.57	"
50[4]	" 1,737.75	104.25	"

Under the FED it is mathematically impossible for American citizens to satisfy the enormous debt owed the International Banking cartel. Admittedly, the FED pays to the U.S. Treasury a pittance of its annual profit but that doesn't mitigate against the scam.

Earnings on U.S. Government securities held by the 12 Banks of the FED amounted in 1972 to $3,771,209,607. These earnings provided the bulk of System income for the year — $3,792,334,523 ...$3,231

---

[3] At no time can the debt be paid off with the money in circulation!

[4] When the debt (in the above hypothetical) is carried to the 50th year, all the money in circulation is insufficient to pay interest alone much less the principal.

million was paid into the U.S. Treasury last year as "interest on Federal Reserve notes."

FED BOARD OF GOVERNORS,
to Senator Alan Cranston, 6-20-73.

Compound Interest: nothing more surely typifies JEWISHNESS than compound interest. Albert Einstein, JEW, said whoever invented the formula was a genius. Charles Lindbergh, Sr., Thomas Edison, and all who detest USURY say "compound interest is Satanical." For example, when you contract for a $40,000 home mortgage payable in 30-years at 15% interest. At the end of the term you will have paid the bank $182,080.80 P&I. All the banker does is make a ledger entry. If you must sell your home before term (Americans move every 7-years on the average) you find there is little equity to show for your monthly mortgage payments. *It takes 24-years to pay-off just one-half the principal!* Most of your money in the early years goes toward interest (interest deductions allowed are negligible). Upon purchasing another home you must commence new mortgage payments all over again. If you are unlucky and can't meet the payments your friendly banker forecloses and walks away with your down-payment and whatever else he can filch.

Fractional Reserve System — Bankers' Gravy Train

The Federal Reserve Board of Governors (FBG) determines the reserve requirement for member banks — thus determining the amount of money placed in circulation. Suppose a bank has Reserve Deposit

Credits of $10,000. If the Reserve Ratio is 15% it can create loans totaling $56,666! If the Reserve Ratio is 20% it can create loans totaling $40,000 (Remember pawnshop dealer Amschel Mayer Bauer, JEW, Frankfort, Germany).

Here is how the theft works:

1)   When   Rockefeller's   Chase-Manhattan   Bank requires $5-million currency, it simply enters a credit of $5-million to the U.S. Treasury.

2)   The treasury delivers government securities in that amount to the bank. The bank pays for them with a check drawn on credit based on the new securities just delivered from the treasury!

3)   Using these new securities (or commercial paper) ChaseManhattan orders the currency from the New York FED which in turn orders the Bureau of Printing and Engraving to print the new currency.

4)   Upon completing the transaction — which cost the bank not one penny — Chase-Manhattan can advance to its customers up to $45million (10% Reserve Ratio) in new credit at the prevailing interest rates. All of this new credit is created out of thin air!

> The banks — commercial banks and Federal Reserve — create all the money of this nation, and the nation and its people pay interest on every dollar of that newly created money. Which means that private banks exercise unconstitutionally, immorally, and ridiculously the power to tax the people. For every newly created dollar dilutes to some extent the value of every other dollar already in circulation.
>
> JERRY VOORHIS, U.S. Congress, CA-D., 1946.

No one has the right to be a moneylender save him who has it to lend.

THOMAS JEFFERSON.

PATMAN: Mr. Eccles, how do you get the money to buy those two billions of government securities?

ECCLES: We created it.

PATMAN: Out of what?

ECCLES: Out of our right to issue credit money.

HOUSE BANKING AND CURRENCY COMMITTEE
hearing, 1941.

It is the influx of this fiat money that causes the American citizen's hard-earned cash to lose its purchasing power. That is inflation. That is usury. That is how TALMUDIC KHAZARS have debased U.S. currency.

When a bank makes a loan it simply adds to the borrower's deposit account in the bank...The money is not taken from anyone else's deposit; it was not previously paid into the bank by anyone. It's new money, created by the bank for the use of the borrower.
SEC'Y TREASURY ANDERSON, "U.S. News & WR", 8-3159.

In purchasing offerings of Government bonds the banking system as a whole creates new money, or bank deposits. When the banks buy a billion dollars of Government bonds as they are offered...the banks credit the deposit account of the Treasury with a billion dollars. They debit their Government bond account a billion dollars, or they actually create, by a bookkeeping entry, a billion dollars.
MARRINER ECCLES, Chairman Board of Governors, FED, 1935.

The government should create, issue and circulate all currency and credit needed to satisfy the spending power of Government and the buying power of consumers. The privilege of creating and issuing money is the supreme prerogative of Government.

ABRAHAM LINCOLN.

Can anything be more absurd than that a nation should apply to an individual (Rothschild) to maintain its credit, and with its credit its existence as an empire, and its comfort as a people...

BENJAMIN DISRAELI, JEW,
Prime Minister, Great Britain.

The United Nations Rip-Off: Henry Morganthau, JEW, Secretary of the Treasury under FDR ("Some of my best friends are Communists") appointed his protege Harry Dexter White (Weiss), JEW, UnderSecretary of the Treasury. White, later exposed as a Soviet spy, stole U.S. Treasury plates giving them to Bolsheviks in the Soviet Union. This explains why millions of JEWS who illegally entered the United States during WWII arrived with healthy bankrolls and proceeded to purchase American property and businesses while Aryan Americans were fighting genocidal wars in Europe. White, at the Bretton Woods Agreements (1944), was credited with creation of the World Bank; and the International Monetary Fund, designed to "stabilize the International economy." Americans contribute billions of tax-dollars annually to these U.N. (One World) related organizations which extend low interest rate loans to foreign governments for "development purposes." In fact loans are issued to assure that foreign states will have funds available to satisfy loans previously contracted with International Bankers. In effect, the U.S. Government guarantees these foreign loans made by International Bankers in event of default! Thus, Bankers enjoy any profits resulting from their high-risk loans while America takes any losses. For many years Robert Strange McNamarra presided over the World Bank. Recently (1997) he apologized to the American people for his lies and mismanagement, as U.S. Sec'y of Defense, of the Viet Nam "police action." White's mentor, Henry Morganthau, Jr., JEW, is best remembered for the Morganthau Plan designed to reduce Germany to a pastoral state. When told his plan would cause millions of German deaths he said, "What the hell do I care about the German people!"

CONGRESSIONAL RECORD (Excerpted)

LOUIS T. McFADDEN, Chr. House Banking & Currency Committee:

Mr. Chairman, we have in this country one of the most corrupt institutions the world has ever known. The Federal Reserve Board has cheated the United States out of enough money to pay the national debt...Mr. Speaker, it is a monstrous thing for this great Nation to have its destiny presided over by a treasonous system acting in secret concert with International pirates and userers. Every effort has been made by the FED to conceal its power. But the truth is the FED has usurped the government of the United States. It controls everything here. It controls foreign relations. It makes and breaks governments at will. (10 June 1932).

Mr. Chairman...there is a condition in the United States Treasury which would cause American citizens, if they knew what it was, to lose all confidence in their government...a condition President Roosevelt will not have investigated. Mr. Morganthau has brought with him from Wall Street James Warburg, son of Paul Warburg, head of the Manhattan Bank (and chief architect of the Federal Reserve System)....James

Warburg is the son of a former partner of Kuhn-Loeb Co., a grandson of another partner, and a nephew of a present partner. He holds no office in our government but...is in daily attendance at the Treasury, and that he has private quarters there. In other words, Kuhn-Loeb Co.) now occupies the United States Treasury. (29 May 1933).

Mr. Chairman, understanding that Henry Morganthau, who is related to Herbert Lehman, Jewish governor of New York, and is related by marriage or otherwise to the Seligmans of the International Jewish firm of J&W Seligman, who were publicly shown before a Senate Committee of Investigation to have offered a bribe to a foreign government; and to the Warburgs, whose connection through the Kuhn-Loeb Co., and the **Bank of Manhattan** and other foreign and domestic institutions under their control, have drained billions of dollars out of the U.S. Treasury; and to the Strausses, proprietors of R.H. Macy & Co., of New York, which is an outlet for goods dumped upon this country at the government's expense... and that Mr. Morganthau is likewise related or otherwise connected to the Jewish Banking Community of New York, London, Amsterdam and other financial centers, and that he has as his assistant presiding over public funds, Earl Bailie, a member of the firm J&W Seligman, bribe givers as aforesaid — it seems to me that Henry Morganthau's presence in the United States Treasury, and the request now give him $200-million of the people's money for gambling purposes, is a striking conformation of other speeches I have made on this floor (24 June 1934).

Some people think Federal Reserve Banks are United States Government institutions. They are not Government institutions. They are private credit monopolies which prey upon the people of the United States for the benefits of themselves and their foreign customers; foreign and domestic speculators and swindlers; and rich and predatory money lenders. In that dark crew of financial pirates there are those who would cut a man's throat to get a dollar out of his pocket; there are those who send money into states to buy votes to control our legislation; and there are those that maintain an international propaganda for deceiving us...that will permit them to cover up their past misdeeds and set again in motion their gigantic train of crime... (10 June 1932)

Congressman Louis T. McFadden is a true American hero. His investigations struck directly at the heart of the ILLUMINATI which, in the 1930s, was plotting the war against Germany and Hitler's economic barter-system. McFadden received scant attention from the press although he endured a barrage of threats, obscene phone calls, and had been shot at. At a banquet in our nation's capitol where he was key-noted to speak upon the full implications of his investigations of the FED he, enjoying good health, suddenly was seized with paroxysms and died on the spot. There was the usual bungled autopsy that follows the deaths of U.S. government personages.

The privilege of creating and issuing money is... The supreme prerogative of Government.

ABRAHAM LINCOLN.

CONGRESSIONAL RECORD HOUSE
INVESTIGATING COMMITTEE

Secret Minutes of Federal Reserve Banks Disclose Clandestine and Illegal Behavior.
(Excerpts 24 May 1977)

Rep. REUSS, JEW, Chrm. Committee Banking and Financing.

We have tried everything from moral suasion to attempts at complete audit of the FED by the General Accounting Office. Our efforts — handicapped by *the FED S all-encompassing claim of independence* have yielded only sporadic results. We have never been able to obtain full and complete information about the various activities of the FED. (REUSS EXPLAINS THAT AFTER MUCH EFFORT HIS COMMITTEE WAS ABLE TO GET PARTIAL MINUTES OF

SEVERAL FED MEETINGS FOR THE YEARS 1972-75, Ed.)

What these minutes reveal about the operations of the FED...is disturbing. Even with 904 deletions (in the minutes) made by the FED dealing with "sensitive matters" these minutes raise the most serious questions about the use of power and money.

The minutes reveal:

1. When Congressional legislation that would have subjected the FED to close scrutiny...was under consideration, the FED used the Board of Directors of its Reserve Banks in a lobbying campaign against the legislation (the FED contacted major corporations who depend upon banks to conduct business urging the corporation executives to threaten withdrawal of political contributions if their Congressmen supported legislation to investigate the FED!) (EXTORTION).

2. The FED encouraged Commercial Banks to make loans to favored recipients while denying it was doing so. (COERCION). 3. The FED permitted a Board of Governors director to vote on matters in which his law firm had vested interests. (COLLUSION).

3. The FED made unsubsidized loans to its own employees. (MALPRACTICE).

4. The FED permitted Directors to vote themselves gifts., (EMBEZZLEMENT).

Anyone of these activities by itself would be cause for concern. Taken together they form a pattern of decision for public accountability. *They show a history of behind the scenes manipulation to ward off legitimate investigations by Congress.* (End Report)

The above report resulted in the dismissal of Chairman of the Board of Governors, Arthur Burns (Burnstein), JEW, who was discreetly kicked upstairs by the ILLUMINATI and made Ambassador to Germany! The Committee avoided disclosure of TREASONOUS ACTIVITY engaged in by the FED, during the years covered by the report (See Chapter 3: ILLUMINATI), when the FED was busy financing Soviet industry during the "Cold War", and our men were dying in Viet Nam.

> There can be no doubt of the fact that finance has already more than half enslaved the world and few, if any, individuals, corporations, or even nations can afford to displease the Money Power.
> PROF. FREDERICK SODDY, M.A., F.R.S.., Oxford.

CONGRESSIONAL RECORD
House of Representatives

HENRY GONZALES, Chairman House Banking Committee.

Mr. Chairman, we are being held hostage President, Congress, and the People by this runaway Board of Governors... I have been a member of the Banking Committee for 20-years... and at no time have we ever had a Chairman or any member of the FED Board show a willingness to show an accounting of its methods, judgments, policies, and procedures... made in camera... in the so-called Open Market Committee (FOMC), which is really a secret committee which in effect determines the policies that can make or break any administration in power...Mr. Volcker says, "These policies (his) will result in the dimunition of the standard of living for some Americans." Well, which? David Rockefeller? Chase-Manhattan Bank had a lot to do with determining the very resolution passed out of this House with respect to Poland (Poland could not repay its debts to American banks)...and Congress reacts immediately: Five Billion Dollars to the *International Monetary Fund (IMF)* so it can help payments to Chase-Manhattan Bank!...Mr. Volcker does not cut-back there...that is not inflationary. But he says such things as home-loans, loans to the U.S. farmer...or to small U.S. cities for drainage...for food-stamps...that is inflationary and must be cut out. (2 March 1982).

If the FED is, as the Governors claim, a governmental agency and not an unconstitutional usurper acting illegally, then whenever the FED creates money as it does in order to would dictate that in such a case the debt would be canceled and the bonds destroyed like burning a mortgage when the house is paid off. But this does not happen.

REP. JERRY VOORHIS, CA-D, *"The Mysteries of the FED"*, 1981.

Heads of the world's Central Banks are themselves not substantive powers in world finance... they are the technicians and agents of powerful, dominant men: investment bankers who raised them to power and can just as easily throw them down. POWER is with the unincorporated Investment Bankers behind the scenes. These formed a system of International cooperation and dominance which was more private, more secret than that of their agents in the Central Banks.

PROF. CARROLL QUIGLEY, *"Tragedy and Hope"*.

Carroll Quigley, a proponent of One World Government, was considered an "insider". His book was meant to be a paean to the ILLUMINATI but he told too much. Initially, the book was firmly suppressed and pulled from the stacks. Quigley, a Professor at Georgetown U., died shortly thereafter. President Clinton, in his acceptance address, referred to Quigley as *"my mentor"*.

Congress can pass laws affecting the general economy after long and serious debate; but the FED can sit in a brief session and nullify all of these entirely.

DR. M. A. LARSON, *"The FED and Our Manipulated Dollar."*

Only the Federal government can take a perfectly good piece of paper, smear ink on it, and make it absolutely worthless.

LUDWIG VON MISES.

With the understanding that commercial banks, as a Chase-Manhattan; and International Bankers as Kuhn-Loeb Co., are integral parts of JEWRY'S World Banking Empire, let us take a look at an investigation by the State of

New York of some commercial banks:

NEW YORK STATE ASSEMBLY

WILLIAM H. HADDAD, Attorney, State of New York.

Mr. Chairman, it is the purpose of this report to outline the pervasive deliberations of two committees (for the Banks). Other evidence comes from the examination of the records...of Chase-Manhattan Bank which voluntarily allowed us to review *selected (Bank) material...* shortly before they, and all banks, simultaneously stopped cooperating with this inquiry.

There is no doubt that all these men knew precisely what was happening in this City... The banks were clearly over-extended in City Securities and in view of the bankers' unanimous belief about the eventual default of the City, the pressure on these banks to unload their debt-paper by any means must have been irresistible...

The banks bailed out in three ways: 1. They sold extraordinary amounts of Municipal Securities from their own portfolios. 2. They did not replace matured-out Municipal Securities - a reversal of previous practices. 3. They sold *for the first time* new and older City Securities to non-institutional and non-professional investors *without disclosing the risk they foresaw...*

Precisely, the banks sold New York City securities to small individual investors and they did so without disclosing their inside information as to the City's financial condition.... In one classic situation a doctor had recently sold her apartment... went to a bank rather than her broker to invest money... she was sold securities the bank was unloading... Yet the bank never disclosed this fact to her.... In her view the bank was a neutral and impartial middleman acting on the highest ethical principals.

Some of the banks were required to unload their portfolios because their poor investments in REITS, tankers, and under developed countries placed them in a financially precarious position. According to the minutes at the second meeting held at Gracie Mansion (the Mayor's dwelling) Mr. Horowitz, Solomon Bros., pointed out "The City has lost the institutional market... although the banks will continue their assitance, out-of-city-banks have stopped buying the City's obligations".

In the minutes of the Chase-Manhattan's Planning Committee was the statememt: "We are continuing to sell New York City obligations at every opportunity". The strategy called for sales even if a loss was sustained. Thank you. **(End Excerpts Haddad Report)**

You will not be surprised to learn that the Securities Exchange Commission (SEC) exonerated all parties of culpability involved in the promotion and sales of the worthless New York City Municipal Bonds. This is not an isolated case. More, it is an indictment of the mind-set of International Bankers who always place monetary profit above ethics.

Tob Shebbe Goyim Harog!

TALMUD: Sanhedrin.

The Tree of Liberty is nourished with the blood of tyrants; It is its natural manure.

THOMAS JEFFERSON.

The State monetary authorities can supply the needs of the People and provide for all work useful to the State to a limit imposed by the availabilies of raw materials and the People's brain-power and muscle-power, without having to ask permission from the Usurer.

EZRA POUND, "Impact".

The panic of 1907 was caused by the deliberate contraction of the currency and credit; the panics of 1920-21 and 1929-35 were due to the same identical cause. There can be no doubt about it; and those behind it went so far that they openly disclosed to the country the plan and purpose, which forever put the plan on public records. It can never be erased.

ROBERT S. OWEN, U.S. Sen., Congressional Record, 3-18-32.

The record shows that in May 1920, by a drastic increase in its rediscount rate (interest rate the FED charges banks) one of history's sharpest declines in business activity and collapse in prices was deliberately brought about. The result was a desperate depression America never recovered from, despite FDR's liberal New Deal, until the creation of WW II and U.S. factories started to churn again. *This was the ILLUMINATI ploy to prepare America for war with Germany which was happy and prospering after Hitler kicked out the JEW usurers and Marxists.*

> By all these means we shall so wear down the goyim that they will be compelled to offer us international power of a nature that will enable us without violence gradually to absorb all the state forces of the world and to form a super government.
>
> THE PROTOCOLS, Section V.

SOME ACCOMPLISHMENTS
OF THE FEDERAL RESERVE SYSTEM

	1913	1982
Federal Debt	1.2 Billion	1.5 Trillion[5]
Pers. Inc. Tax	3.0 Million	200 Billion
Value of Dollar	100 Cents	7 Cents
Property owned by FED	negligible	700 Billion
Cost loaf of bread	10 Cents	65 Cents
Cost ton of coal	14 Dollars	35 Dollars

Because Congress did not delegate its legislative authority over Standard weights and measures, today: One ton = 2000 lbs. One foot = 12 inches. To pay-off a One Trillion Dollars debt at the rate of One dollar per second would require 31,682 years (not including interest).

---

[5] 1998Federal Debt is over <u>6-Trillion dollars!</u>

What about "successful" Americans who have retired with generous annuities, and pensions? The system has been pretty good to them you say. Yes, that is their reward for going along with the system, not raising any dust. Not asking any questions. *"Kissing ass"*. What they *have done* is mortgage the United States of America in exchange for a condominium on the golf course. Their sons, daughters and grandchildren will foot the bill as miscegenated brown sheep under One World Dictate. Never forget: DEBT IS SLAVERY! And, unless you are a banker, you pay it back in blood, toil, tears and sweat.

> By the end of this decade we will live under the first One World Government that has ever existed in the society of nations.
>
> POPE JOHN PAUL II,
> "Keys of this Blood", by Malachi Martin

CHAPTER 5

SPIROCHETES OF JEW SYPHILIS

The development of society is subject not to biological Laws (Nature) but to higher social laws. Attempts to spread to humanity the laws of the animal kingdom are an attempt to lower the human being to the level of beasts.

INSTITUTE OF ACADEMY OF SCIENCES, U.S.S.R.

Marxist theory is this century's most influential system of thought.
ZBIGNIEW BRZEZINSKI, "Between Two Ages."

The Hatred that formed the core of Marxism is present in the new religion (Freudianism) also. In both cases it is the hate of the outsider for his totally alien surroundings, which he cannot change, and therefore must destroy.

FRANCIS PARKER YOCKEY, *Imperium.*

In the language... of myth, vomit is the correlative and inverse term of coitus; and defecation is the correlative and inverse term to auditory communication.

CLAUDE LEVI-STRAUSS, JEW, Freudian.

The Old Testament apocalyptics of Marxism...the anthropomorphic symbolism of Freud sat well with a religious people looking for a replacement for a dying, anachronistic faith. It was a godsend when Boas arrived...and obligingly declared that all races are equal.

WILMOT ROBERSTSON, *The Dispossessed Majority.*

THE 20TH CENTURY is called the bloodiest century. It also has been called the AGE OF LIES because KHAZAR JEWS devised a program, backed by immense financial resources, through which they took control of America's MASS-MEDIA (*the technology that made those remarkable systems possible — printing, electric light, radio, television, photography, motion-pictures, recording, transistors, computers, satellites, etc. — are all Aryan inventions*).

The capture of America's communications systems by an alien nation is a theft of such critical implications that it boggles the mind. The free-flow of ideas and information envisioned by our Founding Fathers, essential to our Republic is filtered first through the minds of TALMUDIC MEDIA MOGULS who promulgate only what they want you and your children to know. The First Amendment to the Constitution of the United States has been abrogated. America dies from lack of FACTS. Instead, mass-media propaganda, misinformation, disinformation and filth is the deadly poison daily fed to the West: "applause tracks" included.

Therefore, when the charlatans MARX, FREUD, and BOAS (all JEWS) emerged from the ghettos of Europe, it was to be expected that they would be bank-rolled by the ILLUMINATI and promoted enthusiastically by America's mass-media as saviors of Western Civilization! When in fact THEY WERE ITS INTENDED DESTROYERS. Their apparent objectives concealed their subterranean goals.

MARX attacked the Natural order of Mankind — rule by the Best. FREUD aimed at poisoning the Aryan mind. BOAS attacked the White gene-pool. Research produced by these Satanical quacks supporting their hypotheses was totally subjective. Facts were considered irrelevant: the end justified the means. It is improbable that they actually believed their own theories. In one of his widely known letters to Engels, his coconspirator, Marx accurately describes Das Kapital as "full of shit." Surely Freud and Boas had similar opinions of their own thaumaturgical garbage. In the end they were simply KHAZARS engaged in a battle of envy, hate and revenge against the Aryan West. William G. Simpson, *Which Way Western Man?*, refers to their TALMUDIC ideologies as "spirochetes of JEW syphilis."

MARXISM

KARL MARX, JEW (1818-1883), was born in Germany, grandson of a rabbi; he converted to Protestantism, married a Gentile of petite nobility; then, suffering cultural alienation, he abandoned his wife, family and Christianity. His compulsion was to destroy the Aryan society that had rejected him. His contribution to the World Revolutionary Movement was immense.

Marx's strategy was to instill HATRED between the classes where it was non-existent before. The theme underlying his political ideology is: *all History, all Life, is economic class warfare.* The two warring classes are the Proletariat (labor), the good guys; versus the Capitalists (Bourgeoisie), exploiters of the proletariat. Capitalism is evil. Therefore every vestige of Capitalism must be eliminated: "Expropriation of the expropriator" (what's yours is mine); and "all infected animals" will be destroyed (i.e, Tob Shebbe Goyim Harog!). The "Dictate of the proletariat" will be established, Marx promises, which eventually will give way to a stateless, classless, godless society wherein everyone is equal (no Christians allowed, however' and "anti-Semitism" (HATE) is a crime!). Marx anticipated Franz Boas, JEW, in his conviction that *Man s accomplishments are simply a reflection of environment.* Ergo, qualities of human intelligence, personality, behavior, emotional and spiritual life, are determined by Man's economic position. *Man, he assures us, is an animal shaped by lust for money: the Idea of State and Nation (Race) is ludicrous.* There are only self-interested individuals, classes and groups that hate one another.

MARX formulated his anti-nature ideology by borrowing, out of context, ideas from two Aryan philosophers: the great Georg W. Friedrich Hegel (1770-1831); and Ludwig A. Feuerbach (1804-1872), who is remembered primarily for his influence on Marx and Sartre.

HEGEL believed that Man's salvation would come through Reason. He believed that Reason operated according to the Dialectical Method, in which an Idea (Thesis) is challenged by its opposite (Antithesis), and the two subsequently metamorphose into an interfused Whole (Synthesis). Hegel saw this method working in logic; in World history; in management of the State; and in the establishing the Spirit of the Age. Hegel, an idealist who would have ridiculed Marx, believed the Dialectic *produced harmonious and continuous evolution within the Nation-State and between its component parts*. FEUERBACH, a materialist, said man is what he eats: matter in motion, nothing more. This concept appears, also, in Freud's and Boas' rantings.

Marx stated there is no God therefore man is not accountable for his acts to some divine Judge. Man is without soul or free-will therefore without significant individual value. He is an evolutionary animal dependent upon his mind (Reason) for salvation. Marx believed Man's destiny is determined solely by his environment (*Marx, apparently, never learned of his nemesis,* Gregor Johann Mendel (18221884), after whom *Mendelism* is named — the study of all things Genetic). In nature everything is evolving because everything is determined by its opposite: ergo, the thesis synthesizes with the antithesis thus becoming a new and different thesis — this process repeats itself *ad infinitum*. In society, therefore, conflict (Dialectical Materialism) is inevitable, essential and continuous until the entire structure (State) collapses. Because this fate is inevitable, and change is progress, why wait? Revolt. Now. Destroy! Kill! Bourgeoisie v. Proletariat = Revolution = dictate = ONE WORLD JEW GOVERNMENT. The ILLUMINATI sponsors Marxists/ Anarchists.

> There are times when creation can be achieved only through destruction. The urge to destroy, then, is a creative urge.
>
> MICHAEL BAKUNIN, Marxist.

"Bourgeoisie" is a JEW code-word for successful goyim: more specifically, for successful middleclass WHITEMEN. The Bourgeoisie, according to Marx, possess everything but are entitled to nothing. While the proletariat possess nothing but are entitled to everything. This is also a Christian concept: "The last shall be first." Albeit, Marx neglected to mention that the Dialectic insists the proletariat, too, shall be replaced! The masses are too ignorant to question the Pied Piper, but they very much like the idea of immediate EQUALITY (see de Tocqueville).

The victory of the proletariat will abolish all classes except for one: "The dictate of the proletariate." And what or who is that? The Dictate are privileged JEWS who will preside over the proletarian State. The State will own the farms businesses, industries, palaces, town-houses and dachas, expropriated from the filthy bourgeois! The Dictate will also own the Gulag, which will be filled with prols. As George Orwell, perspicaciously pointed out in his book *Animal Farm*: *Every one is equal — but some are more equal than others.*

> Marxism is simultaneously a victory of the external, active man, over the inner, passive man; and a victory of reason over belief... Americas is undergoing a revolution...(that) unmasks its obsolescence...by the year 2000 it will be accepted that Robspierre and Lenin were mild reformers.
>
> Z. BRZEZINSKI, "Between Two Worlds";
> CFR/TRI, Prof. Georgetown U.,
> advisor to U.S. President Jimmy Carter.

> We Jews, we the destroyers, will remain the destroyers for ever. Nothing that you do will meet our needs and demands. We will forever destroy because we need a world of our own...

MAURICE SAMUELS, "You Gentiles" (1924).

F. P. Yockey, in his suppressed book *Imperium*, notes that MARXISM is seriously flawed because MARX, being a JEW, could not understand the real differences between CAPITALISM and SOCIALISM, which emanated from the WESTERN CULTURE-ORGANISM. *Capitalism and Socialism are how a Nation (Family, People, Race) feels, thinks, and lives*, and secondarily are ECONOMIC CONCEPTS. One is past history; the other, WESTERN SOCIALISM, represents the future of the West, and the end of JEWRY on Western soil.

The Age of Reason produced CAPITALISM in the West, the IDEA of rugged individualism: "Every Man for Himself." Freedom from authority: "Don't tread on me!" At the same time, paradoxically, it was understood, that these rugged individuals should act in the best interest of the Nation-State. To the West ECONOMIC CAPITALISM meant: free trade, no personal income-tax, no state interference in money matters, private ownership, etc. USURY, however, was relegated outside the Pale, and proscribed.

Capitalists found no fault with economically defeating, within the law, opposing economic groups. That was considered "healthy competition." European States, goaded by Bankers, also competed with one another. Often with disastrous results. During WWI it became painfully clear that the IDEA of "rugged individualism" worked against the ARYAN NATION and its individual States.

WESTERN   SOCIALISM,   unlike Marxism/Communism and Capitalism, emanates not from Reason alone but from the ETHOS OF THE WEST. It expresses the instinctive and Intuitive feelings UNIQUE to the Aryan Nation. Its Idea is the Musketeers' cry: "One for All and All for One!" The ingathering of the White Nation-States into ONE CULTURAL ORGANISM — its own territory and its own State in which to house, protect, and nurture the Nation — precludes Marxist inspired class warfare and hate-struggles between its component parts. The ECONOMY springs from the CULTURE. MONEY becomes merely a tool, a means of exchange, a storage of value — not an ILLUMINATI weapon.

> To Socialism money-possession is not the determinant of rank in society any more than it is in the Army. Social rank in Socialism does not follow Money but authority (ability).
> FRANCIS PARKER YOCKEY, *Imperium*

World-class thinkers of all disciplines agree, MARXISM and the Age of Reason have come to an ignominious deadend. No intelligent person took MARX seriously. His Old Testament idea that work is evil — and New Testament idea that men and races are equally endowed — opposes Nature and the very Soul of the West. The carrot offered "Workers of the World" was immediate EQUALITY in exchange for their dumb obedience. After the "expropriation" they would "lose their chains" and retire into La-La land; to be served and supported forever by survivors of the hated middle-class! (as in the United States, Europe, and South Africa today).

As a propagandist — a seducer of innocents, sophists, Liberals and born losers — MARX was superb. His place in history assured.

3-million unarmed middle-class Russians (priests, proprietors, artists, scientists, farmers, managers, et al.) were slaughtered in the initial thrust of the BOLSHEVIK REVOLUTION, and 31-million died in the aftermath of its JEW TERROR.

Marxists, Bolsheviks, Communists denounce "capitalist pigs." While from behind the scenes — in the on-going battle to implement the PROTOCOLS OF ZION — all wars and revolutions are financed by JEW CAPITALISTS.

> Today it is estimated even by Jacob's grandson, John Schiff (Kuhn-Loeb Co.), a prominent member of New York Society, that the old man sank about $20-million for the final triumph of Bolshevism in Russia.
> CHOLLY KNICKERBOCKER,
> "N.Y. Journal-American", 23-49.

FREUD

Today, Sigmund Freud, JEW (1856-1939), is known only for his anti-cultural significance. And for the severe damage he inflicted upon the Western psyche before his hoax was revealed. Freud like Marx attempted to lump all men together as equals, stripped of any noble or spiritual, significance. *The two JEWS simply used different methods to accomplish a singular purpose, the ILLUMINATI purpose: Destruction of the West.*

When Freud was a young doctor a Viennese psychologist described to him the case-history of a patient who, while under hypnosis, related a traumatic event in her life that continued to cause her anxiety. Upon being released from hypnosis her anxiety was completely cured. Freud, like Saul of Tarsus, JEW, on the road to Damascus, suddenly saw "possibilities" and opened a "head-shrinking" business. He abandoned the use of hypnosis and invented psychoanalysis. A method of consultation in which patients, reluctant to reveal their intimate personal problems (resistance), transfer their emotional ties to the analyst.

PSYCHOLOGY is the study of neurosis, psychosis, perversion, and the normal mind. PSYCHOANALYSIS is a treatment. But of what? Symptoms can be diagnosed but the root cause, like the wind, can't be seen. Brain diseases, are physiological, and tangible. But mind diseases originate in the genes and the Soul of Man, two areas Freud knew nothing about, and cared about even less. Psychiatric "couch sessions", like seances (rap sessions) and tea-readings, are clothed in an ambiance of mystery and occult nomenclature. Actually analysis is little more than the power of suggestion. Everyone knows "confession is good for the soul." And a placebo may accomplish miracles. But the Freudian "cure" began with the premise that everyone is neurotic: either perverted or inverted. Ergo, Aryans are sick, too! Just like us JEWS.

> The fundamental problem is that psychoanalysis is the product of JEW animus toward Western Civilization. The unconscious desire of the JEWS is to unmask the respectability of European society...which closed

JEWS out...by dredging up sordid and infantile sexual aberrations.
HOWARD SACHER, JEW. One of the original Freudians.

Ergo, revelations by credulous patients, duped into compliance, relieve the analysts' inferiority-complexes! JEWS (Psychoanalysts) are easily converted to a JEW system.

Since they are unable to understand or participate in Western society they have no choice but to oppose it.
SIGMUND FREUD, JEW, "The Resistance to Psychoanalysis."

Another problem is that JEW psychoanalysts, who more often than not are mentally abnormal, are licensed to determine who is "normal." This is reminiscent of *The Blind Men and the Elephant*. Then there is the "couch problem." Paternity and molestation Law suits against analysts, whose practice is to relieve vulnerable patients of sexual anxieties, are as frequent as L.A. muggings. This is like hiring the pedophiles Woody Allen, JEW, and Roman Polanski, JEW, to baby-sit.

The madness continues as Freud focuses on the Western Soul. He finds it strictly mechanical and totally predictable: *Spiritual impulses are simply sexual impulses*. Therefore, in Freud's TALMUDIC brain all men are EQUAL because they are all sexually neurotic. And he decides what is neurotic! To Karl Marx, Beethoven's *9th Symphony* was Bourgeoisie duplicity. To Freud it expressed Beethoven's latent lust for Schiller. Obviously, *Cultural Man*, the JEWS' enemy, must be eliminated by turning him into an economic robot and animated genitalia!

> A generation ago the leading theory about schizophrenia was...(that it was) caused by cold and distant mothering, itself the mother's unconscious wish that her child had never been born... 20-years later that artifact of the Freudian (JEW) era is entirely discredited.
>
> U.S. NEWS & WORLD REPORT, 4-21-97.

Freud's gimmick: that the Aryan Soul is mechanical, allowed him to invent diseases of the Soul which only he and his JEW disciples could diagnose and cure: neurosis, complexes (especially guilt, and inferiority), repression, perversion, fixation, penile envy, etc. Part of the "cure" was DREAM ANALYSIS, which contains common reoccurring patterns. These patterns have convoluted, esoteric interpretations. But, only *caballa* members understand them and only they can effect the thaumaturgic "cures." The DREAM WORLD reflects Soul "anxiety." For example, to dream of the death of a family member meant you hated one or both of your parents. Freudians conceived another "Original Sin": *all children are sexually perverted*, therefore, because Child is father to the Man, everyone is sexually perverted. EVERYONE IS SICK!

Freudianism is Kabbalistic, encompassing the occult, Satanism, phallisicm, necromancy, numerology, etc., all emanating from Hebraic superstitions, Talmudic lore, and from Freud's cocaine-diseased brain.

Hollywood finds sit-com material

Ever since Sigmund Freud declared that all young boys want to kill their fathers and copulate with their mothers

JEWS have been been waging war against the traditional Aryan family...The latest poison...comes from Drs. Louise B. Silverstein and Carl P. Auerbach (JEWS) in their article "Deconstructing the Essential Father." They write:

"In contrast to neo-conservative perspective, our data on gay fathering couples have convinced us that neither mother nor father is essential"... they agree that children need some "responsible care-taking" adult, but that "one, none, or both...could be a father or mother" with equal degree of effectiveness. Furthermore they deny that "heterosexual marriage is the social context in which responsible fathering is most likely to occur." Silverstein and Auerbach infer that LOVE shared by natural parents and their children is no greater than that shared with foster-parents — whether queer, straight, or the same race. In their MARXIST/LIBERAL/ TALMUDIC world, all "caretakers" are equal. Therefore, natural families are equally irrelevant.

REVIEW: THE AMERICAN PSYCHOLOGIST (1-6-99), official journal of the American Psychological Association.

When the Berlin Wall fell (1990) Marxism went down... Freudianism, too, despite its continuing influence...has also come tumbling down. Today the official line is that psychoanalysis is not really a science after all but rather an art form...comparable to flower arrangement or macrame?

JOSEPH EPSTEIN, JEW, editor of *The American Scholar*.

BOASISM

FRANZ BOAS, JEW (1858-1942) was born in Germany. As Marx and Freud he was a KHAZAR, distinguished by his repellent physical ugliness. He was not an anthropologist, and where he got his doctorate remains uncertain (Kiel, Ger.?). Albeit, he was appointed professor of Anthropology, Columbia

University, in 1899, remaining there for 40-years. His sponsors undoubtedly were ILLUMINISTS.

Boas' objective was to strike at the heart of the Aryan Race — its gene-pool. To that end he organized the Boas School of CULTURAL ANTHROPOLOGY which presents the doctrine that there are no distinct races; *per contra* it professes that ALL men share EQUAL potential: *racial differences result, largely, from environmental factors rather than from heredity.* This ideology, or pseudo-science, is enthusiastically endorsed by LIBERALS/ MARXISTS/JEWS and is totally disproved by the natural science of Physical Anthropology — accepted by foremost world authorities on the subject. Boas asserts that Race is a myth because the races over eons have intermingled; that mongrel mixtures are better than the parents. They argue that all human blood is the same; all peoples have a common origin; the races are, therefore, akin. No race excels because it is more gifted, or better, but because it has had a more favorable environment and better luck. Because races are equal miscegenation is not only permissible, it is desirable (eliminate the cursed White Race). We are The Family of Man, therefore, ALL MEN ARE EQUAL.

The United Nations gave the Boas Doctrine its unconditional approval:

> The scientific evidence indicates that the range of mental capabilities in all ethnic groups is much the same...As for personality and character, these may be considered raceless...given similar degrees of cultural opportunities to realize their potentialities, the average achievement of members of each ethnic group is about the same.

UNESCO papers, (Excerpt) 1950.

As we have learned, SPIROCHETES OF JEW SYPHILIS (Boasism is one of these) are injected into every society the ILLUMINATI sets out to destroy. But, let me say here and now that *the Boas Doctrine — in its entirety — has been exposed as a fraud!* This will be discussed more fully in Chapter V, *Mendelism*.

Founders of the Boas School of Anthropology were Ashley Montague (Israel Ehrenberg), Raymond Pearl, Melville Herskovitz, Herbert Seligman, Otto Klineberg, Gene Weltfish, Amran Sheinfeld, Isadore Chein, Ruth Benedict, Margaret Meade, and Kenneth Clark. *All but three (Meade, Benedict, and the negro Clark) are JEWS.* Boas was cited by Congress for 46-Communist front affiliations. The subversive activities of Montague, Weltfish, Benedict, and Herskovitz are well known to the CIA, FBI and Congressional investigating committees. All of these MARXISTS/LIBERALS/JEWS, spreading JEW syphilis, established chairs of Cultural Anthropology at America's most prestigious universities.

> During their spurious academic careers Boasites LIED repeatedly, falsified research, bore false witness, slandered, and used all means necessary to achieve their ultimate objective. I knew Franz Boas personally. I was able to observe his influence as founder of the science of anthropology in America. I was also able to observe the increasing degree of control exercised by the Boas cult over students and younger professors until fear or loss of jobs or status was common... unless conformity to the dogma of racial equality was maintained...
>
> DR. H. E. GARRETT, Chr. Dept. of Psychology, Columbia Univ.

PROFESSOR JOHN R. BAKER, Oxford, ("Science and the Planned State") quotes Boasite and Communist scholar Triofim Lysenko, U.S.S.R., who declared that science must be made to support Communist theory; that facts regarding chromosomes and heredity must be suppressed because *"from its conception (genetics) leads to reactionary ideas about race... and it is possible to defend the false basis of Mendelism only by lies."* In the Soviet, proponents of genetics were executed, or imprisoned in the Gulag. (Anti-Semitism was made a crime). The distinction between Mendelism (Nature) and Marxism (ideology) is expressed best in the following lines:

> "Beauty is Truth and Truth is Beauty — that is all ye know upon this earth and all you need to know."
>
> JOHN KEATS, "Ode on a Grecian Urn."

During the WWII Era, MARXISM/LIBERALISM/JEWRY equated Mendelism with Nazism, "racism", and the alleged "Holocaust." Consequently, throughout the West, the Anti-Defamation League of the B'nai B'rith (Sons of the Covenant) made it *verboten* to discuss Genetics in public forum. By the 1980s, however, the vast benefits being made available to Mankind through Mendelism were described in the most prestigious scientific journals, lectures, and so on, making it impossible for the mass-media to conceal the FACTS any longer; one of which is: the Races are inherently unequal. *This irrefutable fact strikes at the heart of MARXISM/ LIBERALISM/JEWRY and their effort to miscegenate the Races and create One World ILLUMINATI Government.* As one might expect the mass-media,

Christian Church, JEWRY and academia continue to promulgate the false doctrines of BOASISM and ignore or decry Mendelism.

> Marxists are self-confessed partisans, their "science" subordinate to their (ideological) commitment. That can hardly do less than prejudice their analysis, their data, hinder free inquiry, and distort their conclusions.
>
> PROF. A. JAMES GREGOR,
> *The Mankind Quarterly* (Spr. '62).

The BOAS proposal that Mankind is composed of interchangeable races equally endowed with courage, intelligence, character, ability, discipline, ambition, morals, etc., would have caused the signers of the U.S. Constitution to grab their rifles. Moreover, the Founders believed in meritocracy NOT rank-in-reverse: *privates running the army, and media-moguls running the U.S. Congress.* Founders expected America always to be a bastion of the West. Not a racial refuse dump. FRANZ BOAS, JEW, more than any other individual, destroyed the Founders' visions.

BOASISM seeks a Communist equality — not equality of opportunity or equality-of-merit but of *results* — which requires transferring money from achievers, who earned it, to the incapable, indigent and "disadvantaged." Since achievers resist dispossession the government is given more regulatory and police powers. The under-achievers — a large votingbloc — very much favor receiving your tax-dollars from politicians who will give away anything (of yours) for a vote. How else can degenerates like U.S.

Senator Ted Kennedy remain in office? In the U.S., today, 60% of the National Budget goes toward Welfare. Distributors of this immense wealth are low IQ Negroes (the "rising middle-class") employed by local, state, and federal governments at high IQ salaries.

> My house is a decayed house, and the JEW squats on the window sill, the owner, Spawned in some estamint of Antwerp, Blistered in Brussels, Patched and peeled in London...
>
> T.S. ELIOT, from "Gerontion."

The 1950 UNESCO Statement denying Race as a factor (see above), was denounced by the world's most distinguished scientists, and by men in the streets who knew race when they saw it. In 1952 UNESCO retracted its statement acknowledging finally that "Races are 'real' and not mere "artifacts of classification." But, true to its Marxist orientation, UNESCO conveniently forgot its apology. Its original (1950) position as stated now appears in almost all reference books.

Similar misinformation (LIES) occurred in the pivotal and tragic U.S. Supreme Court case *Brown v. The Board of Education*, 1954, which decided against segregation of the Negro. The case was presented by Thurgood Marshall, Negro, Consul for the NAACP, supported by the NAACP staff of JEW lawyers. BOASIST Professor Kenneth B. Clark, Negro, performed as chief witness. Clark presented research data from his experiments with black and white dolls, and the reaction of Negro children to those tests, "proving that segregation inflicts injuries upon the Negro."

He almost had the justices in tears. Problem was, the research was DONE INCORRECTLY and THE CONCLUSIONS WERE SPURIOUS.

> I am forced to the conclusion that Professor Clark misled the court....In short, if Professor Clark's tests do demonstrate damage to Negro children, then they demonstrate the damage is less with segregation and more with congregation (integration)...Did Professor Clark know that his previous tests indicate that according to his own criteria Negro children are less damaged by segregation than by congregation?... From Professor Clark's experiments, his testimony, and finally his essay... the best conclusion that can be drawn is that he did not know what he was doing; and worst, that he did.
> DR. ERNEST VAN DEN HAAG, Professor of Social Philosophy, NYU, *Villanova Law Review* (VI, 1960).

> The problem we faced was not the historian's discovery of the truth... it was not that we were formulating lies... we were using facts... sliding off facts... quietly ignoring facts and above all interpreting facts in a way... to get by those boys down there.
> DR. A. H. KELLY, expert employed by the NAACP, in a confession before the American Historical Assoc., 1961, regarding the infamous desegregation case.

Marshall went on to become a member of the U.S. Supreme Court where his colleagues voted his opinions the worst in Court history. Clarke continued the JEWS' tool to the bitter end.

The disasters visited upon White America, and upon Negroes, and the disasters yet to come, resultant of the Supreme Court decision to miscegenate the races, are almost incalculable.

CHAPTER 6

THE "HOLOCAUST" HOAX

Spirochetes of JEW Syphilis (Continued)

The Holocaust was the murder of 6-Million Jews, including 2-Million children. Holocaust denial is a second murder of those same 6-Million. First their lives were extinguished then their deaths. A person who denies the Holocaust becomes part of the crime of the Holocaust itself.

> DAVID MATAS, JEW, Senior Counsel,
> "League for Human Rights," B'nai B'rith.

The policy pursued by the Third Reich resulted in the killing of 6-Million JEWS of which 4-Million were killed in the extermination institutions.

> INTERNATIONAL MILITARY TRIBUNAL,
> Nuremberg, Germany.

My objection to the Nuremberg Trial was that while Clothed in the form of justice they were in fact an instrument of government policy determined once before at Teheran and Yalta... a blot on the American record we shall long regret...which violates the fundamental principal of American Law that a man cannot be tried under ex post facto statute.

> U.S. SEN. ROBERT TAFT, "Profiles in Courage,"
> by J. F. Kennedy.

So far as the Nuremberg Trial... I dislike extremely to see it dressed up with a false facade of legality.

> HARLAN FISKE STONE, Chief Justice U.S. Supreme Court.

The statements admitted as evidence were obtained from men who had first been kept in solitary confinement (up to) five months...The investigators would put a black hood over the accused's head and then punch him in the face with brass knuckles, kick him and beat him with rubber hoses...137 Germans out of 139 cases had their testicles smashed beyond repair...(Other methods used were) Posturing as priests to hear confession and absolution; torture with burning matches driven under the nails; knocking out teeth and breaking bones; near starvation rations; threatening to deport accuseds' families to the Soviet side... The "American" investigators responsible (who later functioned as prosecutors at the Nuremberg Trials were, Lt. Col. Burton Ellis (Chief of the War Crimes Committee) and his assistants: Capt. Raphael Shumacher, JEW; Lt. Robert E. Byrne; Lt. Wm. R. Perl, JEW; Mr. Morris Ellpowitz, JEW; Mr. Harry Thon; Mr. D. Kirschbaum, JEW; Col. A.H. Rosenfield, JEW, Legal Advisor to the court.

E. L. VAN RHODEN,
Simpson Army Commission, Dachau, 1948.

The entire atmosphere here is unwholesome... Lawyers, clerks, interpreters, and researchers were employed (JEWS) — who became Americans only recently — whose backgrounds were embedded in Europe's hatred's and prejudices.

JUSTICE WENNERSTRUM,
Nuremberg Military Tribunal.

The JEW against the Goy is allowed to rape, cheat and perjure himself.

TALMUD: Babba Kama.

TOB SHEBBE GOYIM HAROG! (The best of the Gentiles is to be killed!)

TALMUD: Sanhedrin.

THE "HOLOCAUST" must be viewed in context: against the back-ground of world history, the TORAH, the TALMUD, and Rothschild's World Revolutionary Movement (WRM). It is necessary to comprehend the KHAZAR JEWS' congenital hatred of Gentiles, with their most rabid hatred reserved for the Aryan nation.

The ILLUMINATI set up the chess-board for WWI, their profits assured, when a corrupt U.S. Congress enacted the Federal Reserve Act (1913). The murders of Archduke Francis Ferdinand and his wife, by Gavrilo Princip, Serb FREEMASON, precipitated the War. BOLSHEVIK inspired treason destroyed Russia's ability to continue the war. German troops, then, were transferred from Russia to the Western Front. The war was being won by Germany when Chaim Weizmann, JEW (later, first President of Israel) made a quid pro quo agreement with Britain: *JEWS would bring the United States into the war if Britain would guarantee JEWS (KHAZARS) a "Homeland in Palestine" (Britain double-crossed the Arabs with the Balfour Declaration, 1917).* JEW lies about German "atrocities" brought America into the war. Following the "Armistice," and the betrayal and defeat of Germany, terms of the infamous Treaty of Versailles (The "Kosher Treaty") almost destroyed the German people. BOLSHEVIKS moved in for the kill, attempting to establish a Soviet Dictate in Germany as they had in Russia. But the German People tossed them out. Then, to the astonishment of the world, Chancellor Adolph Hitler, who emphasized genetics and the homogeneity of the Aryan race, led Germany to an amazing spiritual and economic recovery. However, JEWS consider nationalism, racial pride, and family, threats to their "Chosen" status; that is, their "right" to embed themselves among their cattle and suck their vital juices undetected. The WORLD JEWISH CONGRESS (organized in

Geneva, Switzerland, by "American" rabbi Stephen Wise) Declared War on Germany (1933): manifest in money manipulation, slander, libel, assassinations, boycott of German products, sabotage, etc. JEW mischief is seen in the Lindbergh kidnapping/murder case (see: Isador Fisch, JEW); the Hindenburg Zeppelin tragedy and other crimes against Aryans of German descent here and abroad, as the ILLUMINATI prepared for WW II. Germans, thereafter, considered JEWS not only alien intruders but enemies of the State. The CULTURAL schism between Aryans and JEWS worked to the advantage of ZIONISTS in their efforts to induce KHAZAR JEWS everywhere to "return" to Palestine. *Thus, we find ZIONISTS collaborating with the Third Reich, and other European governments to remove JEWS from soon to be incinerated Europe.*

Hitler's "unforgivable sin" was not his policy to colonize JEWS — they had been kicked out of every European state at one time or another. WWII was fought because Hitler's *Juden Frei* MONETARY POLICY completely by-passed Rothschild's central banking system. Germany's new Reich's Bank abandoned international gold reserves; issued its own interest-free currency (as Lincoln had done) — backed only by the productive capacity of the German People. In retaliation the INTERNATIONAL BANKERS refused to accept the Deutsch Mark on the foreign exchange. *Germany, then, simply bartered her products, by-passing the middleman.* Visible to the entire world, Germany had defied the ILLUMINATI, dug herself out of a pit of debt and despair, thrown off her shackles and became the most prosperous State in Europe. JEWS knew their worldwide banking empire was jeopardized. General George Catlett Marshall, U.S. Sec'y of State, records in his memoirs that in 1938 — three years before Pearl Harbor — "American" Bernard Baruch, JEW, confidant of Wilson, Roosevelt, Eisenhower, Churchill and many other power-players, stated, *"We're going to get that fellow Hitler! We're not going to let him get away with it...we're going to destroy Germany's barter system!"* But other world leaders paid Hitler well deserved tribute:

> A change in Germany's monetary system caused her to turn from abysmal depression to a glorious economy...which caused England's WWI leader, Lloyd George, to call Hitler, 'The greatest statesman living and the German people the happiest on earth.'
>
> HUGO R. FLACK, "The Great Betrayal."

> While all those formidable transformations were occurring in Europe, Corporal Hitler was fighting his long wearing battle for the German heart. The story of that struggle cannot be read without admiration... If our country were defeated I hope we should find a champion as indomitable to restore our courage and lead us back to our place among nations.
>
> WINSTON CHURCHILL, "Straight Speaking"
> by Francis Neilson.

> Mariner Eccles of the Federal Reserve Board, U.S.A., and Montague Norman, JEW, of the Bank of England decided, not later than 1935, on the joint policy of killing Hitler's financial experiment by all methods including war if necessary. Norman's job was to engineer Hitler into the dilemma of having to reverse his financial policy or commit an act of aggression.
>
> "THE WORD," English monthly, C. C. Vieth.

> The fight against Germany has been carried on for months... by every

JEW in the world.... We shall let loose a spiritual; and material war of the whole world against Germany. Germany's ambition is to become a great nation again... our JEWISH interests on the other hand demand the complete destruction of Germany. The German nation is collectively and individually a danger to us JEWS.

V. JABLONSKY, JEW, Representative French Zionist Congress, from his article in "Natcha Retch", 1932.

Let me take you back to 1913... If I had stood here then and said to you...the Archduke would be killed and that out of all that followed came the chance, the opportunity, the occasion for establishing a national home for JEWS in Palestine...you would have looked at me as an idle dreamer. Has it ever occurred to you how remarkable it is that out of this welter of world blood there has arisen this opportunity? Do you really believe this is an accident?

LORD MELCHETTE, JEW, Pres. English Zionist Federation, 1928.

As you remember, Rothschild planted the BOLSHEVIK/COMMUNIST STATE in Russia (1917), totally depended upon his central-banking system. The U.S.S.R. was a Bolshevik dagger pointed at the heart of Europe. Hitler's strategy was to defeat the U.S.S.R. Liberate the Great Russian people from KHAZAR/JEW domination — creating a new Euro-Slavic trading partner. Then, by deporting alien races, Hitler intended to create a united Europe with an Aryan population base.

Germans despised and feared Communism. They had witnessed the horrors of the Bolkshevik Revolution, in which the cultural-stratum of Russia, and Eastern Europe had been virtually annihilated. Germans were angered too by the slaughter (1918) of the Russian Royal Family: The Czar, Czarina (a Catholic German princess), their four young daughters, and 12-year old son. All had been hacked

JAMES W. VON BRUNN

and shot to death, by JEWS, their bodies dismembered, thrown into a pit, then covered with lime (Skeletal remains were recovered, c.1990).

Before WWII, Hitler had established himself as the arch enemy of Liberalism, Marxism, and Jewry — precisely the three driving forces...that had ridden into power with Franklin Roosevelt's New Deal (Democrats).
WILMOT ROBERTSON, *The Dispossessed Majority*, 1976.

The first spectacular triumph of the non-Christian Eastern European Democrats was Roosevelt's recognition, less than 9months after his inauguration, of the Soviet government of Russia... November 16, 1933 — at midnight! ...a date our children will long have tragic cause to remember. That was the date Soviet Foreign Commisar, Maxim Litvinoff (Finkelstein) JEW, plunderer of Estonia and the Soviet's first agent for socializing England, sat down with President Roosevelt — after Dean Acheson (the "Red Dean") and Henry Morganthau, JEW, had done the spadework of propaganda and made the deal that has led the American people and our once vast resources into a social and economic calamity...
PROF. JOHN O. BEATY, *The Iron Curtain Over America*, cite. V. La Varre, *American Legion* Magazine, August 1951.

Some of my best friends are Communists.
FRANKLIN DELANO ROOSEVELT.

I have said this before, but I shall say it again, and again, and again. Your boys are not going to be sent into any foreign wars! (America elected FDR 3-weeks later.)
FRANKLIN D. ROOSEVELT, 1940.

The whole story of Germany's appeal for negotiations and our curt refusal and severance of diplomatic relations was not published in 1937 and 1938 when Germany made her appeal, but was withheld from the public until ferreted out by the House Committee on un-American Activities after WWII... and released to the press more than 10-years after the facts were so criminally suppressed.

DR. JOHN O. BEATY, Colonel U.S. Army Intelligence.

The victory of Communism in the world would be far more dangerous to the United States than the victory of Fascism. There has never been the slightest danger that the people of this country would ever embrace Bundism or Naziism... But Communism masquerades, often successfully, under the guise of democracy.

SEN. HOWARD TAFT, *Human Events*, 28 March 1951.

What has been called the "Jewish problem" is seen for the first time. Not race, not religion, not ethics, not nationality, not political allegiance, but something that includes them all, separating the JEW from the West — Culture.

FRANCIS PARKER YOCKEY, *Imperium*.

There is overwhelming evidence that Hitler did not want a European war. He made many attempts to convince Britain to join Germany in the destruction of Communism, the Soviet, and re-unification of Aryan Europe. But, the ILLUMINATI — not the English people — control Britain. In America, the Polish Ambassador, Count Jerzy Potacki, complained that American radio, film and press were "almost 100% JEWISH controlled," and they "clamored for war against Germany." They wanted to exacerbate the Polish Corridor dispute with Hitler, which he was negotiating. Potacki identified the "Americans" behind this campaign as Herbert Lehman, JEW, Governor of New York; Bernard Baruch, JEW, advisor to the President; Henry Morganthau, JEW, Sec'y Treasury; Felix Frankfurter, JEW, U.S. SupCrt. Rabbi Steven Wise. They acted, Potacki said, as defenders of democracy but were "connected by unbreakable ties to international JEWRY."

Following the declaration of war against Germany (WWII) an ominous pause developed. Both sides haunted by ghosts of WWI waited, hoping for someone, something to prevent another blood-bath. Up front the "enemies" fraternized. David Irving (*Churchill's War*), documents the PM's frustration with the "Phoney War." He sought blood, and glory — and he had promises to keep. His advisor, Professor Frederick Lindemann, "German" JEW, proposed that the British initiate terror bombing of civilians. This proposal was given "top priority by the British Government." Hitler, who had inveighed against air campaigns against civilian targets, would be forced to retaliate.

> Prime Minister Neville Chamberlain stated that "America and the world JEWS had forced England into war."
> JAMES FORRESTAL, U.S. Sec. Nav., *The Forrestal Diaries*.

Initially, "Churchill's War", went badly for Britain. On cue, Chaim Weizmann, JEW, ZIONIST, the ILLUMINATI point-man, once again slithers onto the scene.

> We managed to bring the United States into the First World War and if you tow our line over Palestine and the JEWISH fighting force, then we can persuade the JEWS of the United States to drag the United States into it again this time.
> WEIZMANN letter to Churchill, Weizmann Archives, Tel Aviv.

JEW success is measured by the number of crosses marking Aryan dead in battlefield cemeteries stretched across the globe.

With this glimpse, denied us by the MEDIA, of the ILLUMINATI'S order-of-battle, i.e, the POWER OF MONEY; SPIROCHETES OF JEW SYPHILIS; and the intertwining of MARXISM/LIBERALISM/JUDAISM we are now better able to understand the HOLOCAUST HOAX in context. L'INFAMIE!

The "HOLOCAUST" is defined as: The Extermination of about 6-Million or more JEWS Resultant of NAZI Policy.

Since WWII, literally tons of evidence relating to the "HOLOCAUST" has been studied by world-class scholars. There is NO evidence supporting the "HOLOCAUST" as defined:

THERE WAS NO POLICY TO MASS MURDER JEWS. NO ORDER WAS GIVEN TO MASS MURDER JEWS. THERE WAS NO BUDGET TO CARRY OUT SUCH A POLICY. THERE WERE NO MEANS (GAS CHAMBERS, etc.) TO CARRY OUT MASS MURDERS.

Revisionist Historians have concluded that a total of about 300-thousand JEWS died of all causes during WWII. There was *no* JEW "HOLOCAUST." There *was* a German Holocaust!

"HOLOCAUST" LIES were invented for the following reasons:

1)   Initial Phase (c.1930): Invent German atrocities to condition America for war. Create JEW solidarity behind ZIONISM. Cover-up Bolshevik JEW atrocities in Lenin Russia.

2)   WW II Phase (c.1940): Invent "HOLOCAUST" to transform Germany into a PARIAH among nations; justify incinerating Germany; justify ex post facto Nuremberg trials. Hang, thus silence, German leadership.

3)   Post War Phase (on-going): Cover-up ILLUMINATI activities.. Cover-up JEW/ALLIES WWI & WWII atrocities/treason. Provide a raison d'etre for "missing" European JEWS (now in U.S.A.). Extort 100+ Billion dollars in "reparations" from Germany. Discredit WESTERN CIVILIZATION before the World. Paralyze the WEST'S WILL to act in its own interest. Create The United Nations. Allow JEWS to dominate U.S.A. Instill guilt among children of the WEST, thus lowering resistance to drugs, immorality, miscegenation, Marxism, and other forms of JEW SYPHILIS. Equate love of race, family, Nation, with Nazis, ergo: "hateful." Establish the State of Israel: genocide of Palestinians. Create "HOLOCAUST" religion as a cottage industry. Lay the foundations for WW III.

MANKIND, initially, was infected with "HOLOCAUST" SYPHILIS during JEWISH HIGH HOLY DAYS, October 1942. Rabbi Steven Wise, President of The World JEWISH Congress (WJC), and confidant of U.S. Presidents Wilson and Franklin D. Roosevelt, publicly announced: Germany is engaged in a program to exterminate European JEWS... but for economic reasons had abandoned mass gassings in favor of injecting poison by syringe! Millions of JEW corpses were then rendered into bars of soap!

The Allies (U.S.A., U.S.S.R., Great Britain and France), offering NO bona fide evidence, issued a Joint Declaration, December 1943, supporting the outrageous LIES mouthed by rabbi Wise. In private high-ranking British and American officials, as we now know, unsuccessfully attempted to quash the Declaration which stank of WWI atrocity propaganda (including the soap lie) for which the Allies had apologized to Germany.

Let it ALWAYS be remembered it was RABBI STEPHEN WISE, Khazar leader of American JEWRY, and of the WORLD JEWISH CONGRESS, who created the "HOLOCAUST" HOAX, abetted by Allied Leaders (Churchill, Roosevelt, and Eisenhower) whom Bernard Baruch, JEW, negotiated with, groomed, and elevated to center stage in the ILLUMINATI war to destroy the West.

> From time immemorial...the Jews have known better than any others how falsehood and calumny can be exploited... that in the BIG LIE there is always a certain force of credibility ...Is not their very existence founded on one great lie... that they are a religious community and not a race... Schopenhauer called the Jews "The Great Master of Lies."
> ADOLPH HITLER, Chancellor of Germany, *Mein Kampf*.

About two months after the Joint Declaration the British Ministry of Information dispached (2-29-44) a Top Secret letter to the British Broadcasting Corp. (BBC), and to high-ranking ministers of the Church of England on the need to divert public attention away from Red Army atrocities by faking Axis war crimes.

> We know the methods of rule employed by the Bolshevik Dictator in Russia (U.S.S.R.) itself... from the writings and speeches of the prime minister himself during the last 20-years. We know how the Red Army behaved in Poland in 1920 and in Finland, Estonia, Latvia, Galacia, and Bessarabia only recently. We must, therefore, take into account how the Red Army will behave when it overruns Central Europe. Unless precautions are taken, the obviously inevitable horrors which will result will throw an undue strain on public opinion in this country. We cannot reform the Bolsheviks but we can do our best to save them — and ourselves ("Perfidious Albion!") — from the consequences of their acts. The disclosure of the last quarter century will render more denials unconvincing. The only alternative to denial is to distract public attention from the whole subject. Experience has shown the best distraction is atrocity propaganda directed against the enemy... your cooperation is therefore earnestly sought to distract public attention from, the doings of the Red Army by your whole-hearted support of various charges against the Germans and Japanese which have and will be put into circulation by the Ministry.
>
> ZUNDEL "HOLOCAUST TRIALS",
> Defense Exhibit, Toronto (1-785).

It has been observed quite accurately that the heart of the "HOLOCAUST" HOAX is the AUSCHWITZ-BIRKENAU-MAJDANEK "Death Camp" complex. Here the greatest number of JEWS (4-Million) allegedly were murdered: Here the alleged NAZI killing apparatus was most efficient. Here Germany allegedly revealed her diabolic racial soul. "Eye-witness" testimony by the many Auschwitz survivors provided the Nuremberg Tribunal with "moral" justification required to pronounce Nazi Germany guilty of "Crimes Against Humanity." At

Auschwitz the "HOLOCAUST" myth became Reality, and Germany, cultural gem of the West, became a Pariah among World Nations.

In *Judgment at Nuremberg* the International Military Tribunal quoted at length from the Rudolf Hoess Affidavit to support the extermination HOAX. Yet, Sergeant Bernard Clarke, British Intelligence, described how he and five other soldiers brutally tortured Hoess (4-5-46), former commandant of Auschwitz, to obtain his "confession", in which Hoess states: JEWS were being exterminated as early as 1941 in three camps: Treblinka, Belsec and Wolzek; and 2-3-Million JEWS perished at Auschwitz.

> "Certainly, I signed a statement that I killed two and a half million JEWS. I could just as easily have said five million JEWS. There are certain methods by which any confession may be obtained, whether it is true or not."
>
> RUDOLF HOESS, NAZI, before he was hanged.

While under torture, and threatened that his wife and children would be deported to Siberia, Hoess invented the name "Wolzek" to inform posterity (YOU) that his "confession" was false: the extermination camp "Wolzek" never existed!

The Nuremberg Tribunal also regarded as essential the testimony of Rudolf Vrba, JEW, who was prisoner for two years in Majdanek and Auschwitz before escaping. His dictated report to the JEWISH Council of Slovakia, corroborating the "HOLOCAUST" scenario, formed the basis of the War Refugee Board Report (1944). Professor

Vrba, who wrote the autobiography, "I Cannot Forgive", now teaches in British Columbia (died 2000). Book reviews praised Vrba for his "meticulous and almost fanatic respect for accuracy." But during the ZUNDEL TRIALS, Vrba confessed he had fabricated his entire "gas chamber" thesis out of thin air. He had never seen a gas chamber. "I have taken licentia poetarium," he whimpered. This typical JEW "eye-witness", was believed at Nuremberg when he calculated that in 24-months (April 1942April 1944) 1,765,000 JEWS were "gassed" at Birkenau alone including 150,000 JEWS from France! Today, all historians (including "HOLOCAUST" expert, Serge Klarsfeld, JEW, in his "Memorial to the Deportation of the Jews from France") agree that fewer than 75,000 "French" JEWS had been deported to ALL German camps. The reason Vrba saw no gas chambers is that there were NO gas chambers — anywhere — as you will soon learn. Nevertheless, the "Spielbergs" continue to LIE to our children.

At Nuremberg, Chief U.S. Prosecutor, Robert Jackson (Married to a JEWESS), announced to the world that Germans used a "newly invented device" to instantly "vaporize" 20,000 JEWS near Auschwitz "...in such a way that there was no trace left of them." The Washington. D.C. "Daily News" (2-2-45) quoted "eye-witness reports" that Germans, at Auschwitz, used an "electric conveyer belt on which hundreds of persons would be electrocuted simultaneously...then moved on into furnaces. They were burned almost instantaneously, producing fertilizer for nearby cabbage fields." All proven lies. Arnold Friedman,

JEW, Auschwitz survivor, testifying for the Crown (Prosecution) in the recent Canadian Zundel trials, stated under oath that "fourteen foot flames" and clouds of smoke erupted from crematoria chimneys; that greasy smoke and the stench of burning human flesh hung over the camp for weeks; that one could tell whether skinny Polish JEWS or fat Hungarian JEWS were being gassed by the color of the smoke! When the Defense produced Topf & Sons in Erfurt patent descriptions of the Auschwitz crematoria, it showed — as with ALL modern crematoria — the impossibility of it emitting smoke, flames and stench. Thus, demolishing "eye-witness" descriptions appearing in virtually all "HOLOCAUST" horror stories.

Auschwitz, throughout the war, was subjected to intense AERIAL SURVEILLANCE because Buna rubber, a German patent, and other war materials were manufactured there. State-of-the-art, detailed, AERIAL PHOTOGRAPHS of the Auschwitz complex reveal no lines of prisoners awaiting execution; no piles of corpses; no huge stacks of coal; no chimneys belching flames and smoke nor other signs of massexecution described by JEW "eyewitnesses"; and congenital liars like TAMUDISTS Elie Weisel; Simon Wiesenthal; Hollywood's Steven Spielberg, et al.

IVAN LAGACE, manager of a large CREMATORY, Calgary, Canada, testified under oath (Zundel Trials) that the Auschwitz cremation story is technically impossible. "It is preposterous" and "beyond the realm of possibility" that

10,000 or 20,000 corpses could have been burned daily in open pits and crematoriums at Auschwitz. For Professor Raul Hillberg, JEW, to declare 46 retorts at Birkenau could cremate 4000 bodies per day is "ludicrous." Lagace testified that a maximum of 184 bodies, per day, could have been cremated at Birkenau. It takes about 2½-hrs. just to burn one corpse. Crematories cannot run 24-hours straight time.

In 1988, FRED A. LEUCHTER carried out on-site forensic examinations of alleged GAS CHAMBERS at Auschwitz-Birkenau Majdanek "Death Camps" in Poland. Leuchter, Reg. Engineer, State of Massachusettes, is consider America's foremost expert on gas chambers. He is consultant to the State of Missouri, and South Carolina penal systems. At the ZUNDEL TRIALS, in sworn testimony, substantiated by video-tapes shot on location, and in a technical report, Leuchter demolished the "HOLOCAUST" HOAX by proving the sites were not used and could not have been used as execution gas chambers: their construction was totally inadequate: not properly sealed or ventilated, with primitive plumbing, and no way to efficiently introduce the gas. If the alleged "gas chambers" had been used escaping fumes would have killed German patients in the adjacent hospital, prisoners at work, and German camp personnel. Independent laboratory analysis of forensic samples Leuchter had removed from walls and floors of the "gas chambers" proved that the pesticide ZYKLON-B (hydrocyanic acid) had not been used — as reported by eye-witnesses — to gas millions of JEWS at the Auschwitz complex. Leuchter pointed out that traces of Cyanide (Prussic Acid), if introduced into rocks, concrete, and metal, would last for eons of time.

DR. W.B. LINDSEY, a research chemist for 33-years with DuPont Corp., testified that based on a thorough onsite examination of the Auschwitz complex: "I have come to the conclusion that no one was willfully or purposely killed with Zyklon-B in this manner. I consider it absolutely technically impossible."

A confidential forensic examination and report commissioned by the Auschwitz State Museum (JEWS), and conducted by the Institute of Forensic Research, Krakow, has confirmed Leuchter's findings that only minimal or no traces of cyanide compound can be found in the sites alleged to have been gas-chambers.

WALTER LUFTL, Austrian engineer, and former president of Austria's Professional Association of Engineers, conducted on-site investigations of the Auschwitz complex. In a 1992 report he said the alleged mass extermination of JEWS in Auschwitz "chambers" was "technically impossible."

> At Auschwitz, but probably overall, more JEWS were killed by 'natural causes' than by 'unnatural' ones.
>
> DR. A. MAYER, JEW, Princeton U.
> "Why Did the Heavens Not Darken?"

> Britain's chief rabbi wants the "6-Million" figure revised: Its important to find out how many people presumed dead are still alive. It is far more important to unite families than to live with a figure arrived at quite arbitrarily.

DR. JONATHAN H. SACKS, JEW,
The Crescent Magazine, 515-96

For 45-years following WWII the monument at Auschwitz read:

"FOUR MILLION PEOPLE SUFFERED AND DIED HERE AT THE HANDS OF NAZI MURDERERS BETWEEN 1940-1945."

In 1982, Pope John Paul genuflected before the monument and blessed the "4-Million dead." Embarrassingly, he received no hint from Yahweh that 8-years later Yad Vashem Holocaust Center, Israel; and the Auschwitz State Museum, would concede: "The 4-Million figure was greatly exaggerated." The death toll inscribed on the monument was hastily removed. JEWS suggested 1.1-MILLION dead was more likely.

Despite an almost 3-Million reduction in the number of JEWS "murdered" the Cabalistic 6-Million figure remains inviolate to keep intact Germany's reparation payments to Israel. ODDLY, it seems to infuriate JEWS to learn their relatives were NOT gassed, but are alive and well — many employed in America's mass-media, and the U.S. State Department.

Then (1995), Russia released the official Auschwitz Death Registers (one month missing) which lists a grand total of 74,000 deaths from all causes! (including German personnel who died there)

None of the above reported by the Marxist/LIBERAL/JEW media, (Please see Chapt. 10, Parasitism, USA).

You may recall the testimony of Joseph G. Burg, JEW, witness for the Defense, Zundel Trials. Burg stated that JEW "HOLOCAUST" survivors invented the gas-chamber stories:

> If those JEWS had sworn before a rabbi wearing a skullcap then those false statements, those sick statements, would go down by 99.5%, because the superficial oath was not morally binding on JEWS.
>
> J. G. BURG

> ...my promises (to a Gentile) shall not bind... my vows shall not be reckoned vows... nor my oaths oaths... every vow which I make in the future shall be null from this Day of Atonement until the next.
>
> TALMUD: Kol Nidre Oath.

Elie Wiesel JEW, Nobel Peace Prize winner, President Clinton confident, testified that for months after German troops in the Ukraine shot JEW partisans "geysers of blood spurted from their graves and the earth trembled" ("Spielbergism").

A German court, ruling for the defense, in a case involving the authenticity of ANNE FRANK'S DIARY, found that the Diary had been written by one individual — presumably Anne Frank. Several years later German Federal Crimes Office (BKA) certified that extensive sections of the Diary had been written in ball-point pen — a device not marketed until 1950!

This deception, in addition to discrepancies and

impossibilities within the Diary itself, reveal the LIE. Anne was simply exploited — as are all children who find the Diary mandatory reading at their schools. David Irving, British historian, calls the Diary "worthless research material." We should note, here, that Anne and her father were imprisoned at Auschwitz. When Soviet troops approached she was sent to Bergen-Belsen for her safety. Unfortunately she died there of typhus. Her father, Otto Frank, JEW, survived. With no visible source of income he died many years later in Switzerland — a wealthy man.

Yad Vashem Holocaust Remembrance Authority concedes that SOAP was NOT rendered from JEW corpses. "Why give them something to use against the truth?" asks VIP Schmuel Krakpowski, JEW.

The Allied War Commission determined early on there were NO execution gas-chambers in any of the 13 concentration camps located in Germany and Austria. An official document to that effect is signed by the Commission, dated 1 October 1948 (official copies available). The so-called "DEATH CAMPS" were conveniently located behind the Iron Curtain. Investigation of these camps was not officially permitted until the collapse of the U.S.S.R. in 1990. By then the "HOLOCAUST" was accepted as TRUTH by the goyim sheep.

What about all the corpse photographs TV threatens you with daily?

During the final months of the war Allies took command

of the skies. Highways, bridges, railroads, powerplants, live-stock, farmers in their fields were targeted. "Kill whatever moves!" (Gen. Chuck Yaeger, USAF, denounced that order as an atrocity). German transport was severely curtailed. Vital supplies were prevented from reaching the camps. As the Eastern Front rolled back prisoners from those areas, especially women, opted for transfers to German camps rather than fall into Soviet hands. Bergen-Belsen, for example, designed to accommodate 3,000, was inundated with *over 50,000 prisoners*. Systems in ALL the camps broke down. When the Allies took over they were greeted with horror scenes (replayed countless times on screen, stage, and television): the sick and dying and emaciated corpses covered the ground. Tragic. But they had not been murdered as we have been conditioned to believe. They died slowly from starvation, lack of medicine, and disease — TYPHUS raged through almost all camps. To complete the macabre scene the U.S. Army 45th Division, liberators of Dachau, gathered together 560 uniformed German guards, *nurses* and *doctors* and machine-gunned them to death.

The INTERNATIONAL COMMITTEE of the RED CROSS (ICRC), and the Catholic Church, whose members frequented all camps, reported NO mass executions, and do NOT mention gas chambers. Adolph Hitler, a Catholic, has not been excommunicated! Churchill, Truman, Eisenhower, Marshall, De Gaulle, and other Allied leaders DO NOT mention a "HOLOCAUST" in their memoirs.

The U.S. State Department's refusal, 1939, to permit JEWS on board the passenger ship *St. Louis* to disembark in U.S.A. territorial waters was, we now know, a smoke-screen to divert America's attention from the mass immigration, *sub rosa*, of JEWS to our shores. The vast majority of Americans, as people everywhere, didn't want Europe's JEWRY. But Europe's JEWRY wanted the United States. Franklin D. Roosevelt, effete Ivy League traitor, was fond of saying, "Some of my best friends are Communists." He had plenty of them. Before, during, and after WWII U.S. Liberty ships and cargo vessels, after unloading troops and supplies in European ports, returned to the United States crammed with "gassed" KHAZARS. They simply disembarked, fading into the alley-ways, undergoing no naturalization process. And they weren't poor waifs. As described, above, Harry Dexter White, JEW, Under-Secretary of the Treasury, stole U.S. Treasury engraving plates, then gave them to the Soviet Union which printed millions (billions?) of dollars in U. S. paper currency. This money found its way into the pockets of the new "American" JEWS. After the war, White, exposed as a Soviet agent, was scheduled to appear before a Senate investigating committee when he conveniently died! FDR's confidant Henry Morganthau, Jr., JEW, Sec. U. S. Treasury, sponsored the *Morganthau Plan*, which called for transplanting German industry to the Soviet Union. When told this would result in the mass starvation of Germans he replied: "Who the hell cares about the German people?"

Frederick Lindemann (Lord Cherwell), JEW, Churchill's

Zionist watchdog, cared a great deal! Only three months before Germany's surrender (5-5-45), acting upon Lindemann's directives, British and American planes attacked DRESDEN, Germany (2-13-45), a defenseless city packed with refugees, which was observing Christian ASH Wednesday. Over 200,000 men, women, and children were incinerated in fire-storms generated by concussion and phosphorus bombs. Later, photographs of the victims, stacked like cordwood, were super-imposed on Auschwitz "Death Camp" photographs (more Spielbergisms). Most of the airmen were unaware that Saxony was the heartland of their own Anglo-Saxon ancestors.

"Mad Dog" Ilya Ehrenburg, JEW, Minister of Soviet Propaganda under Stalin, promoted the rape of German women by promising the troops "that blonde German hag is in for a hard time!" He sought the extermination of the entire German people. "Germans are not human beings... nothing gives us so much pleasure as German corpses!" (*Pravda* 4-14-45).

Soldiers of the Red Army! Kill the Germans! Kill ALL Germans! Kill! Kill! Kill!
ILYA EHRENBURG, who received the Order of Lenin, and the Stalin Prize. He willed his papers to the Yad Vashem Holocaust Museum, Israel.

The interests of the revolution require the physical annihilation of the bourgeoisie class... Without mercy, without sparing, we will kill our enemies in scores of thousands... let them drown themselves in their own blood. For the blood of Lenin, and Uritzky, Ziniviev and Volodarsky, let their be floods of blood of the bourgeosie — more blood! As much as possible!

GRIGORY APFELBAUM (Zinoviev), JEW,
Soviet Secret Police.

The longer the rotten bourgeoisie society lives, the more barbaric will anti-Semitism (anti-JEW) become everywhere.

LEON TROTSKY, JEW,
Supreme Commander Soviet Red Army.

General DWIGHT EISENHOWER (appropriately named "The Swedish Jew" by fellow West Point cadets) was promoted over the heads of many more qualified officers for a reason. He agreed, apparently, to exchange America's honor *quid pro quo* for 5-Stars and glory. After the war, at the dedication of a New York City park honoring the Bernard Baruch family, key-note speaker Gen. Dwight D. Eisenhower, USA-Ret., admitted:

> As a young unknown major I took the wisest step of my life. I consulted Mr. Baruch.
>
> (General Dwight D. Eisenhower, U.S. Army),
cited by A.K. CHESTERTON,
op. cit., *The New Unhappy Lords*.

Bernard Baruch, KEHILLA, became wealthy dealing in war materiel ("A little bird told him"). Wars were his specialty. During WWII, he was called "the most powerful figure in America" (Congressional Record). Winston Churchill also took that "wise step." The mortgage on Winnie's Chartwell estate was inexplicably satisfied by South African gold dealer Sir Henry Strakosch, JEW (Baruch confidant) after Winnie had spent a week-end at Bernie's NYC mansion. Then came WWII (Pls. see:

Churchill's War, by David Irving)

EISENHOWER dumbfounded and infuriated Allied generals when he ordered victorious American troops to HALT at the Elbe River, pursuant to his agreement with Bernie Baruch, KEHILLA, permitting JEWS and Asiatics, for the first time in history, to plunder and rape the very heart of Europe. This action divided Germany (bulwark of Christendom), precipitated the Cold War, and caused the murder of over 10-Million ethnic Germans following Germany's unconditional surrender. America gave to the Marxists not only the ancient city of Berlin with its priceless archives, but also the important rocket production plant at Nordhausen, the great Zeiss optical and precision-instrument works at Jena; and the first Jet airplane plant at Kahla. Everywhere, America surrendered to the Marxists thousands of planes, tanks, and jet fighters, snorkel submarine plants, as well as research centers, scientific personnel, patents, and other treasures (*Congressional Record*, 3-19-1951). Captured German scientists, NOT the Soviets, beat the USA into space! JEWS (Beria, Andropov) had murdered all Gentile scientists. There was NO advanced technology. Soviets were incapable of producing engines for their own tanks much less sophisticated rockets and jet engines (the U.S. designed and built almost all Soviet tank-engines enabling the USSR to win the key battle of Kursk). Arming the USSR with state-of-the-art technology, per Baruch/Roosevelt/Truman instructions, produced the Cold War — a banker's bonanza — pitting America's pocketbook against the Soviet threat.

Eisenhower, his obligations in mind, treacherously ordered American and British troops to execute OPERATION KEELHAUL driving millions of Russian anti-Communists out of the United States and Europe into torture and death in the Soviet Union. Official Soviet statisticians (10-11945) state a total of 5,236,130 anti-communists were turned over by Ike, and admitted that three-million of these were immediately murdered AFTER THE WAR. The victims were anti-Communists: soldiers, prisoners of war, and men who had been recruited into American service, fighting valiantly under our flag; and civilians: old men, women and children who had tried to escape the BOLSHEVIKS. All had voluntarily surrendered to American forces after being promised protection under articles of the Geneva Convention.

> There have been few crimes in history more brutal and more extensive than this forced repatriation of anti-Communists, to which Dwight Eisenhower committed the honor of the United States. Dragging the honor and reputation of our country through pools of bloody betrayal...
> ROBERT WELCH, *The Politician*,
> Pres, John Birch Society.

The MEDIA announced that 40-thousand Polish army officers and civilian elite had been murdered in KATYN FOREST. Germans, accused of the crime, were sentenced at Nuremberg and imprisoned or hanged. Later, the Katyn Massacre was proven a BOLSHEVIK crime. The numbers murdered were reduced to 14,300. Evidence (as with the Czar's family) points to JEW RITUAL MURDERS.

Victims of the Nuremberg Trials were judged during the

JEWISH HOLY DAYS and were hanged on HAHANNA RABA (16 October 1946), the day YAWEH pronounces final judgment.

While the Nuremberg Tribunal prepared to convict Germany for "Crimes Against Humanity," U.S. planes dropped atomic bombs on defenseless Hiroshima, and Nagasaki, Japan, murdering over 110,000 non-combatants. As many died later of radiation poisoning.

> The JEW against the Goy is allowed to rape, cheat, and perjure himself.
>
> TALMUD: Babha Kama.

> Israelis and American JEWS fully agree that the memory of the Holocaust is an indispensable weapon... one that must be used relentlessly against our common enemy... JEWISH organizations and individuals thus labor continuously to remind the world of it. In America the perpetuation of the Holocaust memory is now a $110-million-a-year enterprise, part of which is U.S. government funded.
>
> MOSHE LEDHEM, JEW, *Balaam s Curse.*

> The British (Bank of England) offered to stop the war (1939-40) if Germany would agree to a Gold Standard and international usury. While Germany offered to stop the war if the British would allow her to develop her barter-trade system and give her back some of her colonies and territory.
>
> C. C. VIETH, British Member of Parliament.

The sudden collapse of the U.S.S.R. (c.1990) provided public access to secret files; to so-called "Death Camps"; and to former Soviet agents. Continuing research, has resulted in Up-dated Statistics relating to JEW deaths during WWII:

The World Center of Jewish Documentation, Paris, incapable of telling the whole truth, has nonetheless revised figures downward, stating: 1,485,292 JEWS died of all causes in WWII. The World Jewish Congress, and Yad Vashem, insist that 6-Million JEWS were murdered by Germans — yet they admit almost 3-Million fewer JEWS died at Auschwitz than previously claimed! Over 4-million JEWS claim reparation payments. However there were never more than 3-million JEWS under German control at any time.

Die Tat, Zurich(1-19-95), base their conclusions on statis-tics provided by the International Committee of the Red Cross, places the total number of civilian dead (not all JEWS) resultant of NAZI political, religious, racial persecution at 300,000 to 350,000.

Revisionist Historians conclude that the TOTAL number of JEWS dead from all causes during WWII are 250,000 to 300,000. The majority of these died from typhus. (See, *The Patton Papers* (pp 353-4) in re JEW filthiness).

To put these figures in perspective remember that about 700,000 civilians died during the siege at Leningrad, and over 200,000 died at Dresden ("strafe everything that moves!"). It is estimated that over 10 to 15-Million Germans died during WWII.

WORLD JEW POPULATION Published Figures

1938 A.D. 16,599,250 (*The World Almanac*[6])
1948 A.D. 15,600,000 to 18,700,000 (*New York Times*)

Professor Arthur R. Butz, Northwestern University, Evanston Illinois, was the first to professionally research and document European JEW population shifts during WWII and the impossibility of the so-called "HOLOCAUST." In his highly regarded book, *The Hoax of the Twentieth Century*, 1975, Butz concludes that about one-million JEWS died of all causes during WWII. He wrote his tome 10-years before the Zundel Trials which, among other revelations, demolished the execution gas-chambers myth.

"HOLOCAUST" MEMORIALS[7] erected by ILLUMINATI all over the World intended to cast a permanent Stigma on the Aryan Race stand instead as MONUMENTS TO MANKIND'S CONGENITAL LIARS: THE JEWISH RACE.

Throughout history, JEWS have been diagnosed as congenital LIARS. It is not surprising to find their holy book bearing false witness, charging the Romans with committing a HOLOCAUST:

> The TALMUD...(claims) that the number of JEWS killed by the Romans after the fortress (Bethar) fell (135 A.D.) was 4Billion, "or as some say" 40-million, while the MIDRASH RABBAH reports 800-Million martyred JEWS. In order to reassure us that these figures are given in earnest the necessarily accompanying events are set forth: The blood of the slain JEWS reached to the nostrils of the Romans' horses

---

[6] Also see *Guiness Book of Records*.
[7] Hitler anticipated the JEW "Big Lie," Chapt. X, *Mein Kampf.*

and then, like a tidal wave, plunged a distance of one mile or four miles to the sea, carrying large boulders along with it, and staining the sea a distance of four miles out. The JEWISH children of Bethar, according to TALMUDIC literature were of course not spared by the Romans, who were said to have wrapped each one in his scroll and burned all of them, the number of these school children having been either 64-Million or at least 150,000...

ARTHUR R. BUTZ, Assoc. Prof. Engineering, Northwestern U.,
The Hoax of the Twentieth Century.

93 CHOOSE SUICIDE BEFORE NAZI SHAME
93 Jewish girls and young Jewish women, the pupils of the teacher of Beth Jacob School of Warsaw, Poland, chose mass suicide to escape being forced into prostitution by German soldiers, according to a letter from the teacher, made public yesterday by Rabbi Seth Jung, Jewish Center, New York City.

ASSOCIATED PRESS, 8 January 1943.

I lied. I lie all the time. I was brought up to lie. I was told that is the way to get along in life.

MONICA LEWINSKI, JEWESS,
Bill Clinton's desk mate, 1998.

History shows us that JEWS are compulsive LIARS. It is a genetic characteristic that all JEWS share. All JEWS know the "HOLOCAUST" is a lie — because they understand one another. Therefore all JEWS must be held accountable. Ponder carefully the following contemporary newspaper item:

PBS DOCUMENTARY CLAIMS BLACK U.S. ARMY UNIT FREED JEWISH INMATES FROM GERMAN CONCENTRATION CAMPS. NICE STORY BUT NOT TRUE SAY THE SOLDIERS.

It was a rare moment: Jessie Jackson surrounded by whitehaired Holocaust survivors. The occasion was a black-Jewish celebration of "Liberators," the PBS documentary about all black U.S. Army units that, according to the film, helped capture Buchenwald and Dachau. The sponsors of the screening TIME-WARNER and a host of rich and influential New Yorkers billed the film as an important tool in rebuilding of a black Jewish alliance... E. G. McConnell, an original member of the 761st Tank Battalion (featured in the film) says... "It's a lie — we were no where near those camps when they were liberated." Nina Rosenbloom who co-produced the film says Mr. McConnell can't be trusted. "You can't speak to him because he's snapped. He was hit in the head with shrapnel and was severely brain damaged." Mr. McConnell, a retired mechanic for Trans World Airlines laughs when told of her statement. "If I was so disturbed why did they use me in the film?" he asks. "It's totally inaccurate," says Charles Gates, the former captain who commanded C Company. "The men couldn't have been there because the camp was 60-miles away from where we were on liberation day." According to him tanks of the 761st were assigned to the 71st Infantry Division whose fighting path was 100-160 kilometers away from the camps. Several Holocaust survivors are quoted in the film saying they were liberated by blacks in those units. Ms. Rosenbloom angrily denounces the film's critics as Holocaust revisionists and racists. "These people are of the same mentality that says the Holocaust didn't happen!"... The "Liberators" fueled by the public relations success is gaining momentum. Copies of the documentary will be distributed to all New York City junior and senior high schools. The cost of the schools project is being picked up by investment banker Felix Rohatyn... although several philanthropists are vying for the honor of buying tapes for the schools. The film will be used to "examine the effects of racism on African-American soldiers and on Jews who were in concentration camps... to explain the role of African-American soldiers in liberating Jews from Nazi concentration camps and to reveal the involvement of Jews as 'soldiers' in the civil-rights movement." Peggy Tishman, a former president of the Jewish Community Relations Council is sticking by the documentary. She says, "The documentary is good for the Holocaust. Why would anybody want to exploit the idea that the film is a fraud? What we're trying to do is make New York a better place for you and me to live." She claims the accuracy of the film is not the issue. "What is important is the way we can bring Jews and Blacks into dialogue. There are a lot of truths that are very necessary. This," she says, "is not a truth that is necessary!"

JEFFREY GOLDBERG, JEW, *The New Republic*.

The greatest deception is self-deception. We will explore that JEWISH vulnerability by examining GENETICS. For it is NATURE that inevitably will destroy YAHWEH'S "Chosen People."

CHAPTER 7

MENDELISM

All is race; there is no other truth. It is the key to history. And every race must fall which carelessly suffers its blood to become mixed.

BENJAMIN DISRAELI, JEW, Prime Minister of England.

Liberalism is a disease whose first symptom is an inability to believe in conspiracies.

FRIEDRICH WILHELM IV (1795-1861).

I knew Franz Boas personally. I was able to observe his influence as founder of the science of anthropology in America. I was also able to observe the increasing degree of control exercised by the Boas cult over students and younger professors until fear or loss of jobs or status was common... unless conformity to the dogma of racial equality was maintained...

DR. H. E. GARRETTT, Chr. Dept. of Psychology,
Columbia Univ.

In studying racial differences in living men, physical anthropologists are relying ...more and more on research in blood groups, hemoglobin and other biochemical features... In them racial differences have been found, just as great as the better know... conspicuous anatomical differences... not only variations in bone and teeth evident in fossil man, and those of the surface features of living men... by which we can distinguish races almost at a glance, but also subtler differences seen only on the dissecting table or through the eyepieces of microscopes. DR. C.S. COON, Pres. Amer. Assoc. of Phys. Anthropologists.

Whatever may be the sociological value of the legal fiction that "all men are born free and equal" there can be no doubt that... in its biological application ...this statement is one of the most stupendous falsehoods ever uttered....

DR. EARNEST A. WOOTEN, Prof. Anthropology,
Harvard Univ.

Man's genetic constitution determines his environment. The egg comes before the chicken. Does anyone believe that an area of the city inhabited by... Chinese would become a slum reeking with poverty, crime, and immorality?

PROFESSOR HENRY E. GARRETT.

The entire egalitarian camp of anthropologists... is very largely JEWISH and almost to a man... related to the Communist conspiracy to... destroy our whole social order. The high proportion of JEWS in the egalitarian camp is highly suspicious for in all human history there has been no other race that believes in its superiority so fanatically as the JEWS.

W. G. SIMPSON, *Which Way Western Man* (1970).

GREGOR MENDEL (1822-1884), was an Augustinian monk born in Brunn, Austria. His discovery of the first laws of heredity (1865) laid the foundations for the Science of Genetics. He demonstrated that hereditary material passing from parents to offspring is particulate (relating to minute particles in nature); and consists of an organization of *living units*. These units, now called genes, are found in all forms of life, from viruses to man. Genes, arranged within the nucleus of each cell, including the sex cells, convey an assortment of the parents' genes to the offspring. *The genes, interacting with each other, determine the development and specific character of each individual.* Environment does play a role in the development of each individual, but it is a small role. The old adage holds: *You can t make a silk purse out of a pig s ear.*

The entire GENOME, the body's "biological instruction manual" consists of 50,000 to 130,000 genes arranged along 46 chromosomes (including two chromosomes, x and y, that determine sex) that are composed of 3-billion pairs of nucleotides, the basic building blocks of DNA (Deoxyribonucleic Acid) which, in every cell, transmits hereditary patterns. As molecular scientists further divide nucleotides we approach the realm of nuclear physics and quantum mechanics in which molecules are broken down into infinitesimal (millionth of a millionth of an inch) quarks — and even smaller particles of matter — which metamorphose into varying wave-lengths of electrical energy. At this point science enters the realm of metaphysics where (I speculate) the stuff genes are made of exchanges energy with the Universal Force (probably in direct proportion to each person's pecking order on the evolutionary scale). If true, is not this interchange of energy Man's SOUL?

IDENTICAL TWINS. Many new facts are available resultant of the technological explosion. Mass techniques, for example, permitting group studies at the genetic level, reveal the effects of racially interacting genes. Now, *scientists attribute no less than ninety per-cent (90%) of differences in our ABILITY to heredity.* The studies of vast numbers of "Identical Twins" prove *what our Aryan ancestors knew intuitively*: that Nature prevails over nurture. Identical Twins begin life with identical arrangements of genes in their germ plasm. When reared apart — fed, housed and educated *in totally different environments* — exhaustive studies show that *invariably Identical Twins develop the same illnesses, share the same interests and have, among other similarities, the same level of emotional and mental properties* that determine their social behavior, character and development. Such qualities exhibit virtually NO environmental influences. These studies alone dealt the SPIROCHETES OF JEW SYPHILIS a mortal blow. Genes make us what we are. And they make us unequal: individually and racially.

MUTATIONS

In depth research shows that genetic mutations, most of which are lethal (90%+), appear to a certain extent in all people. However, some ethnic groups exhibit not only a higher occurrence of genetic defects, *they also may suffer genetic mutations peculiar to their race.* For example, Tay-Sachs disease, and sickle-cell anemia are, respectively, JEW and Negro genetic diseases. While it pleases Liberals to believe all men are created equal, it appears that some races, genetically at least, are "more equal than others."

4-F. During World War I, 30% of eligible American males were declared unfit for military service because they failed mental and physical standards. During WW II, that rejection number rose to 40% — among which more than a million were psycho-neurotics; for similar reasons 300,000 soldiers were culled out along the battle lines. During the Korean war the number jumped to 52% even though *standards had to be lowered! Perhaps this is the reason the Star of David appears so infrequently among the white crosses marking America's fallen war heroes.*

BIRTHS

In the United States 25 out of every 100 children born are so deformed as to be called monsters — many of these are resultant of *regression*. Of the seventy-five who survive twenty-eight are social failures within 15-years, largely because of genetic degenerative diseases. *This translates into a Fifty-three percent (53%) reproduction failure rate! Degenerative disease cases escalate exponentially as America's complexion grows darker.*

MENTAL HEALTH

In 1960, forty-seven percent (47%) of all U.S. hospital beds were occupied by mentally ill patients. Michael Gorman Executive Director, National Committee on Mental Health, estimated that no less than 10% of the entire population would spend time in mental hospitals. He described it as "an epidemic sweeping the land". Equally disturbing is the problem of FEEBLE-MINDEDNESS (the mind failing to develop): The adult idiot has the intelligence of a child 2-4 years old; the imbecile 3-7 years old; the moron 7-12 years old. A grade-level of intelligence above these groups is the "childlike" "dull normal" who are allowed to hold government jobs and vote. Heritability of feeble-mindedness is widely recognized. Worse, these goatish *degenerates breed within the group, out-producing intelligent couples three to one.* It is revealing that the proportion of feeble-mindedness in the United States in 1960 was thirty (30) times greater per capita than in Germany (apparently Hitler's elite Waffen-SS troops, before they were hanged, procreated Alpha children). It is safe to guess that U. S. statistics in this regard show the problem has worsened. It is well known that our insane asylums are overflowing. Liberals see this as a "discrimination" problem.

Ergo, morons of grotesque appearance and behavior are released to their home environments where they roam their neighborhoods like goblins on Halloween.

The ILLUMINATI sought to suppress all information concerning genetics but the "Iron Curtain" parted at almost every level of communications. The JEW mass-media no longer can conceal the devastating FACTS. "Equality" is a MARXIST/LIBERAL/JEW LIE. Genes, not environmental social programs, determine the quality of human life: Physiologically, Psychologically, Behaviorally, Intellectually, and Culturally. Most importantly, Genes relate to the Spiritual Essence of Man in ways we can sense but not see; feel but not touch. Environmental contributions (nurture) are incidental and negligible by comparison.

> Your republic will be as fearfully plundered and laid waste by barbarians in the 20th Century as the Roman Empire was in the 5th, with this difference... your Huns and Vandals will have been engendered within your own country by your own institutions.
> LORD MACAULAY, addressing the U.S.A. 150-years ago.

The truth of his (Supreme Court Justice Brandeis, JEW) conviction that (America's) individualistic philosophy could no longer furnish an adequate basis for dealing with the problems of modern economic life is now generally recognized ...he envisions a cooperative order... Brandeis feels the U.S. Constitution must be given liberal construction.

UNIVERSAL JEWISH ENCYCLOPEDIA (Vol.II).

Scientists must regularly confront these racial or ethnic differences and must deal with them honestly in order to ferret out their origins and implications. It's being naive to deny that certain groups are genetically different from other groups... How many Ashkenazi Jews are there in the National Basketball League?

R. D. BURKE, JEW, Prof. Epidemiology, Einstein College, NY. Quoted by Robin M. Henig, *Washington Post.*

Garland Allen (Prof. Biology) is worried about the possibilities of a new eugenics movement which would echo the wave of restricted immigration and forced sterilization that swept Europe and America in the 20's and 30's culminating in the horrors of the 3rd Reich.

CANDICE O'CONNOR Washington University, St. Louis, Mo.

HITLER was correct in his assessment of the ultimate importance of Genetics. Through applied eugenics (improvement of the Aryan gene-pool) he intended to create eugenically an Aryan Super Race. The "HOLOCAUST" religion was concocted by the ILLUMINATI for many reasons, one was to dissuade the White Nation from pursuing Social Darwinism and Hitlers applied physical anthropology, genetics, and eugenics.

Come to us Children of the West! No longer aspire to dreams of Courage, Conquest, and Glory. Your ancient Heroes and Heroines were simply genitalia in motion. There is no Soul. And Life? Life is simply Money, Lust, and Brotherhood. Come to us Golden Children of the West!

MARXISM/LIBERALISM/JEWRY.

Mankind should not merely go on — but UP! The SUPERMAN I have at heart... and not man: not the neighbor, not the poorest, not the sorriest, not the best... What I love in man is that he is an over-going and a down-going — one who seeks to create beyond himself and to this end is willing that he himself should succumb... Purified races always become stronger and more beautiful... The weak and the botched shall perish: the first principle of humanity.

FRIEDRICH NIETZSCHE.

Every cell, every organism, every race must excrete its waste or die!
WILLIAM GAYLEY SIMPSON, *Which Way Western Man?*

E.A. HOOTEN, Prof. Anthropology, Harvard, who associates crime with genetic factors, states: The country's *"criminal stock must be eliminated."* The only way to curb the proliferation of crime is to *"breed a better race."*

Whereas ASHLEY MONTAGU (aka Israel Ehrenberg), JEW, Boasite, states, *"There is not the slightest evidence to believe that anyone ever inherits a tendency to commit criminal acts."* This, despite mountains of evidence linking genetic defects with criminality. In truth, crime has escalated in the U.S.A. precisely because the Boas School of Anthropology set the guidelines for criminology in the United States.

If what I fear is true... our nobly intended welfare programs may be encouraging... retrogressive evolution through disproportionate reproduction of the genetically disadvantaged.
Dr. WILLIAM SHOCKLEY, Nobel Laureate,
Stanford Univ. in *Scientific American* (Jan. 1971).

A dog that can count to ten is a remarkable dog, not a great mathematician.
GRANDAD, from "Down on the Farm".

Nature teaches that all progress comes through the physical improvement of the breed. Men are not disembodied and denationalized intelligences operating without relation either to their forbears or their posterity. All natural evolution has been effected through certain races: so long as they kept their virility unimpaired human achievement remained cumulative. But once the purity of the blood and the capacity for healthful breeding of a people were impaired, whether through unhealthy conditions or miscegenation, the race deteriorated and the quality of the individual declined with it.

PROF. ARTHUR BRYANT, "Unfinished Victory".

JEWS are in perfect accord, if it benefits their tribe, when it comes to sending young Aryans to die in no-win wars around the globe. But JEWS go berserk when one suggests that sterilizing the genetically unfit will benefit Mankind. Suddenly all human life — even imbeciles not yet conceived — becomes sacrosanct. *The last thing JEWS want is a strong, healthy Aryan Nation.* The Catholic position on applied eugenics is mired in the same hubris displayed in its confrontation with Galileo. God's SUN, after all won that battle, not the Cardinals!

In the famous case: *Buck v. Bell, U.S. Supreme Court, 1927* the court upheld the State of Virginia law upholding compulsory sterilization of the "feeble-minded". Writing for the court Oliver Wendell Holmes, Jr. ruled that sterilization laws were part of the state police powers and that "three generations of imbeciles are enough."

W.G. SIMPSON, *Which Way Western Man?*

The Scandinavian countries followed suit in 1929, 1934, and 1935. From the turn of the Century to the early 1960s the United States of America had its own eugenics movement, sponsored by many high-ranking educators, scientists, and Supreme Court justices who called for sterilization of genetically impaired Hispanics and Negroes.

Laws to Prevent Transmission of Hereditary Disease were enacted by Nazis (July 1933) to provide for sterilizing those with congenital feeble-mindedness; certain mental diseases such as schizophrenia and manic-depression; hereditary epilepsy, blindness, deaf-mutism; and severe malformations. Culling the unfit has been practiced by vigorous nations throughout history. All farmers and ranchers understand the importance of good breeding. If you expect a vigorous, productive garden you must begin with healthy seeds, then prepare the soil, cull defective plants, and eliminate all weeds. *"Weeds are in the eyes of the beholder!"* protest the egalitarians. Precisely. Each race has instinctive feelings about what is beautiful, productive, important. Our rose may be your weed. *One man's tea is another's poison.* Obviously different races cannot exist harmoniously and productively under the same government. *Western Civilization — White Civilization — if it is to survive — must remove the weeds from its garden. As it must remove SPIROCHETES OF JEW SYPHILIS from its mind.* A necessary beginning is sterilization of the unfit — placing a contraception-chip beneath the skin of the recipient. This must be followed immediately by the colonization of the United States' non-White population.

GENETICS AND RACE

As a social anthropologist I naturally accept and even stress the fact that there are major differences, both mental and psychological, which separate the different races of mankind. Indeed I would be inclined to suggest that however great may be the physical differences between such races as the European and the Negro, the mental and psychological differences are greater still.

Dr. L.S.B. LEAKY, *Progress and Evolution of Man in Africa.*

From the beginning of the thirties onward scarcely anyone outside Germany and its allies dared to suggest that any race might be in any respect or any sense superior to any other lest it should appear that the author was supporting or excusing the Nazi cause. Those who believed in the equality of all races were free to write what they liked without fear of contradiction. They made full use of their opportunity in the decades that followed.

DR. JOHN R. BAKER, biologist, Oxford, *Fellow, Royal Society.*

If all races had a common origin how does it happen that some peoples, like the Tasmanians, and many of the Australian aborigines, were still living during the 19th Century in a manner comparable to the Europeans of over 100,000 years ago?

CARLTON S. COON, Prof. Anthropology, Harvard.

Despite glowing accounts of ancient African achievements over the past 5,000 years the history of Black Africa is culturally blank. South of the Sahara desert, until the arrival of other races, there was NO literate civilization. (No written language, no numerals, no calendar, no system of measurement. The black African had not invented a plow, a wheel, domesticated an animal or a crop).

PROF. HENRY GARRETT,
Head of Psychology Dept. Columbia U.

Races of men are differentiated in the same way as well-marked species of animals.

SIR ARTHUR KEITH, M.D., Rector,
University of Edinburgh.

W. G. Simpson ("Which Way Western Man") comments that the primary object of any nation is NOT to produce a slavish herd of lobotomized sheep *but to produce the greatest number of superior men.* Men with great instinct and intuition, with powerful intellects capable of analysis and creativity; with great courage and noble goals; men of bountiful health and energy; with commanding personalities and magnanimous spirits; who regard themselves with Nietzschean *"love and contempt"*. These are the men who prefer to "die in the saddle rather than nod by the fire". These are Titans, part God part Man — they are the bridge between animal and the Superman to come. It is only by understanding and applying Nature's Laws that a great nation will continue to produce superior men and women and save itself from extinction.

GREGOR MENDEL, studying the reproduction of peas in his monastery garden *discovered the building blocks of all living things,* justifying (largely) Darwin's *Theory of Evolution.* Thereafter, Jehovah's suicidal decree that Man shall have *"dominion"* over Nature was relegated to Fantasy Land. Mankind is subject to Nature's Laws. Man's task is to learn Nature's Laws, and obey them; in so doing man will become ever more perfect. *Mendel's gift to Mankind is the science to create more perfect Living Things! GOD S GIFT TO MANKIND IS MENDEL!*

As we have learned the JEW HATE APPARATUS descended upon MENDELISM burying the Truth for 100-years. Eventually Nature triumphed over ideology, as she always will, destroying Marx, Freud, and Boas in the process. It is now an UNDISPUTED FACT: Environment creates NO innate capacity, but can decide only whether or not innate capacity shall be developed. CAPACITY IS INHERITED!!! *AWAKE TO THE MENDELIAN AGE!*

> Summing up all the genetic experiments where the inheritance was constant and the environment variable, it would hardly be an exaggeration to say the results were negligible.
>
> DR. EDWARD M. EAST, Professor of Genetics, Harvard U.

> Never attempt to teach a pig to sing; It ruins your day and annoys the pig.
>
> GRANDAD, from "Down on the Farm".

EUGENICS is the science of applying the Laws of Genetics toward the improvement of races and breeds. Mankind is capable of passing favorable genetic characters to succeeding generations, while eliminating many unfavorable qualities. Man can achieve even more extraordinary results than he has in the breeding of grains, fruits, vegetables, flowers, livestock, horses and pets. Don't let this shock you. Man IS part animal. Therefore, let us examine some of Mankind's breeding practices.

INBREEDING has been practiced since the beginning of human history. It refers to the mating of close relatives: parents and siblings, brothers and sisters, and first cousins. Contrary to Distorters the only injury from inbreeding results from defective inheritance received: defects which persisted in the stock for many generations but were hidden by more dominant characters. Successful inbreeding requires, for one thing, that defectives be prohibited from breeding.

> Instead of being condemned (inbreeding) should be commended.

After continued inbreeding with the discarding of undesirables an in-bred stock has been purified and rid of abnormalities, monstrosities, and serious weaknesses...

EDWARD M. EAST, Ph.D., LL.D.,
Professor, Genetics, Harvard.

Inbreeding is only disastrous if the ingredients of disaster are already in the stock... close inbreeding of a sound stock, if associated with intelligent elimination of the weakly and abnormal, can be practiced for many generations without any undesirable consequences.

A. A. F. CREW, M.D., D.Sc.,
Ph.D., F.R.S.E., U. Edinburgh.

Ancient India thrived on inbreeding. When the caste system was abandoned India precipitously declined. Spartans, considered the greatest physically of all races, practiced inbreeding, as did their remarkable Attic cousins, the Athenians, who, out of a population of 45,000 free-born males (c.530-430 B.C.), produced fourteen of the most illustrious men in history. In Persia wives of choice were cousins on the father's side. Egyptians and Incas married fathers and daughters, sons and mothers, brothers and sisters this last was considered the best of all marriage unions. During Egypt's greatest Dynasty (the 18th) there were seven brother-sister marriages. Hebrews were not only endogamous they often married within the *immediate family.* For example: Abraham wed Sarah his half-sister; Jacob wed Rachael and Leah, both first cousins. Lot bred with both of his daughters (or was it the other way around ?). Hasting's "Dictionary of the Bible" states JEWS are three times more likely than other races to marry cousins. JEWS also produce a high ratio of defectives because TALMUDIC LAW encourages the genetically unfit to breed this fatal policy seriously contaminated the JEW gene-pool.

Inbreeding is the quickest way to bring latent defects to the surface where they can be identified and eliminated. Also, it is single best method of bringing about uniformity and desired qualities.

> Inbreeding canalizes and isolates health and other desirable qualities, just as it canalizes and isolates ill-health and other undesirable qualities. It stabilizes the germ-plasm and this causes hereditary factors to be calculable. It therefore makes appearance a guide to the individual's hereditary equipment... it acts as a purifier of a stock or family.
> A. M. LUDOVICI, "The Quest of Human Quality".

OUTBREEDING is the mating of unrelated individuals or those having distant family relationships, but within the same racial gene-pool. Outbreeding is a means to widen and enrich the hereditary character-combinations which later inbreeding may be called upon to isolate, stabilize, and bring forth in the progeny. This results in what is called heterosis, or HYBRID VIGOR, due to the combination of the parent's qualities. The deficiencies in one parent may be canceled by excellences in the other parent. Or the good in one parent may be intensified by the good in the other. The three most important factors concerning HYBRIDS, as we touched on earlier, are these:

1) To obtain Hybrid vigor both parents must be unrelated and purebred. The parents' qualities must be compensatory and complimentary.

2) Hybrid vigor when it does occur, is particular to the first cross. Further crossing of Hybrids results in acute loss

of vigor. In short, Hybrids used for breeding are worthless: they cannot pass-on even their own size and vigor.

3)   Hybrid vigor, as good as, or better than, those just described, can be attained through crossing different, but distinct, family strains from within the same breed, or gene-pool. Actually this is a type of inbreeding, prevalent in America where the ancient Aryan tribes (German, Celt, Slav, et al) intermarried, establishing an extra-European gene-pool. This great White gene-pool (from which the Founders and Builders of America arose) is being destroyed by our ancient ENEMIES.

Remember (except when discussing self-fertilization or cloning) in-breeding results when the lines of hereditary qualities are narrowed; out-breeding results when the hereditary network is widened.

CROSS-BREEDING, the most extreme example of out-breeding, occurs when couples from completely different gene-pools mate, such as Japanese and Negro, or Aryan and JEW.

GENETIC DISORDERS frequently resultant of extreme out-breeding and cross-breeding are well documented, including physiological, instinctive, and psychological disorders. The most apparent disorders appear as physical aberrations. Hereditary factors are transmitted to offspring independently. For example, a child may receive pale skin from one parent while retaining woolly hair and Negro features from the other; or the offspring may receive internal organs too small or too large for the rest of the body; or receive arms and legs disharmonious with the torso, making it difficult for the body to function as a synthesized unit. At the very least health and efficiency are impaired and symmetry is lost. The mixing of intellectually superior characters with mentally inferior characters degrades the superior gene-pool. But the problem is even more hideous:

REVERSION within the species sometimes results from extreme cross-breeding. The progeny are throw-backs to a stage much earlier on the evolutionary scale. These degenerates, often monsters, represent evolution in reverse and are never viewed on MARXIST/LIBERAL/JEW TV-programs.

The different races have taken millions of years to evolve: some races evolved slower, or started later, than others. *To cross-breed with less advanced races results in a LOSS to the superior race of hundreds-of-thousands of years of evolution, and imposes physiological and psychological abnormalities which, at this stage of clinical research, appear to be catastrophic.*

> The fact that there are inherited differences in the size of the organs and parts is of profound significance when it is remembered that it involves the inevitable sequel that racial and other crossings can lead to serious disharmony ... between teeth and jaws, between size of body and size of some important organ or organs, disharmony among the various components of the endocrine chain...disharmony is commonly displayed in difficult labor caused by disproportion in the...sizes of the maternal passages...
>
> Dr. A.A.E. CREW, University of Edinburgh.

Really healthy and efficient families are too valuable to be mixed with the sick and morbid; they ought, therefore, as far as possible to intermarry among themselves, as ought also the less desirable.

Dr. FRITZ LENZ, quoted by A.M.Ludovici.

Inbreeding is the surest means of establishing families which as a whole are of high value to the community.

Dr. E.M. EAST & Dr. D.F. JONES,
"Inbreeding and Outbreeding".

Cross-breeding has occurred throughout history. There also have been diseases throughout history. The frequency of mongrelism and diseases doesn't establish their desirability. *History demonstrates that the envious and the less gifted want either to destroy those whom they can never emulate, or to lose their identity through miscegenation with a better breed both being forms of genocide. For under-achievers miscegenation is the yearning to catch and hold a tantalizingly beautiful golden butterfly. But, upon grasping it, they find the lovely colors rub off on their fingers. The mongrel child of a golden-haired, long-limbed Swedish woman is never as lovely or as fit as the mother. The glory rubs off — forever.*

Infants are individuals... from the moment of birth. Indeed many of their individual characteristics are laid down long before birth... Every child is born with a nature which colors and structures his experiences... He has constitutional traits and tendencies largely inborn which determine how, what, and to some extent even when he will learn. These traits are both racial and familial... Racial differences are recognizable by the fourth fetal month... There (are) genuinely individual differences already prophetic of the diversity that distinguishes the human family.

PROF. ARNOLD GESELL, Yale University, Pediatrics.

...it had come to be firmly recognized that the racial factor in blood transfusions was of such practical importance that Dr. John Scudder, with a very distinguished career as surgeon, blood specialist, medical school professor, and director of blood-banks in various parts of the world, and as a blood-bank advisor to our government and to several foreign governments as well, in laying down the rules for the selection of blood donors... specified they should be "of the patient's own race" and preferably "of the patient's own ethnic group."

WILLIAM G. SIMPSON, "Which Way Western Man".

In blood groups, hemoglobins, and other biochemical features...racial differences have been found ...just as great as the better known and more conspicuous anatomical variations. Being invisible to the naked eye they are much less controversial than the latter in an increasingly race-conscious world. To me at least it is encouraging to know that biochemistry still divides us into the same sub-species that we have long recognized on the basis of other criteria.

DR. CARLTON S. COON, Prof. of Anthropology, Harvard Univ.

Dr. Carlton Coon, in his highly acclaimed work "The Origin of Races", names four most important factors in the formation of races: Recombination Mutation Selection - Isolation. RECOMBINATION is an inexplicable interchange of genes from homologous chromosomes forming an independent combination of genes in the progeny not apparent in the parents.

MUTATION is an inexplicable change occurring in the chemical composition of a gene causing it to produce an effect different from that produced by the gene from which it was first derived. Put another way, it is a chemical change in genes that produces a brand new not inherited gene which gets into the racial gene-pool. It then becomes inheritable as all other genes in the gene-pool. 90% of all mutations are useless or harmful to the organism; these are rooted out by *NATURAL SELECTION* (Mother Nature is considerate, never kind). Other harmful mutations, however, may be perpetuated producing organic disorders, as Tay-Sachs disease, sickle-cell anemia, goiters, cleft palates, disfigurements, and many other physiological and psychological afflictions which, by the way, can be virtually eliminated through the application of Eugenics. Moreover, and this is the important point, *MUTATION is the "primary element in evolution" of the species! "Without mutation evolutionary change could never have occurred"*. A richly endowed mutated gene had to come about before any population could develop into a race. That special gene gets into the racial gene-pool and a SPIRITUAL CULTURAL-ORGANISM is created giving that race mastery over competing populations.

ISOLATION *of the gene-pool protects the CULTURAL-ORGANISM from contamination by extra-racial forces.* ISOLATION whether geographical or socio-cultural, is the means whereby a particular population unit or gene-pool, is subjected to the differential selective forces of its own unique climatic and cultural mail. Genetic variations and differences that may arise in one population group are preserved and become characteristic of the group (i.e., elements of a 'race type') through restriction of mating to group members. Continued isolation and inbreeding... thus perpetuates and stabilizes group differences.

DR.DONALD A. SWAN, "The Mankind Quarterly" (Vol. IV, No. 4).

Isolation has been the great factor, or at any rate an essential factor, in the differentiation of the races.

DR. R. R. GATES, Emeritus Prof. of Botany, Univ. London.

Unless a breeding population is contained (Isolated) natural selection may be unable to eliminate old, unfavorable genes from its pool.

DR. CARLTON S. COON, Prof. Anthropology, Harvard Univ.

As you can see the evidence is irrefutable. All credible anthropologists, geneticists and historians concur: *RACES ARE GENETICALLY UNIQUE: physiologically, psychologically, intellectually, behaviorally and intuitively. Genes determine Race. Race determines Capacity. Capacity determines culture. Culture determines environment.* Ergo, Cultures are UNEQUAL in relationship to each other. *Genes are intrinsic to the LIFE FORCE, they are living, evolving, racial entities God-given!*

ADOLPH HITLER was the first great political leader to understand and subscribe to the tenets of MENDELISM: Unique genes produced Western Culture.

Western Culture was produced by Aryan genes. Therefore, Aryan genes are unique genes. (A:B)::(B:C) = (C:A).

Respecting that syllogism, which is predicated on Nature's Laws, Adolph Hitler concluded that *the primary function of the Aryan State (Reich) is to protect, and nurture the Aryan Nation (the White Gene-Pool). Hitler expected to begin his political/eugenic program in Germany, gradually uniting the Aryan family under one State; a concept JEWS considered "anti-Semitic" (a threat to parasitism), and nationalistic (a threat to the PLUTOCRATIC New World Order). MARXISTS/LIBERALS/JEWS (abetted by the Catholic Church) refuse to promulgate Mendelism and demonize those who do (Faith/ Religion, always opposes Instinct/Knowledge).*

50-years after America incinerated the Third Reich, the White scientific community assisted by INTERNET released the GENE from the bottle (having lost MEDIA control of the gene, JEWS now frantically seek control of its use). Today, MENDELISM is improving the life of everyone on the planet. Consequently, pharmaceutical companies, university research labs, pathologists, eugenicists, heads of state (seeking to improve their populations), et al., are actively buying White genes in the market-place. In the private sector Aryan college women, for example, are besieged with offers for their OVARIAN EGGS in exchange for full scholarships and other enticements (You are aware of the ongoing Hollywood defilement of the Aryan womb). Icelanders, whose Viking heritage is remarkable for its unpolluted gene-pool, are marketing their genes, and ovarian eggs the world over. Aryan gene/egg sales will soon be Iceland's largest business! (How many sterile parents do you imagine are scrambling to purchase JEW, or Puerto Rican ovarian eggs?).

The Satanic side to commercialization of Life (TEST TUBE MISCEGENATION) is the *in vitro* cross-breeding of White genes: denying the never-to-be-born White child its natural heritage, while afflicting the mongrel offshoot with loss of racial identity, split personality, and tortured Soul.

NATURAL SELECTION (God's Law), begins with the mating process, during which a compatible couple marry and produce children whom they cherish *and nurture, and who glorify their family. This intra*-gene-pool process eliminates undesirable genetic qualities while perpetuating desirable ones, which are produced by genic recombination or mutation.

> We must undermine faith, eradicate from the minds of the Gentiles the very principles of God and Soul, and replace these conceptions with mathematical calculations and material desires.
>
> PROTOCOL Number Four.

During the Modern Era, Western Culture (Aryan Culture), which overwhelmingly made the most significant contributions to Mankind, is now threatened by Cultural Pathology in the form of alien-parasitic growth within the Nation-State itself. If the parasites are not removed the West will die. This is not a melodramatic observation but is the lesson of history.

In the last decade the Total Fertility Rate (TFR) for Europe plunged by 21%, down from already incredibly low levels, to 1.45 children per woman (it takes 2.1 children per woman just to keep a population stable over time). USA (TFR) has declined in each of the past six-years to an estimated 1.98.

> Current world population is 5.8-billion people. The U.N. minimum projection puts the global population of 2050 at 9.4-billion people a 62% increase. And predicts it will climb to 10.7-billion just after the year 2200 -an increase of 84%.
>
> UNITED NATIONS "World Population Prospects 1996 Revisions".

UNESCO COMMITTEE DRAFTS GENETIC RESEARCH GUIDELINES. ...that declares the genetic material in every human is "the common heritage of humanity"

...The declaration states that human genetics research holds vast potential but must be regulated to protect public health and guard against any practice that "runs counter to human dignity and human rights".

REUTERS NEWS AGENCY, Paris, Washington Times.

THE WHOLE PROCESS OF NATURALIZATION HAS BEEN SO WATERED DOWN IN RECENT YEARS THAT IT MAKES A FARCE OF CITIZENSHIP ...In a rush to ensure more Democratic voters... White House officials exerted unprecedented pressure on the Immigration and Naturalization Service to process applications for citizenship. As a result, in 1996, more than one-million new citizens were sworn in a record number but some 180,000 never underwent proper FBI background checks as required by law...there are no uniform standards for testing (qualifications) for applicants.

LINDA CHAVEZ, Washington Times, 3-16-97.

What does the American Negro have...? His past is a stigma, his color is a stigma, and his vision of the future is the hope of erasing that stigma by making color irrelevant, by making it disappear as a fact of consciousness... I share this hope, but I cannot see how it will ever be realized unless color does in fact disappear: and that means not integration, it means assimilation, it means let the brutal word come out *miscegenation. I believe that the wholesale merging of the two races is the most desirable alternative for everyone concerned*...in my opinion the Negro problem in this country can be solved in no other way.

NORMAN PODHORETZ, JEW, editor of "Commentary" magazine. He is also associated with the "conservative" *Heritage Foundation,* and his wife, Midge Dichter, JEW, is an officer of that organization.

The development of society is subject not to biological laws but to higher social laws. Attempts to spread to humanity the laws of the animal kingdom are an attempt to lower the human being to the level of beasts.

INSTITUTE OF GENETICS OF ACADEMY OF SCIENCES, U.S.S.R.

Love Across Color Lines a Biography: ...Maria Diedrich asserts that Frederick Douglass, far from having broken free of color consciousness, was "torn between two races, tortured by his double consciousness of being both and neither." She sees in him an "ultimate longing for an identification with his father's whiteness." Douglass's love of white women...allowed him "to claim as his the territory from which his father-master had exiled him... (territory) which he could only perceive as white." Pointing out that Otillie Assing (Douglass's mistress) was half-Jewish...(she) reached out to Douglass... "as a white woman with all the privileges of whiteness, yet seasoned with the wisdom of a half-breed." (Assing died a suicide).

MARIA DIEDRICH, "Love Across Color Lines"
(from Washington Post book-review, 6-25-99).

Pope John Paul II... has succumbed ...to the tyranny of evolutionary scientists who claim we are related to monkeys... In a statement the Pope said "fresh knowledge leads to the recognition of the theory of evolution as more than just an hypothesis."

CAL THOMAS, syndicated columnist, Washington Times.

Evolution is a FACT. On the other hand... If Man comes from Apes Why do Apes still live in trees And don't wear pants?

GRANDAD, "Down on the Farm."

To reduce dysgenic agonies for both the genetically disadvantaged and the overburdened taxpayer (I recommend) ...voluntary sterilization... by bonuses... perhaps $1000 for each point below 100 I.Q.

PROF. WILLIAM SHOCKLEY, Nobel Prize laureate, Stanford U.

CHAPTER 8

THE NEGRO

There is absolutely no question of any genetic differential: Intelligence potential is distributed among Negro infants in the same proportion and pattern as among Icelanders, or Chinese or any other group.
    U.S. SENATOR DANIEL P. MOYNIHAN, Democrat/Catholic.

Abstract intelligence is the *sine qua non* for the existence of a civilized society. Fifty years of research in the U.S.A. have revealed regular, persistent, and statistically significant mean differences between Negroes and Whites.
    DR. HENRY GARRETT, head of Dept. Psychology, Columbia U.

Today, psychological and genetic tests place the matter of mental inequality beyond doubt, as far as the White race and Black race are concerned.... the intelligence level of the Negro is far below that of the White.
    EDWARD M. EAST, Prof. of Genetics, Harvard U.

...the size of the brain relative to size or weight of the body is of crucial importance in placing each species or subspecies in its proper place in tables of advanced or less advanced stocks... the average brain of the Negro differs in weight, being 100 grams or thereabouts less than the average of the Caucasoid.... it is quite impossible to maintain the brains are the same when we find a distinct difference of this kind.
    ROBERT GAYRE, M.A., D.Phil., D.Sc., Ed. *"The Mankind Quarterly'*.

1.IQ's of American Negroes are 15-20 points lower on the average than American Whites.
2.Negro overlap of the White median IQ, ranges from 10-25% (equality would require a 50% overlap).

3.About 6 times as many Negroes as Whites fall below IQ 70 (feeble-minded group).

4.About 6 times as many Whites are in 'gifted child' category.

5.Negro lag is greatest in tests of an abstract nature: involving reasoning, deduction, comprehension, etc.

6.Negro-White differences increase with age, the gap of performance being greatest in high school and college.

7.Large and significant differences appear in favor of Whites even when economic factors have been equated.

The above statistics are taken from *"The Testing of Negro Intelligence"*, (Social Science Press), by Prof. Audrey M. Shuey, Chr. Dept. Psychology, Randolph-Macon College. The test comprises 382 comparisons, in which 81 different tests were employed covering a wide sampling of hundreds of thousands. The tests were designed to measure the kind of mental ability necessary to do well in a modern urban, highly literate civilization.

The tests received high praise from Drs. Garrett, Gayre, Josey, Baker, Woodsworth and other distinguished scientists. Nevertheless, *six university presses refused to publish it rather than risk losing their government subsidies.*

The COLEMAN REPORT (1966) was supported by the Federal Government at a cost of $1-million. It researched 600,000 children, K-12, in 4000 demographically representative schools in all parts of the country. *About 15% of Negro children equaled or exceeded the White average; 85% fell below the White average. In order of races Whites were first; Orientals second; Amerinds (the most economically deprived of all) third; Mexicans were followed by Puerto Ricans; and last,*

Negroes. The Coleman Report was buried by LIBERALS/MARXISTS/JEWS.

During the Civil War several thousand Negroes escaped to Canada via the "underground railway". Their descendants have lived in Canada "discrimination free" ever since. Yet their mental test scores are the same as the "oppressed" American Negro.

> The size of the human brain is related to a capacity for performance in thinking, planning, communicating, and behaving in groups, as leader, follower or both... In living individuals and populations differences are found in the regular size of the lobes and in the surface areas of the cortex; the size of the surface area varies with the complexity and depth of the folds on the inner and outer surfaces of the hemispheres. The larger a brain is the greater the cortical surface area, both proportionately and absolutely.
>
> DR. CARLTON COON, Prof. of Anthropology, Harvard.

> The human cerebral cortex is the specific organ of civilization... Foresight, purpose and ideals toward which we strive as individuals and as nations are functions of this cortical gray matter.
>
> PROF. C. JUDSON HERRICK, University of Texas.

F. W. Vint, Medical Research Laboratory, Kenya, Africa, published reports (1934) of "examinations of the cerebral cortex of 100 representative adult native brains (not including samples from prisons or mental hospitals) which were compared with European brains." He found that the "supragranular layer of the Negro cortex was about 14% thinner than Whites".

> The whole anterior frontal area on one or both sides may be removed without loss of consciousness. During the amputation the individual

may continue to talk, unaware of the fact that he is being deprived of the area which most distinguishes his brain from that of a chimpanzee. After its removal there will be a defect but *he may well not appreciate it himself.* The defect will be in his ability to plan and take initiative... although he may well be able to answer the questions of others as accurately as ever.

DR. WILDER PENFIELD, Prof. Neurology and Neurosurgery, McGill University, "the World's top brain surgeon".

Dr. Albert Schweitzer, renounced a world-renowned career in Germany as theologian, author, organist, and authority on Bach, to earn a doctorate in medicine. He then established a hospital in Lamberne, Africa. There, because of his Christianity and humanitarianism, he devoted 40-years of his life tending to Negroes. Dr. Schweitzer, idolized by "liberals", was awarded the Nobel Prize. During his acceptance speech he said *"the Negro is our brother, but he is our little brother... and with children nothing can be done without the use of authority... The combination of friendliness with authority is the great secret of successful intercourse with the Negro."* Following that statement Dr. Schweitzer fell from LIBERAL grace; as did Solzhenitsyn when he called Bolsheviks animals.

No western-trained Negro doctor ever volunteered to help Dr. Schweitzer, and his experience so convinced him of the lack of.... mental standards and character in the pure Negro ...that he never felt it worthwhile training Negroes for higher responsibilities in his African hospital.

H. B. ISHERWOOOD, "On the Edge of the Primeval Forest."

It will be seen that when we classify mankind by colour the only one of the primary races... which has not made a creative contribution to any one... of our civilizations is the Black Race. DR. ARNOLD TOYNBEE, "The Study of History".

A solution to these problems must be found, but it will never be obtained from falsification of the facts of hereditary and racial history.

ROBERT GAYRE, editor. "Mankind Quarterly".

Races of men are differentiated in the same way as well marked species of animals.

SIR ARTHUR KEITH.

The average Negro pupil (I.Q. 80.7) cannot go beyond a national-standard Seventh Grade curriculum; for half the Negro group the Fifth Grade is maximum... only one (1%) per cent (110 I.Q. and over) of the Negroes are intellectually equipped to do acceptable college work. Thirty (30%) of Whites are so equipped.

DR. HENRY E. GARRETT. Head Dept. Psychology, Columbia U.

The differences in thickness of the supragranular layers of the cortex of White and Negro brains is the difference between civilization and savagery.

DR. WESLEY CRITZ GEORGE, Head Dept. Anatomy, U. N. Carolina.

The supragranular layers in the dog are 1/2 the thickness of those in the ape, and the ape's only 3/4 the thickness of White man. The Negro's are 14% thinner than White man.

CARLTON PUTNAM, LLD, Princeton, "Race and Reality".

Negroes are more intelligent in direct proportion to the amount of White genes they carry. (Evidence suggests that) the average I.Q. of Negro populations increases by about One (1) I.Q. point for each one percent of Caucasian genes.

DR. WILLIAM SHOCKLEY, Nobel Prize Laureate, Stanford U.

Dr. Curt Stern, Prof. of Genetics, University of California, reports that *"the Average American Negro gets 3/4 of his genes from his African heritage and 1/4 from White genes."* White genes raise Negro I.Q.; conversely, Black genes dumb-down intellectually superior races. *"Almost White"*, is an oxymoron, because there is no almost White race. Either you're White or you are not White.

As a social anthropologist I naturally accept and even stress the fact that there are major differences, both mental and psychological, which separate the different races of mankind. Indeed I would be inclined to suggest that however great may be the physical differences between such races as the European and the Negro, the mental and psychological differences are greater still.

Dr. L. S. B. LEAKY, "Progress and Evolution of Man in Africa".

I was moved by the message of humanity embedded in its walls. The Olduvai Gorge offers a lesson that no matter how different human beings are on the surface, ultimately we come from the same place. We share a common ancestral home. And in the end, no matter our sex, the tone of our skin or the God we believe in no matter the wide oceans or expanses of land that separate us we are all part of the same human family.

HILLARY RODHAM CLINTON, Washington Times (4-3-97).

It is not in our stars, dear Brutus, that we are underlings, but in ourselves.

WILLIAM SHAKESPEARE, "Julius Caesar".

White South Africans are fleeing the country in increasing numbers mainly because of violent crime the government said this week... A recent crime survey by a S. African banking group revealed that on a typical day 52 persons are slain; 470 seriously injured in assaults; more than 100 women are raped; 270 automobiles are hijacked... and 590 homes are burgled.

WASHINGTON TIMES (10-17-96), Johannesburg Wire Services.

I can conceive of no greater calamity than the assimilation of the Negro into our social and political life as our equal.

ABRAHAM LINCOLN.

There is nothing more terrible than a barbaric slave class, who have learned to regard their existence as an injustice, and now prepare to revenge, not only themselves but all future generations. In the face of such threatening storms who dares to appeal with any confidence to our pale exhausted religions.

FRIEDRICH NIETZSCHE, "The Birth of Tragedy".

Amerinds, alone, populated the Americas until Spanish Conquistadors and Portuguese explorers introduced Negro slaves who mixed their African genes with the Indians. In 1619 about twenty Negro slaves arrived with British colonists and indentured servants at Jamestown, Virginia. At inception every one of the thirteen American Colonies recognized slavery. For census purposes Negroes were counted 3/5th of a man, Amerinds were not counted. Jefferson, who owned over 200 slaves, stated in the *Declaration of Independence* that *'all men are created equal"*. What he meant obviously was, *"Equal before the Law"*: Neither Negroes nor democracy are mentioned in the Constitution. With the coming of the *Industrial Revolution* British textile mills afforded a growing market for American cotton farmers. To meet increasing demand more field hands were required. Nordics refused the jobs. They weren't physically or mentally adapted to laboring under a hot southern sun Negroes were. And they were easily obtainable. African tribal chiefs were the procurers. Their tactics were to burn down neighboring villages then round-up the stampeding Negroes as rancheros round-up spooked cattle. The captives, men woman and children, were then chained together and sold to Arab, Jew, and White slave merchants. The principal unit of exchange, for Negroes being shipped to America, was cheap rum. Tribal chiefs became so addicted to the "ruddy cup" they would routinely sell members of their own family and tribe for it. The greatest number of sailing vessels (15) used to transport slaves were owned by JEWS. Slavery, of course, has appeared in almost all human societies since the beginning of history. Negro Africa is no exception. Today, in fact, Negroes conduct a brisk slave trade in the Sudan, Somaliland, et al.

> Slavery was an important function of African social and economic life.
>
> JOHN HOPE FRANKLIN, NEGRO,
> "From Slavery to Freedom".

In the United States Southern plantation owners paid hard cash for Negroes. *As valuable chattel, slaves were cared for by their owners from birth to death.* In the vast majority of cases slaves were treated humanely, often affectionately. Albeit, Negroes brought their savage genes with them from Africa. Therefore, sanitation, discipline and order had to be instilled and maintained, in that sense Negro lives were regimented. Plantation schools, and Bible studies were available to them. They had to be taught how to work, how to use tools, how to garden, how to perform chores. Even so, *living conditions were much better on the plantation than in black Africa, and individual life-span was longer.* By the time of the Civil War slavery was becoming an economic liability, and challenged by machinery was dying of obsolescence. The war, ostensibly fought to *"free the slaves"*, actually was fought to expand Rothschild's banking empire. Now free, the Negro 200,000 years behind on the evolutionary scale suddenly found himself adrift in the 19th Century White world. All intelligent, conscientious men, White and Black, knew (and know) that the Negro must be sent back to Africa, his homeland, and colonized there with the financial support of the United States government. Four major forces circumvented colonization:

1) Lincoln's murder.

2) The nation was encumbered with war debts.

3) Negroes were a source of cheap labor, and no longer had to be cared for "from cradle to grave".

4) The ILLUMINATI, expected to use the Negro as a "Fifth Column" to destroy Western/Christian Culture.

> Nothing is more certainly written in the book of Fate than that these people are to be free; nor is it less certain that the two races equally free cannot live under the same government.
> (The sentence inscribed on the Jefferson Memorial, Washington, D.C., fraudulently stops at the semi-colon).
> THOMAS JEFFERSON.

> I have urged the colonization of the Negro and I shall continue. My Emancipation Proclamation was linked with this plan. There is no room for two distinct races of White men in America (Whites and JEWS), much less two distinct races of Whites and Blacks... Within twenty years we can peacefully colonize the Negro... under conditions in which he can rise to the full measure of manhood. This he can never do here. We can never attain the ideal union our fathers dreamed, with millions of an alien, inferior race amongst us, whose assimilation is neither desirable or possible.
>
> ABRAHAM LINCOLN,
> Lincoln's *"Collected Works"*.

> We have between us a broader difference than exists between almost any other two races... If this is to be admitted it affords a reason, at least,

why we should be separated.

ABRAHAM LINCOLN, Sandburg,
"Abraham Lincoln, The War Years".

Social intercourse always implies sexual intercourse.

E. A. HOOTEN, Prof. Anthropology, Harvard U.

I did this (rape) consciously, deliberately, willfully, methodically... It delighted me that I was defying and trampling upon white man's law, upon his system of values, that I was defiling his women.

ELDRIDGE CLEAVER, *"Soul On Ice'.*

The inevitable result of racial mixing... is a massive reduction in the proportion of intelligent offspring.

NATHANIAL WEYL, JEW, Educator and writer.

Some races are obviously superior to others. A more thorough adjustment to the conditions of existence has given them spirit, vitality, scope and relative stability... it is therefore of the greatest importance not to obscure this superiority by intermarriage with inferior stock, and thus nullify the progress made by a painful evolution and a prolonged sifting of souls. Reason protests as much as instinct against any fusion, for instance, of white and black peoples...(white) greatness falls whenever contact leads to (such) amalgamation.

GEO. SANTAYANA,
Amer-Span. philosopher, *"The Life of Reason."*

If the Negro is not removed from the United States the future America will be mongrel, such as the peoples of (today's) Egypt, India, and certain Latin American countries... when two races come into contact one will expel the other... or adjust their differences through a process of inter-race breeding... the character of the higher race will tend to be obliterated in the mongrels.

ERNEST SEVIER COX, *"White America'.*

Dr. Carlton Coon... states that while the White and Yellow races were toilsomely evolving, the Negro in Africa "stood still for half a million years"...To be more specific, the Negro's brain is smaller and lighter, less complicated, less developed... The primitiveness of his brain betrays itself in the very speed with which it develops after birth, and then suddenly stops development, leaving him like a "lobotomized European".

WILLIAM G. SIMPSON, *"Which Way Western Man"*.

The Australids, shown to be primitive by their morphological criteria, did not progress on their own initiative beyond the food-gathering status; nor did those classic prototypes of paedomorphosis, the Bushmen or Sanids. A parallel conclusion is forced upon us if we look at the results of cognition and attainment tests carried out on various races living under conditions of civilized life. The Mongoloids and Europids did best in both these types of tests; they were followed (at some distance) by the Indianids, and the Negrids were still less successful. In conformity with these results the races among which civilization originated and advanced were the Mongoloids and Europids... Cranial capacity is, of course, directly related to the Ethnic problem since it sets a limit to the size of the brain in the different taxa; but all morphological differences are also relevant...

DR. JOHN R. BAKER, biologist, Oxford, Fellow of the Royal Society, from his acclaimed (but suppressed) book, "RACE".

It would be absurd to claim any superiority of all Europids over all Negrids on the evidence of achievement in the intellectual field; yet it must be allowed that the contributions of Negrids to the world of learning have, on the whole, been disappointing, despite all the improvements in facilities for their education. American Negroes are better known for their mass appeal in public affairs and popular entertainment than for great achievements in such subjects as philosophy, mathematics, science or technology.

DR. JOHN R. BAKER, biologist, Oxford.

WELLESLEY HISTORIAN CALLS AFROCENTRISM A MYTH: Neither Cleopatra nor Socrates was black. The ancient Greeks did not steal their philosophy from Egyptian priests, and Aristotle didn't loot the library at Alexandria. The roots of Western Civilization cannot be traced to Africa. Nevertheless these are among the claims of the Afrocentrism movement which thrives on many campuses.

MARY LEFKOWITZ, JEW,

professor Greek classics, Wellesley,
Excerpted from the *Washington Times,* 1996.

...the ideal is attained only when a particular region is inhabited exclusively by a people of one ethnic stock who compete solely against each other in the schools and colleges, with the result that an elite emerges which assumes the leadership of the people... the Negro peoples are being made victims of a political philosophy disguised as a desire to promote their welfare which will distort their natural development, rob them of their own self-respect and of satisfaction in their own achievements and ways of life, and do them untold harm...

ROBERT GAYRE, *"The Mankind Quarterly"* VI 4-1966.

More than 70% (1996) of all Negro children are born out of wedlock. Their illegitimacy rate, per capita, is over five (5) times that of Whites. Negroes commit 15 times more murders than Whites; 19 times more robberies; 10 times more rapes and assaults. *There were 629,000 racial attacks (1985), 90% of these were committed by Negroes on Whites.* According to the FBI these figures vary from year to year but across the USA represent an upward trend. *The most ominous crime is the increasing number of White women raped by Negroes. (In sub-Saharan Africa rape is considered normal behavior).*

I did this (rape) consciously, deliberately, willfully, methodically...It delighted me that I was defying and trampling upon white man's law, upon his system of values, that I was defiling his women.

ELDRIDGE CLEAVER, *"Soul On Ice".*

If, hypothetically, all NEGROES and JEWS were to disappear from the United States tomorrow there would be an immediate and glorious renaissance of the America envisioned by our Founding Fathers. On the other hand should the White race disappear *"the home of the free and the brave"* couldn't survive a single day!

The Negro has much to offer. But he never can realize his potential, his manliness, or attain to happiness living within a White society. He is not a parasite by choice. He has dignity a JEW can never possess. *The American Negro should have been encouraged, and helped, to develop a Nation-State uniquely his own in Africa, his ancestral HOMELAND. Instead he was manipulated by the JEW: used in hissweat shops; used to tenant his slums; used as plaintiffs in civil-rights cases to batter down White enclaves that JEWS didn t have the guts to attack; and used to perform as anarchists in the streets to help advance ILLUMINATI aspirations.* Only Louis Farrakhan seems to understand what W. E. B. Du Bois envisioned and Martin Luther King destroyed.

IQ TEST SCORES *are by no means the sole determinants of racial viability and value however important IQ scores are to Western Culture.* Common sense, extra-sensory perception (ESP), courage, loyalty, perseverance and *Soul* that indefinable, mystical essence that provides each race a distinctive character all of these qualities and more, which the Negro possesses to a great degree, can be transformed into his own Nation-State. *The Racial Soul can achieve its destiny only within its own territory, among its own People, wherein it establishes its own culture and its own relationship with the Universe.* Not every race is compelled to fly to the moon. Few men are Titans. All men are less than God. Albeit, for the graceful palm tree and the giant Sequoia to fulfill their destinies in Nature's grand design *each must grow in its own milieu!*

The FACTS are irrefutable: integration with alien races will destroy not only the White race a genocidal TRAGEDY but will deprive Mankind of its greatest benefactor, Western Civilization. When the White Race is lobotomized who will care for the diseased, famine-stricken populations of the World? Surely not JEWS whose practice is to fleece the sheep not feed them. The ILLUMINATI goal is fulfillment of the *Protocols of the Learned Elders of Zion* not fulfillment of Martin Luther King's pitiable DREAM of EQUALITY.

> We are exterminating the bourgeoisie (Aryan) as a class.
> VLADMIR LENIN, JEW, Communist,
> Supreme Dictator, U.S.S.R.

Nathaniel Weyl, JEW, *("The Mankind Quarterly",* XI,# 3, Jan. 1971), using calculations provided by the distinguished British geneticist Sir Julian Huxley, concluded the following:

> If, in the United States, Negroes (average IQs of 80-85) interbreed randomly with Whites (average IQs 100) the next generation of Americans would have an average IQ of 98.46. "What a small price to pay for EQUALITY!" Yet this decline of 1.5% in average intelligence would cause a decline of 50% in the number of people with IQs of 160 plus! "In short it would halve the production of people with the intellectual powers requisite for leadership and creative effort in advanced societies. To this must be added the massive negative effect caused by the shift from assortive to random breeding in terms of intelligence."

It remains to be seem whether or not the Negro living in America has the WILL to demand his own unique Nation-State in Africa or remain forever a slave to

LIBERALISM/MARXISM/JEWRY.

The sole condition required to centralize power in a democratic community is to profess equality.

ALEXIS de TOCQUEVILLE.

I was very much attracted to Dutch girls. I wanted desperately to make love to them...to exert some form of superiority over the White race. That's always the aim, isn't it? For brown skinned men to overpower the White man!

PRESIDENT SUKARNO, Indonesia.

...We want poems like fists beating niggers out of Jocks or dagger poems in the slimy bellies of the owner-jews...

...Setting fire and death to white ass. Look at the Liberal Spokesman for the jews clutch his throat and puke himself into eternity...

Put it on him poem. Strip him naked to the world! Another bad poem cracking steel knuckles in a jewlady's mouth...

LEROI JONES, Negro, "Black Art".

From reeking West whose day is done, Who stink and stagger in their dung, Toward Africa, China, India's strand, Where Kenya and Himalaya stand And Nile and Yang-tze roll:

Turn every yearning face of man.

Come with us, dark America: The scum of Europe fattened here And drowned a dream,

Made fetid swamp a refuge seem: Enslaved the Black and killed the Red And armed the rich to loot the dead;

Worshipped the whores of Hollywood Where once the Virgin Mary stood, And lynched the Christ.

Awake, awake, O sleeping world. Honor the sun;

Worship the stars, those vaster suns Who rule the night

Where black is bright

And all unselfish work is right And greed is sin.

And Africa leads on. Pan Africa!

W.E.B. Du BOIS, Mulatto, *"Ghana Calls"*.

You know what the American Dream really is? 10-million blacks swimming to Africa with a Jew under each arm.

STANLEY KUBRICK, JEW, "Vanity Fair" (7-1-99).

Whitemen will stick it in anything. They would stick it in the crack of dawn if they could reach that high.

GRANDAD, from *"Down on the Farm."*

Negroes are getting lighter. Blackgirls got round heels.

ANONYMOUS.

If you marry marry light !

HARLEM CREDO.

CHAPTER 9

THE ARYAN FORCE

Indo-European languages (Aryan) were at one time associated with a single, if composite, racial type, and that... racial type was an ancestral Nordic.

> CARLTON COON, Prof. Anthropology, Harvard, from his monumental success *"Origin of the Races"*.

Only that is good for a nation which comes from its own core seed, without aping of another. For what is beneficial to one people at a certain historic stage, may perhaps show itself as poison to another. All attempts to introduce foreign novelty to a people in whom a need for the same is not deep within its heart are foolish, and all devices with revolutionary intention are without success, for they are without God who holds himself aloof from such blunderings.

> GOETHE, *"Conversations With Eckermann'*, 4 January 1824.

Material prosperity encourages the preservation, pampering, and reproduction of inferior elements which are parasitical upon rich civilizations. Then some cleaner blooded and crude stock crashes in and wipes the slate clean... we can either prune off our own rotten branches or submit to ruthless cutting down and thinning out by more vigorous conquering stocks.

> DR. ERNEST A. HOOTEN, Prof. Anthropology, Harvard.

Material prosperity encourages the preservation, pampering, and reproduction of inferior elements which are parasitical upon rich civilizations. Then some cleaner blooded and crude stock crashes in and wipes the slate clean... we can either prune off our own rotten branches or submit to ruthless cutting down and thinning out by more vigorous conquering stocks.

> DR. ERNEST A. HOOTEN, Prof. Anthropology, Harvard.

I agree with you that there is a natural aristocracy among men. The natural grounds for this are virtue and talents... the natural aristocracy I consider the most precious gift of nature for the instruction, the trusts, and the government of society...

May we not say, that form of government is the best which provides most effectively for a pure election of these natural aristocrats into the office of government.

THOMAS JEFFERSON, letter to Adams, 28 October 1813.

Aristocracy has nothing to do with Plutocracy. The best are NOT the rich ...the best may rather be among the poorest... character and capacity are what should count.

W. GAYLEY SIMPSON, "Which Way Western Man?"

OSWALD SPENGLER (1880-1936) will emerge from oblivion where he was consigned by MARXISTS/LIBERALS/JEWS, to become the Philosopher of the 21st Century. Spengler demonstrated that the history of World Civilization did NOT advance in a linear manner: beginning in Mesopotamia in some distant era following a Biblical Flood; then producing a sequence of historically related events (omitting Far East history); while *"day by day in every way growing better and better"* until, lo! Mankind arrives at today's *"modern" Western Civilization"* a product of all civilizations that preceded it. Instead, Spengler (*although he was not versed in Mendelism*) proves that *each Civilization appearing on the world landscape emerged from a HIGH CULTURE:* the UNIQUE EXPRESSION OF AN INSPIRED PEOPLE:

Each Culture has its own new possibilities of self-expression ... "There is not one sculpture, one painting, one mathematics, one physics but many, each in its deepest essence different from the others, each limited in duration and self contained, just as each species of plant has its peculiar blossoms or fruit, its special type of growth and decline"(SPENGLER).

Because Cultures are Organic they share the same GENUS. Each High-Culture, therefore no matter how distant from others on the calendar of history experiences analogous *"contemporary phenomena"* which occur in the same relative positions during the Cultures' life cycles and *"therefore have a corresponding significance"*. Spengler shows, for example, that the *"Way"* as prime symbol of the Egyptian Soul; and the *"Plain"* representing the Russian world-view; and the *"Magian"* Arab Culture; and the *"Faustian"* Idea of the West *are inescapably analogous in character yet unique in expression*. Other analogous Cultural characteristics are: racial attitudes, religiosity, techniques, morphology, pathology, and Life-cycles: gestation, birth, youth, maturity, old age, and death. Therefore, while HIGH-CULTURES are of the same Genus EACH ONE is the UNIQUE EXPRESSION of an inspired people. *Each member of that People man, woman and child is one cell in the morphology of the HIGH-CULTURE-ORGANISM. The Soul of the High-Culture Organism is the COLLECTIVE SOULS of the PEOPLE. In sum: a High-Culture is a spiritually endowed organism possessing its own unique self-expression: "its Historical Autobiography is the ZIETGEIST!"* (YOCKEY).

HIGH-CULTURES create Ideas, religions, Esprit, authority, imperatives, armies, wars, heroes, myths, legends, music, art, poems, literature, architectural forms, laws, philosophies, sciences, techniques and States. While certain forms of knowledge and techniques may be transferred over time and space from one Culture to another, every High-Culture, instinctively and relentlessly pursues its own unique SPIRITUAL IDEA: *this inner-compulsion of the organism is its DESTINY.*

WESTERN CULTURE expresses the IDEA of *unlimited progress!* Spengler defines the Soul of the West as, *"The Faustian Soul whose prime symbol is pure and limitlessspace."* Reaching ever toward the Infinite. While many scientists believe the Universe will never be fully understood rationally, Aryan Man's Destiny lies in the attempt. Why? Sir Edmund Hillary looking at Mt. Everest, replied, *"Because it is there."* The ancient symbol representing *Western Imperative* is seen in the Gothic forms of the great cathedrals of Europe, their spires reaching toward the heavens. (Sigmund Freud, JEW, *thought the cathedral spires represented penis worship carved in stone.* Norman Mailer, JEW author, *contemned Western space exploration as insane and immoral).*

The continued development and custody of Western Culture rests in the hands of a relatively small group of extraordinary People. They may come from the most humble or most prestigious of circumstances, but a chance combination of parental genes *endowed them with the character, ability, and intense spiritual quality* that distinguishes them from their peers and from other races. *They are to the Nation what yeast is to the brew.*

Within this thin *Culture-bearing stratum* are the creators, appreciators, and custodians of the Nation's many expressive forms. They also are Nietzsche's "Over-going, and Down-going", the martyrs, race-warriors, protectors of the Western IDEA. Thus, Yockey finds the High-Culture-Organism has 4-strata: 1) The Idea (SOUL). 2) The Culture-bearing stratum that transmits the Idea (BRAIN). 3) The recipients of the Idea who understand, appreciate and take action (BODY). 4) Those incapable of cultural attainment, *"The beast with many heads"* (Shakespeare).

> The individual's life is of importance to no one but himself: the point is whether he wishes to escape from history or give his life for it. History recks nothing of human life.
>
> OSWALD SPENGLER.

The STATE is a political term. Yockey calls it *"the nation in action"*. It is a structure, created by the Culture-Organism to contain, nurture and protect the People and their territory. It changes form as the Culture develops. An apt metaphor for State is *"vessel"*, or *"Ship of State"*. When the State no longer functions or protects the People who created it, the State must be changed or replaced!

> Men are tired to disgust of money-economy. They hope for salvation from somewhere or other, for some real thing of honor and chivalry, of inward nobility, of unselfishness and duty.
>
> OSWALD SPENGLER.

CIVILIZATIONS, sacrificing quality of life for indulgences, grow out of and gradually engulf High-Cultures sending them into decline. Posterity has but a short memory. *The Conquerors and Creators are followed by purposeless progeny. They are soon dispossessed by COSMOPOLITAN PARASITES, who fear High-Cultures (race, family, nation) coveting instead open-bordered, polyglot Democracies, in which they are less visible. MONEY* replaces loyalty, duty and rank; *USURY* produces slavery; entitlement replaces achievement; middlemen replace producers. Heroic deeds give way to acquisition of things; expediency replaces honor; TREASON thrives in high places. *CULTURE DISTORTERS* control education and the press; patriotism is re-named "racism"; "Spielbergisms" become "history"; hedonism, bestiality, promiscuity, *JEWISHNESS* replace high-purpose, chivalry, ethics. Family, People, State dissolve before *EGALITARIANISM / UNIVERSALISM / CATHOLICISM. Racial wars explode. MISCEGENATION destroys the gene-pool. The CULTURE/ORGANISM DIES.*

Strange is it that our bloods, Of color, weight, and heat, pour'd all together Would quite confound distinction, yet stand off in differences so mighty.

SHAKESPEARE, "All's Well that Ends Well".

POPULATIONS *are racially diverse, mongrelized, fragmented, disjointed, friction oriented, counter-productive, aimless in the landscape.* Populations often are cross-bred remnants of once great cultures that declined and died. Other populations through ignorance, perhaps for religious reasons, propagated centuries of genetic defects making them incapable of greatness. Still others, bereft of brains from the start, have scarcely evolved at all on the evolutionary scale.

Populations contribute nothing to world culture. *The ILLUMINATI thinks of them as consumer units.* (see *With No Apologies*, Barry Goldwater, JEW).

A PEOPLE *is a family, tribe, clan, nation, emerged from the same GENE-POOL*, hence, endowed with similar instincts, among which are: love of family, race, nation, country; aggression, survival, the need for territorial exclusivity; a sense of discrimination, and a *sense of high purpose.* A People also share: esthetic appreciation, physical appearance , *esprit de corps,* intellectual and behavioral patterns, and psychological, physiological, and SPIRITUAL similarities. *Only a People can create a HIGH-CULTURE.* WESTERN CULTURE is ARYAN CULTURE, therefore, *the WHITE GENE-POOL is our most precious possession.* White genes make us what we are, and determine our Destiny. *Those who seek to destroy the Whitegene-pool, by whatever means, arecommitting genocide and must be treated as murderers. They are our most dangerous ENEMIES.*

RACE *is a major division of the human species whose distinguishing features are most apparent physically, but are manifest also in intellectual and emotional development; in behavior, temperament, character and SOUL.* These racial features, as we know, are transmitted basically unchanged except for mutations by successive breeding generations over eons of time. Despite denial by purveyors of JEW SYPHILIS, there is absolutely no doubt that *distinct races do exist.* They are *"the raw material contributing to human evolution."*

When races cross-breed their off-spring tend to suffer well known physiological defects, but also psychological disabilities and conflicts, such as: schizophrenia, manic-depression, instability, disorientation, and lack of firm and definite character. *They have divided Souls.* When one studies aWorld Atlas those areas where cross-breeding has been most extreme are the very areas where populations are notoriously miserable, untrustworthy, irresponsible, and poverty stricken. They contribute little or nothing of value to Mankind, for example: modern India and Egypt, Cuba, Hawaii, Mexico, Hispaniola, Surinam, Brazil, Africa, et al. Whereas *countries that are most durable and with the greatest creative output are those with populations displaying little or no racial cross-breeding, such as Europe, China, and Japan.* There is no Family of Man, and no Equality of Men. *There are only Natures Laws which are contemptuous of MARXIST/LIBERAL/JEW/CHRISTIAN posturing.*

To repeat: *a High-Culture (Spiritual-Organism) is unique in its World View: totally distinct from populations that surround it or from aliens that temporarily infest its territory.* HIGH-CULTURE MAN, then, represents the highest form of Life! *While Non-culture man is a biped cipher.*

"The Decline of the West" (*"Der Untergang Abendlandes"*), Oswald Spengler's masterpiece, examines eight High-Cultures that dominated the history of our planet. One of them, Western Culture, still dominates *but suffers from severe pathological problems and is in sharp decline.* Seven other High-Cultures appeared on the landscape of world

history, flourished brilliantly like *novae* in the solar system, then declined and died. These were the: Babylonian, Egyptian, Indian, Chinese, Arabian (Magian), Classical, Mexican (Aztec, Inca, Mayan). *All, except the Mexican, died from within, resultant of CULTURAL PATHOLOGY: usury, parasitism and miscegenation.*

Let me repeat here very quickly we discussed miscegenation earlier the notion that "hybrid vigor" results from haphazard breeding of different racial stocks is *ludicrous!* To get cross-bred vigor to any degree the parents must be unrelated; *pure-bred*; have pedigrees displaying racial superiority, and the parents' good qualities must complement each other. Without pure-bred parents the cross-bred progeny contain little or no merit. Ergo, while the first generation (F1) hybrid may or may not result in increased vigor, *further crossing of the hybrids results in a substantial decrease of vigor in subsequent generations and will obliterate the outstanding qualities of the original pure-breeds. The miscegenation of Whites with Negroes, for example, will effectively breed out of existence blue-eyed blonds, red-heads, and fair-skinned brunettes, along with the higher intelligence their blondness represents. Miscegenation also destroys the Negro race, denying them their Soul, their Destiny, their culture, and their territory.*

> I believe that the wholesale merging(miscegenation) of the two races is the most desirable alternative for everyone concerned.
>
> NORMAN PODHORETZ, JEW,
> editor of "Commentary" magazine.

The most terrible thing in the World is ignorance in action.

GOETHE.

How important a restriction of mixture (is) follows from the Mendelian principal that one act of crossing can undo the work of a hundred generations of faithful inbreeding.

C. D. DARLINGTON,
Prof. Botany, Oxford U.

A people which takes no pride in the noble achievements of its remote ancestors will never achieve anything worthy to be remembered by noble descendants.

THOMAS B. MACAULEY.

A blond and marvelous people arises in the north. In overflowing it sends wave upon wave into the southern world. Each migration becomes a conquest, each conquest a source of character and civilization.

WALTER RATHENAU, JEW,
German Industrialist, c.1925.

Rathenau might have added, *and then* alien parasites engulfed the Aryan States in a sea of HUMAN MUD.

The history of these blond warriors and creators we know them today as Swedes, Danes, Norse, Celts and Germans becomes the history of the many civilizations they founded (Egyptian, Indian, Persian, Greek, Roman, Western, Russian, et al). The Ancients wrote of a golden-haired race of conquerors from the legendary land of *Atlantis* who implanted civilizations in Rome and Greece. Homer's blue-eyed, fair-skinned, gods and goddesses, ruling from Mount Olympus, were images *of these Northmen. Some archaeologists believe Atlantis once was part of the Iberian Peninsula, near Gibraltar. Others say* Atlantis was a peninsula jutting seaward near today's Wilhelmshaven,

Helgoland, Germany – that disappeared during a quake into the Frisian Sea. *Atlanteans* probably were precursors of the Goths, whose chieftains ruled from the *Island of Goth* lying in the Baltic Sea between Stockholm and Koenigsberg. Anthropologists are assembling credible evidence showing that many pre-history Aryan tribesmen migrated out of Northern Europe long before 2000 B.C. establishing colonies as far east as the Urals perhaps into areas of China and Japan.

Archaeological digs and historical data confirm that steady streams of Nordics flowed out of Northern Europe from 2000 B.C. until 1000 A.D. These Aryan tribes appear under different names but they emanate from one White gene-pool. Kassites captured the remains of the Babylonian empire about 1700 B.C. About a century later northern barbarians, called "Hyksos" by Egyptians, captured a faltering Egyptian civilization, invigorated it and ruled it. Aryans conquered India, establishing a caste system (endogamy) to protect the White gene-pool; they then went on to conquer Persia (Iran). Achaeans (Germans) and later Dorians (Celts) conquered Greece and planted the seeds of Classical Civilization there. The Rus and Vikings, sailed the Dneiper, Volga and eastern European waterways, opening up trade routes to the Sea of Azof, and the Black, Caspian, and Mediterranean seas, and as far beyond as their graceful ships would take them. In short, we know that this Aryan (Nordic) proto-race established some of the world's greatest civilizations: Aryan-Indian, Kassite, Hittite, Persian, Mycenaean, Greek, Roman, Keltic, Teutonic, Slavic,

Western Civilization, and Aztec/Mayan/Inca.

> Indo-European languages (Aryan) were at one time associated with a single, if composite, racial type, and that... racial type was an ancestral Nordic.
>
> CARLTON COON, Prof. Anthropology, Harvard.

> Although (Aryans) are stretched across two continents we attribute to them a common ancestry and a common origin...
>
> C. D. DARLINGTON, Prof. Botany, Oxford.

> Aryans appear everywhere as promoters of true progress and in Europe their expansion marked the moment when the prehistory of (Europe) begins to diverge from that of Africa or the Pacific.
>
> Dr. V. GORDON CHILDE, "easily the greatest prehistorian in the world." (Encl. Britannica).

Toward the end of the great migrations, Aryan Gothic tribes (Ostrogoths, Visogoths), feared for their courage and ferocity pillaged and rampaged throughout Europe under names more familiar to us: Franks, Angles, Saxons, Kelts, Vandals, Lombards, Burgundians, Belgae, Jutes, Vikings, Danes, Rus, Germani, Teutons, Normans, *et al.* Then, assuming the upper stratum of each society they conquered, they supplied the leadership, the armies and the laws. *What distinguished this White stock from mere populations was its WILL to fulfill its MANIFEST DESTINY.* This, the ARYAN FORCE, manifest in all aspects of thought and action, impelled the Vikings, in miniscule ships, for example, to brave the ferocious Atlantic all the way to American shores and beyond. Compare this breeding stock to Negroes who never produced a conqueror, an explorer, an alphabet, or even invented the wheel; or to the

ISRAELIS who were lost for 40-years in an area the size of Rhode Island. Ask any general if he would prefer to command an army of Thuringians, or one of JEWS.

Julius Caesar, deep in Gaul (France) conquered the indigenous Celts (Celts). However, those Nordic tribes north and east of the Rhine, which he never conquered, Caesar thought of as *"original"* Celts. The Latin word for original, or seminal, is *"germane"*. So, it was Caesar who first called Germans by that name. The Celts, who are Nordics, later invaded Ireland, Wales, Scotland, and most of the world at one time or another. The so-called *"Black Irish"* (former President Nixon may be one of these) are progeny of Spanish sailors cast upon Irish shores when the Armada was defeated by Sir Francis Drake. President John F. Kennedy, Celt, caused much resentment in powerful quarters, before the JEW built Berlin Wall fell, when he announced: *"Ich bin ein Berliner!"* He spoke for all Aryans.

German Angles crossed the Channel and named the island *"Angleland'*, later corrupted to *"England"*. They had a difficult time there with the Jutes (German), and Celts, so they asked the German Saxons for assistance. The Saxons enjoyed England so much they stayed on. As everyone knows, in 1066 William the Conqueror led his Norman (Nor(th)men), and Teuton troops to victory over the Saxons at the *Battle of Hastings.* To this day the Brits are known as Anglo-Saxons (WASPS: *White, Anglo-Saxon Protestants).*

Today's self-serving British Royal Family is of the

Germanic House: *von Saxe-Coburg-Gotha*. During WWI they felt obliged to change their name to the House of Windsor *("Uneasy lies the head that wears a crown")*.

The English language is Germanic in origin. Germanic languages include: Scandinavian (Swedish, Norse, Danish), Icelandic, Dutch, German, English, and Frisian (Old Prussian, and Gothic are extinct). France was named for the Franks a Germanic tribe. *"Frankness"* was the *sine qua nom* for sincerity, honesty, integrity and character, consequently the *franc* became the French monetary unit. Charlemagne, a Frank, of the Carolingian dynasty, and Emperor of the Holy Roman Empire held court in Aachen, and Aix-la-Chapelle, the German and French names for the same city. The HRE (c. 950 A.D.) mixed Romans, Christians, Germans from Barcelona to Hamburg; from Rheims to Rome.

Palladius, according to Bede, brought Catholicism to Ireland about 430 A.D. The Irish, thereafter, spread the Myth to Europe. When the Saxons finally were converted to Christianity by Frankish arms (800 A.D.) the conversion, Saxons reasoned, made Europe *quasi una gens, "one race"* of Christians (During this same time period, c. 700, Asiatic Khazars converted to Talmudism). *By 1050 A.D. all Christians thought of themselves as a racial family.* As time passed, Christianity took on a territorial meaning. Europe became known as *"Christendom"*, consequently, in Medieval Europe *"race relations"* actually meant relations between languages and culture groups, not breeding stocks.

The Greek word *"Agon"* means fighting or warfare *within the family group,* as opposed to fighting an alien enemy. Thus, Christians engaged in bloody internecine wars *(Agon)* to advance Western IDEALS. *But, before the ILLUMINATI annihilation wars against Europe during the 20ᵗʰ Century, Aryans always united and fought as one people to protect Christendom against the Khazars, Moors, Saracens, Mongols, et al.* Today, the Catholic Church (founded by JEWS) *which owes its existence to Aryan knighthood promotes miscegenation, and denounces Aryan nationalism,* while abetting the state of Israel. The Pope's behavior has precedence. Jesus denied the Gentiles saying, *"I was sent to the lost sheep of the house of Israel and to them alone."* (MATTHEW).

As exploration and expansion continued Aryans established bastions of Western Culture wherever they conquered and persisted: North and South America, Canada, Australia, New Zealand, Iceland, Greenland, and Africa, among others already enumerated, were founded and civilized by these gifted People. *It should be obvious to anyone with a shred of intelligence that once a People have acquired a superior gene-pool they should do EVERYTHING in their power to protect and improve it. The incomparable ARYAN GENE POOL produced multitudes of illustrious men and women. I will parade a few of their names before you as a reminder that they, and you and your children, are members of that same gene-pool if you are White:* Ikhnaton, Mahavira, Sigurd, Grettir, Njal, Arthur, Cuchulain, Ulysses, Pericles, Aristophanes, Aurelieus, Aristotle, Zarathustra, Sappho;

Siegfried, Darius, Alexander, Rurik, Theodoric, Martel, Charlemagne, Roland, Caesar, Cleopatra, Eric, Alaric, Jean d'Arc, Godfrey, Bruce, Luther, Marlboro, Rob Roy, Peter the Great, Pitt, Napoleon, Nelson, Wellington; Erickson, Cortes, Columbus, da Gama, Magellan; Katherine, Elizabeth, Corday, Nightingale; v. Steuben, Washington, Monroe, Jefferson, Hamilton, Madison, Allen, Henry, Hale, Morgan, Frederick, El Cid, Bismarck, Clauswitz; Hus, Garfield, McKinley, Hess, Hitler, Patton, MacFadden, McCarthy, Zundel; Bridger, Coulter, Crocket, Bowie, Houston, Clark, Hickock, Earp, Longbaugh, Oakley; Lee, Jackson, Forrest, Grant, Lincoln, Barton, Custer, Stuart, Chamberlain; Pershing, Mata Hari, Richthofen, Rickenbaker, York, Cavell; MacArthur, del Valle, Crommelin, Rommel, Prien, Nimitz, Lindbergh, Earhardt, Goering, Mussolini, Montgomery, Murphy, Foss, Mindszenty, Pound, Solzhenitsyn; Shakespeare, Petrarch, Dante, Goethe, Voltaire, Schiller, Swift, Emerson, Byron, Keats, Blake, Burns, Wilde, Shaw, Yeats, Melville, Whitman, Poe, Balzac, Hesse, Dostoevsky, Shelley, Eliot, Kipling, Dreiser, Steinbeck, Plath, Hemingway, Roethke, Dinesen, Bronte, Waugh, James, Pegler, Marsden, Mencken, Chesterton; Bach, Foster, Grieg, Wagner, Smetna, Beethoven, McCartney, Tschaikowsky, Rachmaninoff, Dvorak, Lehar, Strauss, Debussy, Chopin, Brahms, McDowell, Elgar, Borodin, Bizet, Herbert, Vivaldi, Verdi, Puccini, Handel; Praxitiles, Rodin, Remington, Mallol, Titian, Da Vinci, Durer, Rembrandt, Brueghel, Monet, Homer, Bierstadt, Wyth, Degas, Goya; Plato, Goethe, Kant, Hume, Schopenhauer,

Spencer, Pascal, Descartes, Carlyle, Machiavelli, Montaigne, Kierkegaard, Nietzsche, Spengler, Santayana, Yockey, Simpson; Kepler, Copernicus, Newton, Swedenborg, Franklin; Shockley, Coon, Ardrey, Oliver, Sombart, Baker; Mendel, Curie, Lister, Pasteur, de Bakey; Gutenberg, Galton, Ohm, Edison, Ford, Carnegie, Krupp, Benz, Chrysler, Diesel; Planck, Goddard, Hertz, von Braun, Humboldt, Richter, Marconi, Goethals, Rutherford, Roebling, Wright, Sullivan; Yaeger, Costeau, Lovell, Glenn, Armstrong, Shepard, Grissom; Traubel, Hess, Sutherland, Swartzkoph, Pons, Lehmann, Caruso, Pavarotti, Wunderlich, Cararras, Pinza, Hines; Barrymore, Cooper, Gielgud, Olivier, Wayne, Astaire; Day, Streep, Hayes, Leigh, Davis, Temple; Griffith, Lean, Wells, Hitchcock, Ford, Bergman; Ripken, Di Maggio, Ruth, Spahn, Williams, Schmidt, Hornsby, Gehrig, Berra, Rose, Wagner, MacGwire; Nicklaus, Jones, Hogan, Palmer, Snead, Norman; Lombardi, Staubach, Montana, Elway, Kramer, Unitas; Hingis, Laver, Borg, Graf, Connors, Court; Bird, West, Bradley, Laettner, Walton, Havlichek; et al.

> Race lifts a man above himself: it endows him with extraordinary I might almost say supernatural powers so entirely does it distinguish him from the chaotic jumble of peoples drawn from all parts of the world... his Race strengthens and elevates him on every hand... he soars heavenward like some strong stately tree nourished by thousands and thousands of roots no solitary individual, but the living sum of untold souls striving for the same Goal.
> H. S. CHAMBERLAIN, "The Foundations of the 19th Century".
> (Chamberlain, British, was Nietzsche's son-in-law).

All great civilizations of the past only perished because the original races died of blood poisoning.

ADOLF HITLER, Chancellor of Germany.

CHAPTER 10

PARASITISM U.S.A.

What has been called the "Jewish problem" is seen for the first time. Not race, not religion, not ethics, not nationality, not political allegiance but something that includes them all, separating the JEW from the West Culture.

FRANCIS PARKER YOCKEY, *"Imperium"*.

Connected amongst themselves by the most obstinate faith, the Jews extend their charity to all of their own persuasion, while toward the rest of mankind they nourish a sullen and inveterate hatred.

TACITUS, *"Historical Works'*.

The Israelis control the policy in the U.S. Congress.

J. WILLIAM FULBRIGHT,
U.S. Senator, CBS *"Face the Nation"*.

The Jewish influence in this country is so strong You wouldn't believe it. We have Israelis coming to us for equipment. We say we can't possibly get Congress to support a program like that. They say, "Don't worry about Congress we'll take care of the Congress.... this is somebody from another country but they can do it.

GEN. GEORGE S. BROWN,
Chairman Joint Chiefs of Staff, 1973.

There are only two groups that are beating the drums now for war in the Middle East, and that is the Israeli Defense Ministry and its amen corner in the U.S. Congress.

PAT BUCHANAN, *"The McLaughlin Group'*, 1991.

Kennedy said, "I wholly agree with you that American partiality in the Arab-Israeli conflict is dangerous both to the U.S. and the free world."...The assassination of President Kennedy... shattered the

possibility that his second term might see Washington start to free itself from the grave burdens of U.S partisanship on the Arab-Israeli conflict.
ALFRED M. LILIENTHAL, JEW, *"The Zionist Connection'*.

TREASON AND SEDITION

As we have seen, wherever JEWS penetrate a Gentile State their single purpose is to suck the vital juices from the host nation and implant their own culture. About 1850 A.D. JEWS set the cross-hairs of their sights on America. During the ensuing 150-years they invaded the United States, hitched their ambitions and hatred to our resources and man-power; then proceeded to entangle America in a series of wars fought only to enrich JEWRY and advance the ILLUMINATI agenda.

Charles Lindbergh published his "Wartime Journals" in which he insisted his non-interventionist (WWII) stand had been fundamentally correct and that the U.S. had actually lost the war... he stressed the irreparable genetic loss... suffered by the Northern European peoples.
WILMOT ROBERTSON, *"The Dispossessed Majority'*.

After WWII an *"Iron Curtain"* settled over Europe. *It was imperative to keep the populations ignorant of the vampires who had feasted on them.* The "HOLOCAUST" HOAX, *a stratagem to cover-up the Holocaust perpetrated against Germany,* emerged like a rabid dog. JEWS invaded the machinery of the United States government. The *"Cold War",* another hoax, appeared on the horizon. Bolsheviks crawled like maggots out of the corpses of Russia and Eastern Europe threatening Main Street, U.S.A.

> Jew immigrants into the U.S. so successfully resisted identification by race (and religion) insisting that they be set down not as Jews but as Germans, Poles, or what not that for many years the various national quotas were taken up almost entirely by Jews; and to this day the number of Jews in the United States is known only by the figures Jews themselves give us.
>
> WILLIAM G. SIMPSON, *"Which Way Western Man?"*

One of those immigrants who, like so many others, "miraculously" escaped the "HOLOCAUST," was Albert Einstein, JEW (1879-1955), a theoretical physicist renowned for his brilliant "theory of relativity" (E=mc2) and for his support of Communism, wrote to Pres. Franklin Roosevelt urging him to initiate a program to develop a U. S. nuclear weapon for use against Germany. Alexander Sachs, JEW, banker, delivered the letter which FALSELY accused Germany of building an atomic bomb. In fact Hitler, while investigating nuclear-power potential, inveighed against ALL weapons of mass-destruction (including the bombing of civilian targets). Roosevelt's advisors, Baruch, JEW; Rosenman, JEW; Morganthau, JEW; Hopkins, Hiss, et al, sold FDR on Einstein's idea. The minds that eventually developed the Atomic-bomb were Lisa Meitner, JEW; Neils Bohr, JEW; Hans Bethe, JEW; Edward Teller, JEW; John von Neumann, JEW; Leo Szilard, JEW; and Enrico Fermi, Aryan, with a JEW wife. Almost all had been educated at the University of Gottingham, Germany; and some had worked at the Max Planck Institute. Meitner had purloined details of successful German fission experiments in Berlin. These were the precursors of nuclear power, and later the A-bomb constructed at Los Alamos under the direction of Dr.

Robert J. Oppenheimer, JEW. Teller and von Neuman left the A-bomb project and began development of the Hydrogen-bomb. Schematics of the A-bomb were quickly duplicated by JEW traitors and given to the Soviet Union. The A-bomb was not completed in time to drop on Germany, much to the chagrin of world JEWRY. But, they were not to be denied a blood sacrifice. Japan, staggering toward certain defeat, would be taught a TALMUDIC lesson. The only strong protest against dropping the A-bomb on Japan was registered by Truman's science advisor Ernest Lawrence, Aryan. There were stronger voices. Obeying his masters Truman ordered the incineration of the undefended cities of Hiroshima (a Christian city) and Nagasaki. Sufficient example of the Atomic-bomb's destructive capacity could have been made by dropping it on an uninhabited area. But the vampires wanted to teach an unforgettable lesson to the honorable Japanese who had allied themselves with Germany. *Be assured, descendants of the great Samurai have NOT forgotten.*

The dangerous extent of Communist penetration into the United States became apparent during the numerous espionage trials following WWII; even the most ignorant goy was beginning to understand the stupidity of America's alliance with "the evil Communist Empire" against Aryan Germany. President Harry Truman, under pressure from the media and his JEW advisors (Rabbi Steven Wise, Sam Rosenman, Eddie Jacobson, the Rostow brothers, Max Lowenthal, David Niles, et al), turned down Canada's request for assistance in its investigation of Communist

Espionage rings operating in Canada and the United States. Truman (who got us into the Korean debacle allegedly to fight Communism, and who attempted to abolish the incomparable U.S. Marine Corps, called the Commie investigations a "Red Herring". Proceeding without U.S. help Canada arrested and convicted a rats-nest of Soviet agents among which were: Sam Carr (Cohen), organizer for all of Canada; Fred Rose (Rosenberg), a member of Parliament organizer for French Canada; and Hermina Rabinowich, liaison with T. S. Communists. All of these "Canadians" were KHAZAR JEWS.

Finally, startled at the extent of subversion whichTruman had scoffed at U.S. intelligence services began (c.1950) to arrest and convict Soviet spies working in the United States, among which were: John Gates (Israel Regenstreif), editor of the Communist "Daily Worker"; Gil Green (Greenberg); Gus Hall (Halberg); and Carl Winters (Weissberg), ALL JEWS.

That same year the first U.S. atomic spies were convicted for espionage, among which were: Julius and Ethel Rosenberg; Morton Sobell; David Greenglass; Harry Gold; Abraham Brothman; Miriam Moskowitz; Gerhardt Eisler; William Perl (Mutterperl) Physics Dept. Columbia Univ. ALL JEWS (*the Rosenbergs were convicted and executed for treason amid cries of anti-Semitism. Soviet files, finally made public in 1997, verified that the Rosenbergs had transferred A-bomb schematics from Los Alamos to the Soviet Union*). As it turned out, these JEWS were relatively minor players in a much deeper JEWISH conspiracy. As we shall see.

While America was engaged in the "Cold War" against the Soviet Union (some Americans were building bomb-shelters in their backyards), Dr. Robert J. Oppenheimer, JEW, head of the Los Alamos Project, and America's most publicized nuclear scientist, suddenly protested further development of the Hydrogen-bomb. He who had been gung-ho to drop the A-bomb on Germany and Japan demanded, to the astonishment of U.S. brass, that the project be abandoned for "humanitarian reasons"! His views were strongly supported in print and deed by U. S. JEWS who (regarding the Soviet Union) had suddenly become deeply religious pacifists. The U. S. Joint Chiefs of Staff knew the Soviets had made a quid pro quo offer to captured German scientists, to wit: their release from certain death in the Gulag in exchange for their scientific expertise. With great effort the Joint Chiefs over-rode Oppenheimer's opposition. The Special Committee of the National Security Council (two Aryans and one JEW) then voted two to one to continue the H-bomb program. The dissenting vote was that of David Lilienthal, JEW, Chairman of the Atomic Energy Commission. The United States managed to produce the H-bomb 11-months before the Soviets produced theirs; thus saving the U.S.A. from Soviet extortion perhaps extinction. Smelling a rat "underneath the piles" the FBI removed Oppenheimer's security-clearance. Reason given: his wife, mistress, and best friends had "extensive Communist affiliations". The ADL and media shrieked bigotry! President Lyndon Johnson, an easily black-mailed slob prodded by Abe Fortas, JEW, and the Rostow brothers, JEWS reinstated Oppenheimer's security-clearance in a grand ceremony, complete with tributes, awards, and maudlin apologies. (Shortly thereafter Johnson's nominee for Chief Justice of the Supreme Court, Abe Fortas, and his partner Louis Wolfson, JEW, were convicted of stock-embezzlement. They did easy time in the same type country-club prison that later housed JEW VIPS like Michael Milken, Ivan Boesky, and other Wall Street junk-bond salesmen and swindlers).

1994, Pavel A. Sudoplatov, former Soviet agent, released KGB files to the U.S. Central Intelligence Agency revealing that the enigmatic Dr. Robert J. Oppenheimer, JEW, was a Soviet spy! Oppenheimer (now decd.) had compromised U.S. security by providing the Soviet Union with detailed U.S. nuclear secrets. Oppenheimer's treason nearly cost the United States victory in the Cold War, and indirectly contributed to the deaths of thousands of U.S. military personnel in Korea and Viet Nam. The news-media has decided to put a lid on this information. Your Congressman plays dumb.

> Let it be remembered that the Attorney General of the United States recently testified that an analysis of 4,984 of the more militant members of the Communist Party in the United States showed that 91.4 percent of the total were of foreign stock (JEWS) or were married to persons of foreign stock.
> PAT MCCARRAN, Chr. Judiciary Committee, U.S. Senate, 1950.

The great majority of JEWS change their names following a precedent set by Lenin (Ulianov) JEW; Trotsky

(Bronstein) Jew; and Stalin (Dzugashvili) Tartar, married to a JEWESS. Today, change-of-identity includes facial surgery vastly improving their appearances enabling them to hide almost unnoticed among the goyim whom they intend to destroy.

SENATOR JOSEPH McCARTHY led the attack (c.1950) on Communists within the U.S. government (called a "witch-hunt" by government prosecutors and the mass-media). McCarthy was warned by friends that he would be attacked from both sides of the aisle. He replied, "The American people will never let me down." He didn't know brainwashed *Boobus Americanus*. McCarthy initiated investigations of the Departments of State, Agriculture, Treasury, and Defense. Eventually, several Soviet agents were arrested, including: Alger Hiss, Currie, Ware, Collins, Duggin, Reno, Remington, Wadleigh, Field, and Whittaker Chambers. Among JEWS exposed as Soviet agents were: Abe Pressman, Abt, Perlo, Silverman, Witt, Gompertz, and White (Weiss), protégé of Henry Morganthau, JEW, FDR's Sec'y of the Treasury.

The ADL resorted to time-tested tactics, demonizing the messenger to distract from the facts. McCarthy had hard evidence that Communists were eroding the foundations of our Republic and betraying U.S. intelligence to the Communist bloc.

He was making real headway when he was accused of making unsubstantiated charges against the integrity of the U.S. Army: viz., falsely accusing U.S. Army dentist Dr.

Victor Perlo, JEW, of Communist affiliations. The charge against McCarthy was blown out of proportion by the media, which demanded blood. In the heat of the nationally televised character assassination the Senator's valuable services to America were ignored. Finally, Senator McCarthy, censured by a servile Senate, was forced into retirement. Perlo (who later confessed to being a Communist) walked, a hero of the Left. A new word of approbation, "McCarthyism" (meaning: invalid, indiscriminate attacks upon a witness) entered the American lexicon. Its true definition is: *He who attacks Commies will be burned at the stake.* An important aspect of this American tragedy was that courtroom opposition to McCarthy was led by Aryan attorneys, many of them Ivy League, Skull & Bones types, vassals of the Golden Rule: He who hath the gold rules.

Recently, the deceased Senator arose from his grave:

McCARTHY-ERA 'SCARE' PROVES FAIRLY ACCURATE: Documents Show Soviet Infiltration

Sen. Joseph McCarthy and other Red-baiters weren't too far wrong about the extensive Soviet penetration of U.S. government agencies... documents released yesterday by the National Security Agency shows... more than 100 Soviet agents had infiltrated the Departments of State, Justice, War, Treasury and even the Office of Strategic Services precursor of the CIA... Previous releases... detailed the discovery of Soviet efforts to steal nuclear secrets and the involvement of Julius and Ethel Rosenberg in the wartime spying effort. "Not everyone accused by McCarthy was innocent," Mr. Radosh said, noting that the backlash against McCarthy' anti-Communist crusade tended to discredit anyone who sought to expose Soviet activities in the U.S.A. But historian David Kahn (JEW), author of *"The Codebreakers",* said he is far more cautious about reviving McCarthy's reputation... "I don't want to go overboard,"

Mr. Kahn said.

The WASHINGTON TIMES, 6 March 1996.

Back in the 1970s (Nam Era) the mass-media, with McCarthyism in mind, protested that domestic spying by the U.S. government threatened "Freedom".

President Ford, always easily persuaded, permitted Attorney General Edward Levi, JEW, to impose "Levi Guidelines" on U.S. investigative agencies. These Guidelines gutted government personnel-security-programs by making those who preached subversion immune from investigation unless they advocated or engaged in specific crimes. In other words the USA is no longer allowed to engage in fire prevention until the fire starts. Which introduces another spy story...

Front-page news, October '98, was the signing of yet another Peace Accord between Palestine and Israel. Yasser Arafat, Arab, lips quivering, spoke of a glorious future of peace and prosperity for their two Peoples: "We Semitic brothers"! Benjamin Netanyahu, JEW, Khazar, noticeably winced.

In the wee hours of that morning after the deal was struck, but before the signing, Netanyahu, Israeli Prime Minister blind-sided the negotiations. He threatened to walk out unless the United States, as part of the Accord, released ISRAELI SPY Jonathan Pollard from prison. Clinton dared not comply. However, to assuage the Israelis, his last act as President was to pardon a rat's nest of JEW thieves, including

U.S. embezzler Marc Rich, JEW, prominent on the FBI's "most wanted" list.

Pollard, is the "American" JEW who sold "*an amazing number of America's top-secrets to Israel.* "Because Pollard has an intimate knowledge of all aspects of U.S. security he remains a risk even while in prison. Alan Dershowitz, JEW, Professor, Harvard Law School, and TV celeb, states: it is a "stain on America" to detain Pollard because "the secrets were sold to a U.S. ally; he has served enough time" (12+ years). Media "talking heads", with their jobs in mind, agree that Pollard, who became an Israeli citizen while in prison, should be returned to Israel for "the sake of peace." Israel, where Pollard is considered a national hero, demands that the United States release their spy immediately. Dershowitz was angered during a CNN interview when the question of JEW dual-loyalty was posed. "That's an old canard," he snarled. "Pollard is just one American Jew who happens to be a spy." Dershowitz, of course, is dissembling. JEWS as all races are genetically unique: genes determine behavior. JEWS have been notorious, historically, for disloyalty to host nations. That doesn't mean all JEWS in the United States pose security risks as Pollard, and the others. It simply means that many JEWS who profess belief in MARXISM/ JUDAISM/ZIONISM are security risks. More specifically, it means that about 98% (ninety-eight per cent) of all JEWS are security risks. The United States of America is discovering what Europe learned long ago": JEWS smile while stabbing their hosts in the back.

Alfred Lilienthal, JEW, tape-recorded (7-4-72) the following interview with two Brooklyn teenagers who belonged to the International Conference of Synagogue Youth:

If Israel and the U.S. get into a war which side will you be on?

This will never happen it couldn't happen.

Do you consider yourself an American or a Jew?

I am an American and a Jew.

But which do you consider first?

I am a Jew before I am an American.

Do you have a dual loyalty? Some people insist that you do.

No, but we do have strong connections with Israel as well as with the U.S., and we have more connections with Israel; because that is our state.

What do you mean? I thought the U.S. was your state?

We live in the U.S. We are proud however that Israel is our state Israel is our homeland and our final goal is to settle there.

Why don't you go there now?

We're not ready to go.

Then why do you stay in the U.S. and use the U.S.?

We must have a country powerful and strong, and we want to build up the U.S. because while we are here we can help Israel. We are here because this is a powerful country and we want to use our influence.

Influence the U.S. in behalf of Israel?

Not only influence the U.S. but influence other American Jews, many of whom are not doing as much as they should.

What is your feeling towards Israel?

Israel is ours. The U.S. is not our state. We are making it our home but a home is not our state.

What happens when people say there are Jews who are using the U.S. and imply it is time you get out?

They would want us to get out that is anti-Semitism.

But you have dual loyalties?

What's wrong with that? Israel can help the U.S. and the U.S. can help Israel... We don't use the U.S. as a base. We are supporting the U.S., we pay our taxes. We don't want to immigrate right now. And don't get the idea we're living off the fat of their land and taking it away that's bigotry, that sounds like anti-Semitism.

Well maybe it is, but don't you feed this anti-Semitism with your ideas?

No. If the U.S. asked us to serve in the army and it didn't involve Israel we would serve. But we can't trust the U.S. to do completely what we want. If the U.S. does not have a favorable policy towards Israel, its up to us to help to build that, and we wouldn't be able to do for Israel what is necessary if we weren't living in the U.S.

ALFRED LILIENTHAL, "The Zionist Connection".

A youthful Pollard could have been one of the JEWS interviewed above. *("Nits grow up to be lice,"* Gen. Sheridan,

USA).

Recently, another KGB document decrypted by the U.S. Venoma program indicates, but does not prove, that David K. Niles (Neyhus), JEW was a high placed U.S. traitor. A long-time protégé of Bernie Baruch, JEW, and of Harry Hopkins, FDR Chief of Staff, *Niles was administrative advisor to Roosevelt and Truman* (Hopkins, *recently exposed as a Soviet spy,* actually *lived in the White House*). When Niles died in 1953 he was described by the New York Times as *"a man of mystery".* The FBI had placed Niles and many of his associates under surveillance Their scenario began when Niles recommended David Karr (Katz), JEW, to Alan M. Cranston for employment. Karr was a staff member on the Communist *Daily Worker*, and PR director of the American League for Peace and Democracy, a Communist front. Cranston, was then a member of the Office of War Information (OWI). Later he became U.S. Senator (CA-Dem.). Cranston published a distorted edition of "Mein Kampf", which he pawned off on the American public as a first edition translation a *"Spielbergism".* Obeying Niles' directive Cranston hired Karr as an official at the OWI. In that capacity he had daily access to the staffs of Presidents Roosevelt and Truman which included Hopkins, Lauchlin Currie, Alger Hiss, Harry Dexter White (Weiss), JEW (all exposed as Soviet agents), and of course to David Niles, JEW. The Venona Files also confirm the espionage activities of Kim Philby, Klaus Fuchs, JEW, and the Rosenbergs, JEWS. The point is, David Niles, has never been investigated by Congress. Truman (who prodded the

U.S. into the Korean debacle) called Niles a "a close friend and trusted associate". The answer to how high-up TREASON went (and goes) in the Democratic controlled White House is locked in FBI files which the Bureau will release unexpurgated only to the U.S. Congress. Congress, who must curry media favor, feigns disinterest (see: Washington Times editorial, 8-29-97).

Before World War II Hitler had established himself as the arch enemy of Liberalism, Marxism, and Jewry precisely the three driving forces... that had ridden into power with Franklin Roosevelt's New Deal.
WILMOT ROBERTSON, "The Dispossessed Majority", 1976.

Some of my best friends are Communists.
FRANKLIN DELANO ROOSEVELT

The whole story of Germany's appeal for negotiations and our curt refusal and severance of diplomatic relations was not published in 1937 and 1938 when Germany made her appeal, but was withheld from the public until ferreted out by the House Committee on un-American Activities after WWII... and released to the press more than 10-years after the facts were so criminally suppressed.
DR. JOHN O. BEATY, Colonel U.S. Army Intelligence.

John F. Kennedy proposed a Peace Plan to the United Nations (1961) calling for the "general and complete disarmament of the United States" a further measure to implement Bernard M. Baruch's plan.
A. K. CHESTERTON, "The New Unhappy Lords."

The depth of penetration of the Allied governments by JEW AGENTS is evidenced by 20th Century wars fought not only to benefit enemies of the West but also by strategies employed to assure Western defeat. We have seen, above, that the White House, and No. 10 Downing Street, capitulated to the ILLUMINATI, aligning themselves with the Soviet Union against Christian Germany. We have seen how Bernard Baruch, KAHILLA point-man, "the most powerful man in America," imposed absolute control over FDR, Churchill, and Dwight Eisenhower, who in concert sacrificed their country's heritage to advance the ILLUMINATI agenda (see Chapt. 6: "Holocaust"). The betrayal of Christendom by Roosevelt at Yalta, and Truman at Potsdam, widely documented, assured a total COMMUNIST VICTORY in WWII and caused the deaths of millions of unarmed Europeans following the war.

> Treason doth never prosper. What is the reason? For when it doth prosper none dare call it treason.
>
> LORD HARRINGTON.

STRATAGEMS of DEFEAT AND NO-WIN WARS

CHINA: Following WWII Mao Tse-Tung, financed by the ILLUMINATI, led his Chinese Communists in an armed conflict against National China under Generalissimo Chiang Kai-Shek, America's ally against Japan. Truman warned Chiang to integrate Communists into China's National government or American aid would be withdrawn. Chiang refused to be extorted, citing his revulsion of the International Banking cartel. Deprived of American assistance, his army bereft of supplies, Chiang Kai-Shek retreated to the island sanctuary of Formosa and dug in. Thus, the U.S.A. deliberately betrayed its former ally Chiang Kai-Shek and GAVE mainland China to Communism. Subsequently Communist China was awarded a permanent seat on the U.N. Security Council, its most powerful chair. Mao Tse-Tung, of *"Little Red Book"* fame, and darling of New York-Hollywood "elite," JEWS, then proceeded to murder 65-million of his countrymen in what David Rockefeller and "Mongol" Brzezinski call "a glorious revolution."

KOREA: Shortly thereafter Truman, with Congress averting its eyes, committed U.S. troops to Korea. The alleged mission was to PREVENT Communism from spreading to South Korea, a peninsula pointed at now disarmed Japan. This "police action" quickly developed into a full-blown but undeclared war. The great General Douglas MacArthur drove the North Koreans, led by Red Chinese officers, toward the Chinese Border amid cries of protest from Wall Street which feared war with "our trading partner" Red China. LIBERALS/MARXISTS/JEWS in America's streets "protested" our victories and exulted in our defeats thus, in patriots' eyes, giving the war a raison d'etre. MacArthur complained that his conduct of the war was compromised by spies within the U.S. government: "The enemy receives my (Pentagon) directives before I do". MacArthur asked Truman to permit Chiang Kai-Shek's troops to fight with Americans against the Red Chinese. Truman refused. MacArthur was denied his request to attack enemy forces massing across the Yalu border in preparation for attack. He was denied his request to gather intelligence by aerial reconnaissance over China. MacArthur soon realized he was expected to win battles but lose the war. Again and again against incredible odds, and at great cost in American casualties, U.S. forces stopped the enemy; but were prevented by President Truman from administering the coup de grace. MacArthur publicly insisted upon victory, infuriating the ILLUMINATI. Whereupon Truman dismissed MacArthur for insubordination. His replacement, General Ridgway said after the war: "The reason we didn't win is because I was under orders not to win". Why has no one been hanged for high treason? Only the ILLUMINATI knows. All of the facts, in retrospect, lead to the conclusion that the U.S. government's purpose in dragging America into Korea was not to defeat Communism but to kill as many American's as possible in an ignoble defeat, get rid of the hero MacArthur as a possible presidential nominee, and lure a disillusioned America into acceptance of One World Government.

VIET NAM. A repeat scenario was played 10-years later under another JEW-pocked Democratic Administration. President Lyndon Johnson, Democrat, in a special address to the American public, reported an attack upon a U.S. naval vessel in the Tonkin Gulf by a North Vietnamese torpedo boat. Johnson solemnly announced that "Communist aggression must be stopped as a threat to American security!" (Later, after 58,152 American dead were just names on a wall, declassified US Navy logs revealed there had been no torpedo attack!). Johnson then ordered 165,000 U.S. forces under General Westmoreland to support a handful of American "advisors" previously ordered there by former President John F. Kennedy, Democrat. The "advisors" assisted inept South Vietnamese in their ongoing racial war against the North Vietnamese, who also happened to be Communists. Once U.S. forces were committed in large numbers the U.S. federal government, as in Korea, prohibited them from attacking specified enemy sanctuaries (staging areas) into which the Communists retreated, regrouped, re-armed and launched renewed attacks. War materiel, shipped via the "Hanoi Run" from USSR to Viet Nam, was produced in Russian plants that had been built by American companies and financed by the JEW owned Federal Reserve System. As in Korea, Marxist spies within the U.S. government released vital information to the enemy. Again the secret policy of the ILLUMINATI was: "containment of Communism" while disallowing an American victory! Denying a final victory over a dedicated and skilled Marxist enemy WAS A RECIPE FOR THE MURDER OF OUR MEN. It meant re-taking the same bloody ground over and over again. Yet, despite treason in high places American troops outnumbered ten-to-one were winning the war. Which is precisely why U.S. MARXISTS/JEWS/LIBERALS so vehemently protested U.S. involvement and that is the only reason we were destroying their comrades... the Communists. The REDS.

Marxist *canaille* on the streets of America (Bob Dylan, JEW; Joan Baez, JEW; Bettina Apetheker, JEW, Mort Kunstler, JEW; Jerry Rubin, JEW; Abbie Hoffman, JEW; "Hanoi Jane" Fonda, Rhodes Scholar William J. Clinton, liars, queers, punks, lesbians, Hollywood JEWS, McGovernites, et al) staged protest parades, threw excrement at police, burned draft-cards, despoiled the American Flag, consorted with the enemy, made a mockery of the courts, smeared our military heroes *literally spitting on disabled vets returning from Viet Nam all with no punishment exacted yet.*

But, when the Hell's Angels, and Pagans motor-cycle gangs bloodied MARXIST/JEW noses the Harley boys were arrested under fake RICO Act charges. At Kent State three of the four rock-throwing psychos slain by the National Guard were JEWS (later martyrized in marble by the University).

Meanwhile the mass-media suddenly reversed its pro-war policy: denying our beleaguered troops moral support from home. The MEDIA heaped calumny on U.S. military leadership; presented biased, horrifying scenes depicting *"the wanton killing of Vietnamese civilians"*, and the *"degeneracy"* of our fighting men and women. Finally the brain-washed, confused, exhausted American goyim forced our government to surrender. We now see a pattern of SEDITION/TREASON. The U.S. government secretly abets Communism around the globe, then sends in the American military to *"contain the Communist menace"*. Thus, Europe, Russia, China, Korea, Viet Nam, Cambodia, Thailand, Japan, the Middle East were turned into killing grounds, and their existing governments destroyed. The ILLUMINATI then moves into the vacuum, establishes central banks, and issues debt-credit to the devastated populations. *There is no doubt these treasonous NO WIN*

U.S. WARS were meant to disillusion the American nation into accepting loss of sovereignty and One World Government (See The Protocols). You can be sure, too, the KHAZARS enthusiastically applauded as heroic Americans died.

U.S.S. LIBERTY: Nothing better illustrates the control JEWS exert over the U.S. Government than the *USS Liberty* atrocity. The *Liberty,* a well known "ferret", or surveillance ship (listed in the standard reference manual *Jane's Fighting Ships)* was a converted WWII *"Victory"* ship bearing an unmistakable silhouette. She was outfitted with sophisticated state-of-the-art surveillance-gear which added to her distinctive appearance. On 8 June 1967, the *Liberty* patrolled international waters off the Sinai Peninsula. The day was warm, with unlimited visibility, a 5-knot breeze, and calm seas. 100-feet above the bridge a 40-square feet United States flag flew from the main mast; a 12-feet tall numeral 5 was painted on both bows and her name appeared boldly on the stern. The *Liberty's* total armament consisted of two twin-mount 50-caliber machine guns sans splinter shields: one fore one aft. At 1130 ISRAELI reconnaissance planes began to monitored the ship closely and continuously for almost 3-hours. At 1405 three ISRAELI Mirage jets appeared in formation, each carrying two 30-mm cannon and up to 72-rockets. Suddenly, without challenging the *Liberty,* they conducted a deadly and coordinated attack on the virtually unarmed ship. The objective, clearly, was to sink the *Liberty* with all hands, leaving no traces. *In retrospect this was deliberate murder.* The first pass knocked out the radio-room killing all hands;

the next pass shot-up all life-rafts. The JEWS made repeated criss-cross attacks blasting *Liberty* from stem to stern. Her decks were awash with American blood which streamed through the scuppers and down the freeboard. *Our flag was shot from the mast.* UNABLE TO SINK HER the JEWS sent in three motor-torpedo boats which riddled the *Liberty* with 20-mm and 40-mm automatic weapons. One of three torpedoes launched struck the ship amidships destroying the communications center. Still, she refused to go down. In 39-minutes 34 American sailors were murdered and 164 wounded. Captain McGonagle, at the onset of the attack, managed to send a "Mayday" which was picked-up 600-miles away by the Sixth Fleet. The flat-top *USS America* launched an attack *but the U.S. planes were called back by the White House.* ISRAELI pilots upon intercepting Sixth Fleet communications (JEW radios were set on USS frequencies) quickly exited the area: JEWS are best at shooting starving Arabs armed with sticks and stones. Captain McGonagle brought the listing Liberty to dry-dock in Malta, thence to Little Creek, VA. Finally the bloodied hulk was scrapped. The crew muzzled. An ISRAELI Board of Inquiry blamed the attack on *mistaken identity:* their pilots had confused the 10,000-ton *USS Liberty* with the Egyptian 2,640-ton *El Quseir,* a troopship!

In the United States strong pressure to support the ISRAELI position was exerted by America's Ambassador to the U.N., Arthur Goldberg, JEW, and Eugene and Walt Rostow, JEWS, *Special Advisors on National Security* to President Johnson. These were the same JEWS who helped mastermind the Viet Nam war (Walt Rostow teaches now at Yale, hotbed of ZIONISM). Chief of the CIA, Richard Helms, *in re* the *Liberty* attack, permitted all U.S. intelligence operations inside ISRAEL to be conducted by the Mossad (the Mossad *is* the CIA). A U.S. Panel of Inquiry, chaired by Rear Admiral I. C. Kidd, USN, declared, *"The attack on the Liberty was, in fact, a case of mistaken identity."* Thus, establishing the official U.S. position.

Over the ensuing years facts creeping to the surface indicate the ISRAELIS knew exactly what they were doing, for example: JEWS claim that they thought they were attacking an Egyptian ship, yet they JAMMED ONLY United States communications frequencies. The *USS Liberty* got off her "Mayday" before the radiomen were killed only because of McGonagle's quick actions and the ship's advanced communications gear.

Apparently this is what happened: The *Liberty* had been ordered by the White House to another sector of the Mediterranean, but the message for undisclosed reasons was never dispatched. Still patrolling off Sinai, the *Liberty* intercepted communications revealing ISRAEL'S sneak attacks on Egypt and Jordan igniting the 1967 war. Meanwhile, with the assistance of U.S. mass-media, ISRAELIS announced to the world they had been attacked by the Egyptians. The White House (double-crossing the Arabs) abetted the ISRAELI LIES. Moshe Dayan, Israeli Chief of Defense, ordered the *Liberty* to be sunk. She knew too much and, more importantly, when she was sunk with all hands the atrocity could be blamed on Egypt, producing another *Lusitania,* Pearl Harbor, or Coventry reaction in America.

ISRAEL did not court-martial the Mirage pilots, two of whom were "American" JEWS trained at the U.S. Air Force Academy, in Colorado. The U.S. Navy warned surviving *USS Liberty* personnel never to discuss the incident. For the first time in American history medals awarded for valor omitted the ENEMY'S name: referring, instead, to a "battle in the Mediterranean." In a ceremony normally conducted with solemnity and dignity at the White House, Captain McGonagle, was awarded our Nation's highest honor, the Congressional Medal of Honor, by a *representative* of President Johnson in an ante-room at the navy yards – as quickly and quietly as possible. As of this date, the U.S. State Department refuses to declassify important documents relating to the *USS Liberty* murders that occurred almost 35-years ago! Declassification would be considered anti-Semitism.

Captain Joe Toth, USN, seeking damages on behalf of his murdered son, Stephen Toth, and two other officers killed aboard the *USS Liberty,* was threatened by the U.S Navy and by the U.S. State Department to keep quiet or suffer the consequences. His widow said:

> First they killed my son, then my husband. The harassment took the form of threats and claims that Joe was damaging national security; and there was surveillance and pressure from people like the IRS. It was too

much for his bad heart. It took a year to kill him, but finally it did.

Ten years later UPI reported (9-18-77) that CIA documents obtained by Egypt through the Freedom of Information Act reveal Israel Defense Minister, Moshe Dayan, KHAZAR, ordered the unprovoked attack. CIA Director Stansfield Turner, goy traitor, questioned on national TV about the CIA documents stated "they have not been authenticated... the ISRAELI attack was an honest mistake".

Nonsense. Prima facie evidence alone reveals the brazen cover-up: It was broad daylight. American sailors, plainly visible, don't resemble Egyptians. Now, ask yourself, who do you suppose controls United States Presidents, Congressmen, admirals, and CIA Directors? Thus, JEW PARASITES murder our People, distort our culture, and trash our Destiny. America's tragic political-military defeats, and acts of sedition and treason which our gutless Congress refuses to investigate are not unrelated events. Rather they are moments, examined in a time-warp, depicting the *continuing decline of Western Civilization.* The evil scenario for these High Crimes is provided by the *Protocols of the Learned Elders of Zion* which, as Henry Ford firmly stated: *fit what went on in the past and they fit what is happening now.* Exactly. The metaphor: *"Ship of State,"* referring to the U.S.A., elicits images of the *USS Liberty* bleeding and listing. So too our Nation bleeds; riddled by parasites; consumed by an ENEMY none dares name.

THE MASS-MEDIA

Occasional cries of Americans demanding justice, are ignored because *the media interprets the 1st Amendment as the right to print only what fits ILLUMINATI objectives.* It is axiomatic, when the *vox populi* is silenced treasonous acts remain unpunished. (We note: "Freedom of the Press" is not granted Nazis, the Aryan Nations, the KKK, etc.).

The MASS-MEDIA shapes public opinion – brainwashing society with mis-information, dis-information, phony polls to move in whatever direction the ILLUMINATI wishes. It has been pointed out that public opinion polls really test media efficacy. The MASS-MEDIA is, in effect, an adjunct of the ILLUMINATI and its spores: CFR/ TRI, Federal Reserve System, Internal Revenue Service, World Jewish Congress, Anti-Defamation League of the B'nai B'rith, the Foundations, et al whose combined influence far exceeds that of our constitutional government. *Only Aryan Americans properly armed and led, have greater power.* THE MASS-MEDIA keeps the three branches of the U.S. government in harness. Nationalistic jurists and politicians are considered politically-incorrect: *branded persona non grata* by the media and ignored, or else they are crucified by it. The two most influential newspapers in the world, meditated over morning coffee by D.C. power-brokers, are the New York Times ("All the News that Fits") owned by the Oakes (Ochs),JEWS, and Sulzberger families, JEWS; and the *Washington Post,* owned by Martha Meyer

Graham (mongrel-daughter of Eugene Meyer, JEW, banker, who purchased the paper as a propaganda organ to drive America into the Wars). Both of these media empires include radio-TV stations, web-sites, and additional publishing ventures. They make or break governments, spread spirochetes of JEW syphilis, create financial panics and wars, and get their instructions from the KEHILLA.

Some additional publications controlled by JEWS include:

the *St. Louis Post Dispatch* (owned by the Pulitzer family, founders of "yellow journalism"); *Philadelphia Inquirer, San Francisco Chronicle, Los Angeles Times, Las Vegas Sun; U.S. NEWS AND WORLD REPORT, TIME, NEWSWEEK; FORTUNE, MONEY, THE NATION; NEW YORK REVIEW OF BOOKS, SATURDAY REVIEW OF LITERATURE, BOOK OF THE MONTH CLUB, ENCYCLOPEDIA BRITANNICA, BOWKERS; NEW REPUBLIC, COMMENTARY, SCHOLASTIC, AMERICAN HERITAGE, STARS AND STRIPES; VOGUE, GLAMOUR, SEVENTEEN, MADEMOISELLE, McCALL S, TEENAGE, LADIES HOME JOURNAL, RED BOOK, COSMOPOLITAN; PEOPLE; NEW YORKER, VANITY FAIR, ESQUIRE, SPORTS ILLUSTRATED; AMERICAN HOME, HOUSE AND GARDEN, FAMILY CIRCLE, ARTS AND ANTIQUES*, etc. Ancorp National Services (Union News), owned by Henry Garfinkle, JEW, is the leading distributor of paperbacks, magazine and newspapers to newsstands and retail outlets. Sam

Newhouse, JEW, owns the third largest newspaper chain represented, at last count, by over 30 dailies.

JEW control is pervasive in book publishing: Knopf, Random House, Viking Press, Doubleday, Dell, Holt-Rinehart & Winston, Grosset and Dunlop, Penguin, Bantam, to name a few. Most book/film reviewers are JEWS, or they work for JEW publications. The same holds true for book, film and television agents. Harry Sherman, JEW, owner of Book-of-the-Month Club, distributes millions of titles yearly to the country's retail outlets. Do you think they distribute material on the ADL hit-list? Try to purchase, at your local book dealer, a copy of David Irving's "Churchill's War"; or Wilmot Robertson's "Dispossessed Majority"; or Ernst Zundel's "Did 6-Million Really Die?" You will come up empty handed. They won't even catalogue them. On the other hand, "Ann Frank's Diary", a proven hoax, is available everywhere. In effect JEWS determine what Americans are allowed to read, hear, see, write and THINK.

> Abraham H. Foxman in his letter to the Editor... accuses me of "anti-Semitism"; he calls me "a well known Holocaust denier and Nazi apologist", and he writes of my "pattern of bias and deceit". Then I see that he directs a league against defamation (ADL). How odd.
> DAVID IRVING, Letters, "Vanity Fair", October 199

Recently, Bertelsmann USA, a German conglomerate, purchased several New York book publishers, creating panic among the Tribe. However, the deal specified that Bertelsmann would no longer publish *"Mein Kampf"*, and the infrastructure of the acquired publishers would remain firmly under JEW management!

A succession of JEW hierarchies during the definitive years prior to, during, and after WWII controlled ALL information broadcast over America s radio-TV networks: William Paley, JEW, CEO at *CBS*; the Sarnoff family, JEWS, headed up *RCA (NBC)*; Leonard Goldenson, JEW, headed *ABC. PBS,* and the Sports Network are also controlled by JEWS, as are the leading Cable Channels: *TNN, CNN, A&E,* the *History Channel* to name a few. Network ownership has changed in some instances due to corporate mergers but the infrastructures remain unassailably JEWISH, for example *The Disney Co.*: Headed by Michael Eisner, JEW, purchased *ABC*; and Sumner Redstone (Rothstein) JEW, purchased *CBS* forming *Viacom,* the world's second largest media conglomerate, spewing its filth into all corners of the world. Highly paid Aryan "Talking Heads" mouthing JEW ideology (Cronkite, Jennings, Sawyer, Cokie Roberts, George Will, Matthews, Brokaw, Rather, et al), performing as Judas goats have led the United States to the brink of catastrophe: a non-winnable war against the Arab states. That which Americans know about their own history, and about JEW history is what the TRIBE allows them to know.

TIME-WARNER COMMUNICATIONS, the world's largest media conglomerate, headed by Gerald Levin, JEW, recently acquired Turner Broadcasting Company. Turner, an uneducated (Brown Univ.) but very successful business entrepreneur, was married to Jane Fonda, Hollywood bimbo. As you remember she was photographed behind enemy lines waving a Communist flag during the Viet Nam war. Afterwards, American troops placed laminated photographs of "Hanoi Jane" in their urinals. Ergo, it's not surprising that Ted/Jane (who are now divorced) merged with *Time-Warner* (JEWS); and then, with much hoopla, donated 1-Billion tax-exempt-dollars to the United Nations: whose objective is ILLUMINATI WORLD GOVERNMENT. Ownership of Hollywood, the theater, Tin-pan-alley, and the recording industry are very nearly a JEW monopoly. To escape anti-trust actions a few obedient goyim are permitted a small share of the loot. Khazars control not only financing, creation and production of the medium, but also own, almost exclusively, the distribution, exhibition and ancillary rights foreign and domestic as well as casting-couch privileges whereon enterprising young starlets are made (and bred).

JEW power in the "entertainment industry" stems from their seemingly unique ability to obtain financial backing. In the final instance, investment bankers, financiers, venture capitalists, almost all JEWS, determine what will be produced. If content does not fit ILLUMINATI prerequisites it gets trashed. There have been no films based, for example, on David Irving's *"The Destruction of Dresden"*, *"Goebbel s Diaries"*; Veale's *"Advance to Barbarism"*; Solzhenitsyn's *"Gulag Archipelago"*; Shakespeare's *"Merchant of Venice"*; Taylor Caldwell's *"A Pillar of Iron"*; or a documentary covering the *"U.S.S. Liberty"* atrocity – a film that would shake the world and hang Congressmen and CIA moles for treason.

JEW contribution to film culture (in addition to on screen copulation and the "laugh-track") is the DOCU-DRAMA, wherein the film documents historical characters and events to provide authenticity but distorts those characters and events to support JEW ideologies. Finally, the docu-drama is sold as authentic history. These half-truths are, of course, LIES which are seriously damaging, as they are meant to be, to the Aryan Nation. *Schindler's List* is an example of a "Spielbergism":

The following is taken from the copyright-page of the First Edition of Thomas Kneally's book, upon which the film *"Schindler's List"* was based. Current editions of the book omit the disclaimers!

> TOUCHSTONE Rockefeller Center
> 1230 Avenue of the Americas
> New York City, NY 10020
>
> THOMAS KENEALLY Schindler's List.
>
> This book is a work of fiction. Names, characters, places and incidents are either products of the author's imagination or are used fictitiously. Any resemblance to actual events, or locales, or persons, living or dead, is purely coincidental.
>
> 1. Schindler, Oskar, 1908-1974 ......Fiction.
> 2. Holocaust, Jewish 1939-1945 ......Fiction.
> 3. World War II, 1939-1945 ......Fiction.

The docu-drama allows director Sir Stephen Spielberg, JEW, uninhibited by historical facts, to spew forth his hatred of Germans. No LIE is too degenerate for this KHAZAR to depict as Fact. Sadly, his rape of the First

Amendment traumatizes young people who believe what their elders tell them.

Vintage U.S. Air Force photographs and interviews with former prisoners reveal that in reality Plaszow Camp was much different from that depicted in the much publicized film, "Schindler's List". For example the house of Cmdr. Goeth, the "maniacal killer", was actually located at the base of a hill making it impossible for him, from there, to casually shoot JEWS located in a compound on top of that same hill. It didn't happen except in Spielberg's malevolent brain. History shows Plaszow as a reasonably comfortable, well managed concentration camp. There were no gas chambers. No crazed Commander. ALL *Spielbergisms!*

Spielberg made his career slandering Germans. It is revealing, therefore, that he (as so many Hollywood JEWS) prefers Aryan women. Thus far the celebrated director has married two of them. Spielberg knows a quality aquiline nose when he sees it. He wants those "hateful, bigoted, maniacal" Aryan genes in his offspring. Recently, the United States Congress, prodded by Senator Arlen Specter, JEW, Democrat, granted billionaire Spielberg One-million dollars of your money to tape the fantasies of newly discovered "HOLOCAUST SURVIVORS" in a continuing effort to extort pity from the brain-washed goyim public. In their greed JEWS forget that more survivors means fewer "victims".

It probably could be shown by facts and figures That there is no distinctly native American criminal class except Congress. MARK

TWAIN.

LIBERALS *feel so good* when they have others to pity! GOD'S CHOSEN, wailing SHOAH, prey on these piteous pitiers like pick-pockets at Macy's. As the dumb goyim flagellate themselves with brotherly love JEWS filch everything of value not nailed down all the while crying anti-Semitism.

MONEY

*C*hutzpah works in the MONEY GAME, too! *Forbes* magazine lists the top 400 U.S. mega-Billionaires and Billionaires (1998). There are 5 JEWS among the top 10-mega-Billionaires; and 15 JEWS among the top 30-Billionaires. Ergo, while claiming to be victims of anti-Semitism and 3% of the population JEWS represent 50% of the richest men in America. The majority of these JEWS were born in eastern Europe proving the Nazis were not as efficient as we have been led to believe. *Vanity Fair* magazine, presenting the "New Establishment" for 1998 lists 12 JEWS among "the top 30 power-brokers in the United States." *Conspicuous by their absence in both of the above polls are members of the International Banking cabal* who own the interest on America's Six-trillion dollar debt. These are the *"dominant men"* President Wilson referred to, who sit on the Boards of Directors of the world's most prestigious corporations; shadowy figures who snap their fingers and Congress jumps.

Usury may be practiced on Christians.

TALMUD: Abhodah Zara 54a.

A special 1950 Federal Census Report... revealed that of The... different U.S. population groups "foreign born Russians" had the highest medium income. The medium income of Americans of white parentage was 40 percent less... "the Russian group contains large refugee and Jewish components".

WILMOT ROBERTSON, *"The Dispossessed Majority'*.

Christian property belongs to first Jew claiming.

TALMUD: Babha Kama 113b.

Jews must divide what they overcharge Christians.

TALMUD: Choschen Ham 183.7.

We now know the "Trickle-down Theory" of financing begins with the Chairman of the FED Board of Governors who provides "Confidential" information, to privileged financiers, which trickles-down to lesser members of the cabal. Would you like to learn 48-hours in advance that the FED intends to lower the prime-rate? Would you like to be an agent on the sending or receiving end, for example, of dollars pipe-lined through the IMF to Russia, or Israel? You too can be in *Forbes 400!*

Why is it that many members of Congress arrive poor and retire rich? Answer: Because their honor is worth less than what they receive from special interest groups. Money buys everything. It "bought" the Lincoln bedroom. It bought the Supreme Court. It bought your country.

JEWISH INFLUENCE?

Not so long ago it was unheard of for Jews to be in the major law firms in Washington, D.C.... Jews were not allowed in any of the major country clubs... I think about what the Jewish position is now in America: The Secretary of State is Jewish... The Secretary of Defense is half Jewish... The Secretary of the treasury is the only one who is Jewish and admits he's Jewish... The head of every major Hollywood studio is Jewish. The heads of all the networks are Jewish. The heads of two out of the four national newspapers are Jewish... The heads of every Ivy League University are Jewish... I tell you how I know beyond a shadow of a doubt that the Jewish position in America has changed dramatically... a close friend had a memorial service at the Chevy Chase Country Club (!). And there was a cantor with a yarmulke giving the service... I cannot describe to you how astonishing a turn of events this was.

> BEN STEIN, JEW, speech at a Jewish pro-life conference at
> Catholic University Law School
> (excerpted from *"The Washington Times"* 11-17-98).

NO ROOM FOR WHITE CHRISTIANS IN IVY LEAGUE RAINBOW

If elite colleges and grad schools enroll 75 percent of their students from the small Democratic minorities while white Christians and Catholics, who make up 75 percent of the population, are relegated to 25 percent of the seats, there is no doubt who is going to run America in the 21st Century.

Buried in the editorial page of the Wall Street Journal (11-16-98) was a remarkable essay (authored by Ron Unz, Harvard Alumnus) which exposes the true and hidden story of who is really "underrepresented" in our elite schools, and who are the real victims of ethnic bigotry in America. According to Mr. Unz, today at Harvard College, Hispanic and black enrollment has reached 7% and 8% respectively, slightly less than the 10% and 12% of the U.S. population that is Hispanic and black. This has been a cause of protests... as Hispanics and African-Americans insist on more proportional representation.

Mr. Unz...goes on nearly 20% of the Harvard student body is Asian-American, and 25% to 33% is Jewish, though Asian-Americans make up only 3% of the population and Jewish-Americans even less than 3%. Thus 50% of Harvard's student body is drawn from 5% of the U.S. population!

When one adds foreign students, students from our tiny WASP elite, and grandchildren of graduates, what emerges is a Harvard student body where non-Jewish whites 75% of the

U.S. population get just 25% of the slots! The same situation... exists at other elite schools... As Hispanics, Asians, African-American, and Jewish-Americans also vote overwhelmingly Democratic, the picture that emerges is not a pretty one. A liberal elite is salving its social conscience by robbing America's white middle class of its birthright, and handing it over to minorities who just happen to vote Democratic...

PAT BUCHANAN, excerpted from *Washington Times* (12-13-98).

The same conspiracy existed in post WWI Germany. Hitler attempted to deport the JEWS. JEWS declared war. America sent troops overseas to kill the Germans! Now the JEWS run America.

TOO-MANY-JEWS POLICY TRIGGERS PROTEST:

The chairman of the House International Relations Committee, Benjamin A. Gilman, wrote to President Clinton yesterday, objecting to a report (anonymous) that senior foreign affairs positions are not being filled because there are too many... 'white Jewish males' in senior State Department positions... The sources were speaking in the context of the Clinton administration's preoccupation with seeking "diversity" ...so that no single sex or ethnic group is overly represented... Nevertheless Mr. Gilman said... "For such a statement to appear, even anonymously, in this day and age is outrageous... *Religious discrimination is totally inappropriate in personnel decision making*" ...Mr. Gilman told Mr. Clinton, "We will be watching your administration's personnel decisions closely on this matter."

WASHINGTON TIMES, by Ben Barber, 1997.

Gilman, JEW, is pulling the old canard that JEWRY is to be identified by *religion*, NOT *race*. When even the village idiot understands Elizabeth Taylor, JEW and Sammy Davis, Jr., JEW, are not KHAZARS and Henry Kissinger, JEW, isn't German. It's a shell game. When hiring or recruitment practices are based on *racial* quotas, and JEWS are under-represented, then one hears God's Chosen wailing anti-Semitism (anti-Race). Parasites are insatiable.

President Clinton *directed by the ILLUMINATI* has appointed more KHAZAR JEWS to vital government positions *(with the disaster that implies)* than any President in U.S. history. Yet, Gilman, the quintessential JEW, like Shakespeare's quintessential usurer, Shylock, demands flesh, flesh and more flesh.

> A Jew remains a Jew even though he changes his religion. A Christian who would adopt the Jewish religion would not become a Jew, because the quality of a Jew is not in the religion but in the race.
> "THE JEWISH WORLD", London, England, 12-14-1922.

CULTURAL INVASIONS

It is said that to enjoy Wagner, Beethoven, and Richard Strauss one need only listen to a composition by Mahler, JEW. Be that as it may, at the podium whatever the program there is almost invariably a JEW conductor: Bruno Walter, Daniel Barenboim, Serge Koussevitsky, Pierre Monteux, Erich Leinsdorf, Eugene Ormandy, George Szell, Arthur Fiedler, James Levine,

Leonard Bernstein, Andre Previn, George Solti, Arthur Schnabel, Leonard Slatkin, Zubin Mehta, et al. The foregoing represent a few of many JEW conductors, since WWII, assigned to direct the world's greatest orchestras. Token Gentiles who are permitted occasionally to wave the baton are considered intruders on what has become JEW turf. Why?

Royalties foreign and domestic from the sales of discs, and tapes are what keep symphony orchestras, conductors, and soloists out of the red. In the United States the RECORDING INDUSTRY is controlled by JEWS. In effect, it is they, abetted by the media, who determine what artists will be hired, starred and fired. Thus, the West's great musical forms have come to be interpreted by JEW conductors and JEW soloists in their kitschy manner. It is they who receive the financial benefits and accolades while *Aryans apparently are incapable of interpreting the great music created by their own race.* This is another example of the culture-clash that polarized Germany.

JEWS aren't content with plagiarizing, appropriating and distorting our music, they have another trick up their sleeves. Invariably a musical tour de force, for example a Mozart recording directed by von Karajan, will feature on the flip-side selections by third-rate JEW composers, as Copeland, Bernstein, and Gershwin. Thus the sanctity of Aryan music libraries, like those of private clubs, and schools, are infringed by the uninvited. To object to such chutzpah invites yelps of anti-Semitism; when in reality the objection is to JEW Culture.

> To be a successful composer of musicals you either have to be JEWISH or gay. I am both.
>
> LEONARD BERNSTEIN,
> Conductor, New York Philharmonic.

> Ye shall be a treasure unto me above all People.
>
> EXODUS 9:15

> The Jews in Europe have a peculiar character and are known for their fraud.
>
> DAVID HUME, Scottish philosopher.

SPACE

The conquest of space has long been the provenance of the West, beginning with the Icarus myth and Da Vinci's Faustian concept of man in flight. The Wright brothers got man off the ground with wings at Kitty Hawk. Goddard pioneered rocketry; German scientists invented jet engines and developed the rocket science that propelled the U.S. and the USSR into outer-space; Werner von Braun and his German-American team at the National Aeronautics Space Administration (NASA) got America to the moon. *The creativity, thescience, the marvelous technology and techniques that brought the solar system within reach was produced by Aryans.* It was they who took the risks, and conquered the sometimes fatal hazards. Then along comes Daniel E. Goldin, KHAZAR/JEW, appointed by President Clinton per ILLUMINATI instructions to head NASA. *Thus assuring Israel of all NASA intelligence that JEW spies don t first steal. Under Goldin the U.S. and Russia (financed by the United States) now cooperate on the space program not the U.S. and Aryan Europe! (The Monument erected on the Moon memorializing space-pioneers neglects to mention Werner von Braun, Aryan).*

PARASITISM, U.S.A. is, of course, an historical *redux.* Theodor Herzl, JEW, pointed out that *anti-Semitism exists wherever JEWS appear because they bring it with them.* Their original mission was to propagate their religion. In this they failed. Few JEWS today claim that messianic mission. Israeli leaders, Prime Ministers Golda Meir, and Benjamin Netanyahu, for example, freely admit they are not *"true believers." But the idea of a mission remains in degenerate form: spoil everything that is not JEWISH.* This they accomplish, whatever their host nation, through a highly organized, clandestine plan of acquire and destroy, fairly described in these pages.

The JEW philosophy is not to "MAKE" (EARN) money but to "GET" money. This is why JEWS are always financiers and middle men, rarely captains of industry, builders and producers. The sturdy, loyal Aryan chooses work that he enjoys and is proud of even if that means "making" a little less money. But with the JEW "getting" money is the major consideration. Ideas of *"creative labor," and "job loyalty"* seem ludicrous to him. Aryans relish dealing with creative ideas, skill, quality *and danger.* JEWS don't conquer wildernesses or launch themselves into space. To Aryans the JOB means everything, not brokering deals and living off the effort of others. Soon the so-called "American" JEW the parasite who made nothing got everything!

We have attempted to show in this chapter a few examples the very tip of the iceberg of what "American" JEWS do best: commit treason and other high-crimes at the highest echelons of government; promote the destruction of the American Ethos by fomenting UNDECLARED NO-WIN WARS (called "police actions") in which thousands of young Americans died needlessly their honor then dragged down Main Street by JEW led canaille; steal America's nuclear program while building the military and nuclear ability of CHINA/ISRAEL/SOVIET; pre-meditated murder of the USS Liberty; continuing "HOLOCAUST" extortion and LIES despite OVERWHELMING EVIDENCE there was no policy to mass-murder JEWS and there were NO gas chambers; capture of America's money (FED), mass-media, government, business, military-industrial complex, and space program. All of this, and more, by an ugly, and hostile tribe living parasitically within the sinews of our Nation.

> Let me issue and control a nation's money and I care not who makes its laws.
>
> AMSCHUL MAYER ROTHSCHILD.

> Kill the JEWS!
>
> SADAM HUSSEIN.

> The "Jewish Problem" is not to be explained ethically, racially, nationally, religiously, socially but only totally culturally... In this

century with the West passing into a unity of Culture, nation, race, society, economics, state the Jew appears clearly in his own total unity: a complete inner stranger to the Soul of the West.

FRANCIS PARKER YOCKEY, *"Imperium".*

This crafty race has one great principle: as long as order prevails there is nothing to be gained.

GOETHE.

As the new millennium appears JEWS are confronted with three terrifying prospects:

1) The Dialectic Synthesis of the West ushering in the Mendelian Age; 2) The cultural-elite of many nations throughout the World have judged that JEWS must pay for their crimes; 3) The World-wide Internet, for the first time in 85-years, lifts the iron curtain of JEWISH censorship from public information. Historical FACTS formerly suppressed are now available here and abroad to anyone with a computer.

In Toronto, Ontario, "HOLOCAUST DENIAL" is treated as a HATE-CRIME punishable by stiff fines and imprisonment. Ernst Zundel's court cases there, blacked-out or distorted in the U.S., constituted high drama. In court Zundel's defense *conclusively proved there were no gas-chambers at Auschwitz.* Nevertheless, *the Judge found Zundel guilty of hate, ruling:* "Truth is No Defense." Before and during the trial hate ran red-hot. Numerous attempts were made to kill Zundel with letter-bombs, clubs and gunshots. Zundel's office was torched causing $600,000 in damage. Neither the government, the media, nor the Canadian police, knowing on which side their bread is buttered, dared admonish the JEWS (see Bibliography). THE WORLD JEWISH COUNCIL, Edgar Bronfman, Chairman, JEW (Seagrams Distillers) exhorts the U.S. and Canadian governments to shut down Ernst Zundel's web-site:

http://www.zundelsite.org

In Germany, Manfred Roeder, continues to protest the HOLOCAUST HOAX in a brain-washed Reich (still occupied by U.S. Negro troops). Roeder, former attorney to Adm. Doenitz, was nearly beaten to death last year by six masked thugs wielding iron pipes. There were no arrests. Instead, Roeder has been indicted, tried and sentenced to three years in prison for denying the "Holocaust."

In the United States of America *JEW crimes against Revisionists also are tolerated by local police as JEW espionage and subversion also is tolerated by the U.S. Congress.*

Resultant of the rising tide of Mendelism, and Revisionism, U.S. JEWS (under the banners of Judeo-Christianity, Democracy and Brotherhood) are intensifying their efforts to solidify their remarkable political gains, miscegenate the races, and establish One World Zionist Government. To facilitate that task they intend to abolish U.S./Mexican/Caribbean immigration restrictions, confiscate ALL guns belonging to American citizens, and trick America into a global war. Jews as always will emerge with the loot while Aryans will do the dying. Remember, the ILLUMINATI'S REVOLUTIONARY ARM is composed of JEWS in DIASPORA: Bolsheviks, "neo-Conservatives", assassins, mobsters, anarchists, con-artists, pimps, from the outhouses of the world.

These, the *canaille,* will foment revolution in America's armed forces, prisons, inner-cities and on Main Street, U.S.A.

TOB SHEBBE GOYIM HAROG!

CHAPTER 11

PATHOLOGY AND SYNTHESIS

PATHOLOGY

Power and law are not synonymous. In truth they are frequently in opposition and irreconcilable. There is GOD'S LAW from which all equitable laws of man emerge and by which men must live if they are not to die in oppression, chaos and despair. Divorced from GODS ETERNAL AND IMMUTABLE LAW, established before the founding of the suns, man's power is evil no matter the noble words with which it is employed or the motives urged when enforcing it. Men of good will, mindful therefore of the LAW LAID DOWN BY GOD, will oppose governments whose rule is by men and, if they wish to survive as a nation, they will destroy that government which attempts to adjudicate by the whim or power of venal judges.

CICERO (106-43 BC).

The Jewish people, taken collectively, will be its own Messiah. It will attain to mastery of the world through the union of all OTHER human races, through the abolition of boundaries and monarchies, which are the bulwark of Particularism, and through the erection of a universal Republic, in which the Jews will everywhere enjoy universal rights. In this new organization of mankind the sons of Israel will spread themselves over the whole inhabited world, and they, since they all belong to the same race and culture-tradition, without at the same time having a definite nationality, will form the leading element without finding opposition. The government of the nation, which will make up this universal Republic, will pass without effort into the hands of the Israelites, by the very fact of the victory of the proletariat. The Jewish race can then do away with private property, and after that everywhere administer the public funds. Then shall the promise of the Talmud be fulfilled. When the time of the Messiah has come, the Jews will hold in their hands the key to the wealth of the world.

BARUCH LEVY, JEW, historian,
from his famous letter to Karl Marx (emphasis added).

In order to possess what you do not possess, you must go by way of dispossession.

T.S. ELIOT, *"Four Quartets".*

Not to know what happened before we were born keeps us forever a child.

CICERO (106-43 BC).

Purified races always become stronger and more beautiful.

NIETZSCHE.

The *raison d'etre* of a Communist government, according to Karl Marx, is to build up a proletarian system of society. When persons or classes of persons are found who cannot be fitted into such a society they are "liquidated", that is they are put to death... In this entirety passionless spirit, Lenin (JEW) and Dzershinsky (JEW) had eliminated the aristocratic and plutocratic classes of Czarist Russia together with tens of thousands of Orthodox bishops and priests after the Revolution of 1917....The great majority perished (simply) because they could not be assimilated by the new proletariat state being created.

F. J .P. VEALE, English jurist, *"Advance to Barbarism."*

JEWS could never have captured America without the compliance of her White leadership which, early in the 20th Century, resided in the sons, grandsons and great-grandsons of the men who pioneered this land. These scions inherited power, privilege and wealth but completely lost touch with the IDEA that made this Nation great: *"the manifest destiny of the White Race."* Consequently, *America was seduced into fighting wars abroad for JEW interests, destroying not only the White seed of Europe, but damaging the ethos of the entire West, thus allowing the ILLUMINATI to burrow deeper and deeper into America's sinews.* The Aryan upper-crust, educated in prestigious prep-schools and Ivy League colleges, was kept totally ignorant of the Laws of Genetics God's Laws; while the TALMUDIC garbage of Marx, Freud, and Boas were proclaimed and promulgated as the path to peace and plenty. Displaying masters degrees and doctorates these brain-washed, socially elite goyim with soft hands and bleeding hearts were complicit in spreading spirochetes of JEW syphilis throughout the West. The results have been disastrous. A HIGH CULTURE as we now know, is the reflection of a UNIQUE PEOPLE. When that People sickens it is reflected in their culture. *No doubt Western Culture is sick. Why?*

Cultural Pathologists exhibit several indisputable FACTS from which one must draw obvious conclusions: *JEWS deliberately prepared Western Man for the 20ᵗʰ CENTURY WARS OF ANNIHILATION by distorting his racial instincts through lies, propaganda, and demonizing the "enemy," and by BUYING Allied political leadership, thus bringing America and Britain into total warfare AGAINST their European family. Germany's High Purpose was to unite Europe against the REAL ENEMY JUDAEO-MARXISTS. The tragic result was TOTAL victory for the KHAZARS and devastating defeat for the Aryan West.* Consider England, c. 1900, a tiny island of approximately 40-million souls, controlling over 80% of the earth (including mastery of the seas). She was the greatest civilizing influence the world had ever known. Today, after fighting two world wars FOR

THE ENEMY, British supremacy of the seas is gone; her commercial and political primacy in Europe are gone; her colonial power is gone; her monetary reserves are gone; and her Aryan breeding stock is seriously depleted. She was kicked-out of Palestine by ungrateful JEWS (armed by American ZIONISTS), her soldiers assassinated, their bodies booby-trapped, her diplomats murdered. England now is owned lock-stock-and-barrel by the ILLUMINATI, and has been forced to accept waves of non-White immigration among her pink-cheeked Teutonic Family in preparation for ONE WORLD JEW GOVERNMENT (Population statistics project London will have a non-white majority by 2010; Britain will have a non-white majority within 100-years).

America fared no better. She won the military debacle FOR THE ENEMY, and lost the Peace. Interest ($245-Billion per annum) on her 6-Trillion Dollar Debt, belongs to the ILLUMINATI. The United States, *"The World's only Super Power,"* is now a JEW colony. White Americans, dispossessed, are merely well paid highly taxed employees. They keep the wheels turning, fight JEW wars and are admonished to relinquish their daughters' wombs to miscegenation.

Quite clearly Mendelism exposed a bleeding wound: When a Culture Organism fails to fight for itself, it fights against itself. It always loses when it fails to fight the REAL ENEMY. Cultural pathologists reveal that *an entire People was led to its destruction,* against its instincts, by self-serving leaders and false propaganda. *Complicit in the destruction of Western Culture the MASS-MEDIA has been found guilty of abetting treason, sedition, murder, genocide and other high crimes.*

> If any question why we died, Tell them, because our fathers lied."
> KIPLING.

> When lo! an angel called him out of heaven,
> Saying, Lay not thy hand upon the lad,
> Neither do anything to him. Behold,
> A ram, caught in a thicket by its horns,
> Offer the Ram of Pride instead of him.
> But the old man would not so, but slew his son,
> And half the seed of Europe, one by one.
> WILFRED OWEN, *"The Parable of the Old Man and the Young."*

Those patriots who died to "Save the World for Democracy" died bravely but in vain. DEMOCRACY, we have seen, is political anthrax used by JEWS to destroy their Gentile hosts by turning the meritocracy pyramid upside down. Thus, through the franchise superior men (UN-common Men) are rendered politically impotent by votes of the numerically superior masses; *they being ignorant, frenetic and compulsive ("the beast with many heads") are easily manipulated by MONEY and the MASS-MEDIA (the Electoral College represents the party bosses and is a sham).* Honest leaders, shunned by media-moguls, are rarely seen or heard publicly. Consequently, they rarely are elected to public office; while pols enjoying MEDIA approval enjoy long careers at the public trough, and in back-rooms selling America's heritage to the highest bidders. The rule of thumb is: if the candidate has media approval he's been bought! Thus, in a nation where quantity is valued over quality, and equality over merit every segment of the culture is degraded.

The Liberal axiom that *"This is a nation of Laws"* (under which all men are equal) lost its validity when *"all men" was interpreted by U.S. judiciary to mean "all races."* The Founders, as their writings clearly document, contemned the notion of racial equality even as they contemned the notion of democracy. But the visions of our Aryan Founding Fathers meant nothing to the JEWS, or to the legislators and jurists that the ILLUMINATI so regularly blackmailed, extorted and bought.

Ergo, Constitutional amendments, liberal enactments and interpretations of the law have nullified government as envisioned by the Founders, literally turning the Law of the Land against the White race *("We the People")* the very People it initially was crafted to protect. (On a global scale, too, Democracy is disastrous for Whites who comprise only 10% of the World Population).

The gradual dismemberment of our Constitutional Republic was performed gradually and deliberately. The America we were raised to love and respect and to which we pledge our allegiance has carefully been preserved in its panoply, monuments, and historic places. But, as we shall see, that's largely an illusion. The vision of Washington, Adams, Jefferson and Franklin has been distorted beyond redemption. *"An Enemy Hath Done This!"* (Ezra Taft Benson). *Inside the heart of the nation feeds a disgusting, salivating leech.*

The First *U.S. Constitution (1787)*, signed by the Framers, preserved in vacuum under glass, was abrogated in 1861 when a federation of northern states waged total war against outnumbered southern states of the union which subsequently were torched and broken. The northern onslaught, based upon bankers' greed and political expedience, was cloaked in the hypocrisy of racial equality: the manumission of Negro slaves who then were segregated in JEW-owned tenements, their low intelligence exploited in sweat-shops. *A Second Constitution* took effect when Rothschild's hand-picked pols, at gun point, imposed the 14th and 15th Amendments (1865 and 1868) which effectively revoked the Constitution the traitors had sworn to defend. A Third *Constitution* appeared, under the auspices of President Woodrow Wilson, Democrat, when Congress, controlled by Wall Street, enacted:

1) the *unconstitutional* Federal Reserve Act (1913) giving control of America's MONEY to Rothschild;

2) the first U.S. Income Tax (16th Amendment) designed to pay for ILLUMINATI'S World War I, and *"Save the World for Democracy!"*; and

3) the democratic election of Senators (17th Amendment) replacing the Republic with a democracy. The *fourth Constitution (1931)* came into effect under Franklin D. Roosevelt, Democrat. The war criminal and his "Communist friends" promptly established a *"dictate of the*

proletariat." Henry Morganthau, JEW, Secretary of the Treasury, *ordered American citizens to sell all of their gold* to the U.S. Treasury at BELOW international gold prices! The "cheap gold" was then bought by International Bankers to bulk-up for the world war they were planning. This theft of American gold by International Bankers became known as *"the Great Bank Heist of 1933"* (Revilo Oliver). When *the economy was not allowed to recover* from the FED-created depression Bernie Baruch, JEW, head of the War Industries Board *("most powerful man in America"),* put starving Americans to work preparing for another war against Aryan Europe. Soon U.S. sheep were led to the killing-fields of World War II and ordered to destroy Herr Hitler's *Juden Frei, Wucher Frei,* monetary system and slaughter as many Aryans as possible. Having *saved the world for DEMOCRACY* (MARXISM/LIBERALISM/JEWRY) America became an entry in the ILLUIMINATI checkbook. Successive Democratic administrations invited hordes of JEWS and other non-White immigrants into the United States for one reason alone they vote the Democratic/Communist ticket. This form of *Gerry manding* on a national scale changed the political and racial complexion of our constitutional republic into a Marxist-style welfare state wherein everyone is equal but some are more equal than others. The Fourth *Constitution* emanated from THE FAILED REMOVAL FROM OFFICE of impeached President WILLIAM CLINTON, Democrat (c. 1999), revealing the utter contempt JEWS have for the U.S. Constitution, and the Code of Laws upon which jurisprudence rests. The Senate and the citizens of the

United States also were on trial albeit vicariously. Eventually both were exposed as *self-serving, superficial, venal and devoid of honor.*

The House Judiciary Committee, containing a Republican majority (all Aryans), risked their political careers voting to impeach a popular President; while 16 Democrats (5-Whites, 5-Negroes and 6-JEWS) unanimously voted to keep the security risk and compulsive liar in office *(95% of all Negroes and 90% of all JEWS voted to elect him president.* Negroes wistfully call him *"the only black President. "* They love his lies and his blues saxophone). Impartial jurists agree that Clinton lied while under oath, committed perjury before a Grand Jury, and willfully obstructed justice. Senator Robert Byrd, *"dean of Democrats"* and *"Constitutional expert, "* emotionally stated on national TV that Clinton was guilty of high-crimes, requiring his removal from office. American citizens military and civilian are serving hard-time for lesser offenses. Shortly after impeachment by the House Judiciary Committee Clinton appeared in the Rose Garden (abutting the Oval Office where he and Monica Lewinski, JEWESS (a security risk), had performed fellatio/cunnilingus with Lincoln's bronze bust as witness). The Yale liar addressed the audience: He was *"confident in the future. "* He would *"continue the peoples' work. "* A careful observer expecting signs of remorse could discern, instead, suppressed euphoria on the President's face! A *"little bird"* had whispered something into his ear. Vice President Al Gore, in on the secret, hugged the impeached President, assuring him of his loyalty (even as "Red" Dean Acheson, Yale, had sworn never to turn his back on Alger Hiss). *Two days later Senator Byrd reversed his position on impeachment! "The little bird"* had whispered in his ear, too! *"Sources close to the White House"* told the writer that Senator Byrd and Senate Majority Leader Trent Lott were ordered by Leslie Gelb, JEW, Chairman, Council of Foreign Relations, to exonerate Clinton of all articles of impeachment. Lott, a former college cheer-leader, did a frantic back-flip. *The Fix was on!*

> Politicians are not born, they are excreted.
>
> CICERO.

The United States got exactly what she fought for in World Wars I and II, manifest in CLINTON'S ACQUITTAL and in America's moral degradation (Clinton's public approval ratings remain high despite the fact that he is a self-serving liar, draft-dodger and security risk). The U.S. Senate sent a clear message to the World (and to our children): under the Constitution of the United States of America it is permissible to LIE under oath; perjure oneself before a grand jury; obstruct justice; and LIE TO THE NATION. Which elicits a question: Why honor the MARXIST/LIBERAL/JEW Government of the United States of America?

As the State crumbles and anarchy nears, government grows paranoid and George Orwell's "Big Brother" appears. To wit:

Two-million telephone conversations are intercepted

annually by law-enforcement officials, and 400-million by employers. Over 30-million workers are subjected to employer electronic surveillance. An American facility in Menwith Hill, Yorkshire, England, monitors every telephone call, Fax, wire, E-mail originating in U.S.A., Europe, Africa, West Asia, and the mid-East; collecting over 2-million an hour (17.5 billion in 1991). Over 13,000 of these "private communications" were winnowed out for high-level scrutiny.

The Al Gore Commission recommends the acquisition of 1,000 CTX-5000 Hi-Tech bomb detection baggage-scanners for the nation's terminals at $1-million each plus $100,000 annual service charges (wearing a Zionist face the USA now has many enemies).

The Committee for Economic Development composed of seventy-five of the nation's most important corporate directors, presented (1962) a plan to eliminate American farms and farmers. Strictly a profit/loss study it ignored the disastrous affect upon the quality of the White gene-pool (reminiscent of the Army Corps of Engineers' plan to remove inconvenient bends in America's rivers, digging convenient shipping channels, then losing it all to accelerated currents eating out banks, cover-vegetation, and trees). Rural areas always have produced America's healthiest, sanest, most patriotic young people and our best militiamen. *Today only 2% of all Americans live on farms, a 28% reduction since the turn of the century.* 2000 A.D., about five multinational agro-companies control 95-96% of the

World's corn and wheat crops. Three companies control 80% of the U.S. meat-packing industry. The danger of corporate-consolidation lies *first,* in its power to control supply, as the Bolsheviks did in the Ukraine, and as Jimmy Hoffa did through control of the Teamsters Union (Sid Kroshak, JEW, controlled Hoffa); *second,* monopolies can eliminate small producers by paying less than production costs for their products; and *third,* mega-corporations control prices by eliminating competition in the market place. In 1996, 1,471 corporate mergers were achieved by *congressional lobbyist* who are expert at selling America's heritage for personal profit.

The *Fourth Amendment,* guarantees *"the right of the people to be secure in their persons, houses, papers, and effects against unreasonable searches and seizures..."* The IRS (Internal Revenue Service) *modus operandi* includes consistent violations of the 4th Amendment. The IRS is the enforcement unit of the Federal Government, working closely with the FED, ADL and Treasury, to coerce and punish politically incorrect American citizens. In 1992 IRS seized 3,253,000 bank accounts and paychecks (50,000 seizures were incorrect or unjustified). Each year the IRS imposes over 1,500,000 liens (an increase of 200% since 1980). The Fifth Amendment, among other guarantees, proscribes taking life, liberty property without due process yet over 35% of American tax-payers received no warning from the IRS before liens were placed on their properties. Many didn't learn of the leans until they were arrested.

Joining the IRS in its attack on the U.S. Constitution are the ATF (Bureau of Alcohol, Tobacco, and Firearms); the FBI (Federal Bureau of Investigation); the DEA (Drug Enforcement Agency), and other enforcement bodies too numerous to mention (all abetted by the mass-media and the Anti-Defamation League). As with the IRS, these quasi-legitimate government organizations are regularly commandeered by forces within the government to harass and destroy the politically incorrect. Randy Weaver, for one, was centered in their cross-hairs. Weaver believed in *Christian Identity*, a White supremacist group. He and his family moved to Ruby Ridge, Idaho, to escape racial pollution. He believed his Aryan forefathers had provided him certain inalienable rights among which are: freedom of speech; and the right to keep and bear arms (included in the First and Second Amendments, respectively). He was mistaken. When Weaver failed to appear in court to settle a minor firearms violation (he owned a sawed-off shotgun) the FBI used this as an excuse to stake-out the racialist's wilderness cabin. Weaver's 14-year old son and his dog were about to go hunting. The dog ran toward the woods barking. The agents killed it. The boy fired randomly. The agents killed him. Mrs. Weaver, holding an infant in her arms, peered out of the cabin door. FBI sniper, Lon Horiuchi, literally blew Mrs. Weaver's head off.

The following year, 1993, ATF/FBI agents attacked the Branch Davidians, a religious commune in Waco, Texas. David Koresh, the leader, preached the wickedness of America; condemned its evil government; predicted

Apocalypse, now. These concepts annoyed persons in high places. Employing standard JEW tactics (*L Infamie!*) Koresh was demonized, accused of *"heinous crimes,"* including pedophilia and importing methamphetamine from Mexico. The Federal Government, however, refused to provide Koresh due process to prove his guilt or innocence. They wanted Koresh and his followers taken out 127 men, women and children. 76-ATF/FBI agents plus a US. Army tank, deployed to spread C-S gas (banned by U.S. treaty), smashed into the frame building which burst into flames. 82 Branch Davidians died in the holocaust, including 30 women and 25 children, a tiny Dresden. Janet Reno, Clinton's Attorney General who supervised the operation, said she was very sorry.

Timothy McVeigh, decorated infantryman, served in the Gulf War. The demonizing of Arabs, Iraqis and Saddam Hussein had been so exaggerated that McVeigh was astonished to "find out they are normal like me and you." He wrote, "They hype you to take these people out. They told us we were to defend Kuwait where the people had been raped and slaughtered. All lies. War woke me up." Disillusioned, McVeigh quit the army. He became interested in conspiracy theories. He was angry at the federal government's treatment of Weaver and Koresh and countless other Americans. He felt the need to wake-up the public. Unwisely, blowing-up the Federal Building, Oklahoma City, which housed ATF offices, was McVeigh's message. He quoted at his trial:

Our government is the potent, the omnipresent teacher.

For good or ill it teaches the whole people by its example."
L.D. BRANDEIS, JEW, U.S. Sup. CT.

The Powers of Darkness are at work elsewhere. NATO, plus a few reluctant UN forces (extorted by U.S. MONEY), spent billions of dollars in an undeclared war against Serbia for forcibly ejecting an ethnic Albanian minority (Muslim) who refused a government edict to leave Serbian soil (Kosovo). Nationalism / patriotism is anathema to JEWS wherever it appears. They intend to eliminate it in Serbia even if it means killing every Serbian man, woman, and child (Christians). The U.S. State Department describes its actions as "an object lesson to all racists (sic) unwilling to accept diversity." If left unchecked some proud nation might once again eject the parasitic JEWS. For that reason an INTERNATIONAL WAR CRIMES TRIBUNAL has been established in The Hague to litigate HATE CRIMES. *The Chief Justice as one might imagine is a JEW!*

These same Allies, today shedding crocodile tears over the harsh expulsion of Muslim Kosovites from Christian Serbia, were themselves complicit in the rape, torture and expulsion of over 15-million unarmed ethnic Germans from Eastern Europe immediately AFTER WWII lands they had occupied in some areas for over 1000-years. Of these over 2-million (perhaps 5-million) were murdered by Partisans (Bolsheviks) *with the compliance of Allied Commanders* who were NOT tried for "CRIMES AGAINST HUMANITY." Rather, for over 50-years the MONEY-driven governments of Russia, England and the United States have hidden their ethnic-cleansing of

Germans behind the monstrous "HOLOCAUST" LIE.

How predictable that the ILLUMINATI shows NO interest in millions of people being slaughtered today in: Chechnya, Tibet, Rwanda (Negroes), South Africa (Whites), et al., whilst discovering "compassionate" reasons for killing Serbs it's called GREED, a synonym for ONE WORLD GOVERNMEN T. The New York Times (7-8-98) reports that Kosovo is the site of a 3.5-TRILLION DOLLARS mineral-deposit (lead, zinc, coal). Aha! Establishing "democracy" in Kosovo will enable Uncle Sammy to assist "compassionately" in the disposition of Serbia's former treasure trove. Long before Serb corpses stiffened International Bankers were sniffing around. It's not compassion; it's MONEY.

American soldiers at risk in Kosovo were told by Secretary of Defense Cohen, JEW, "you are peacekeepers preserving our democratic way of life," i.e., if some little guy disapproves of DEMOCRACY the USA will deploy Stealth Fighters, Cruise Missiles, etc. to bomb the hell out of his donkey carts. Witness, Iran, Iraq, Libya, Lebanon, et al, all "anti-Semitic" Semites.

> It matters not whether you win or lose; It matters only whether I win or lose.
>
> SAMMY GLICK.

History's oft repeated lesson re-visited in Serbia is that defying Nature's Laws (forcing incompatible ethnic groups together jamming square pegs into round holes) results in disaster. Homogeneity doesn't create wars, as JEWS would have it. Forcing together diverse ethnic groups creates wars. The Laws of Genetics God's immutable Laws have reduced MARXISM/LIBERALISM/JUDAISM to absurdity. Most evident in America's DIVERSE SOCIETY where prisons and asylums are overflowing, ugliness proliferates, and murder/violence/sex Hollywood-style has become Main Street, USA.

Aryan children, thrust into the trench warfare of integrated schools, crave their own society and territory the America created by their forefathers: they want WHITE schools, teams, dances, hang-outs, music, religion. They want WHITE standards of beauty and excellence not TALMUDISM, Afrocentrism and "fail/pass" equality. The FEDERAL GOVERNMEN T, by *denouncing these genetic instincts, applies severe psychological pressures ON THE CHILDREN.* MARXISTS/DEMOCRATS continue to cram square pegs in round holes:

26.3-million immigrants (1990) live in the U.S., up from 9.6-million in 1970. This represents 42% of the total increase in the poulation since 1990. Overwhelmingly they vote Democratic! *85% of all immigrants are non-White.* They reproduce 3.5-times faster than Whites. 6-million of their children are mongrels. 33% of all U.S. Public School Students are minorities. Each school desk they occupy is one less desk for Whites.

120 different languages are spoken. SAT scores are a joke. America's once great public-schools have been destroyed by egg-head MARXISTS/LIBERALS/JEWS. *U.S. college freshmen rank LAST among the "industrial nations" in science and mathematics.*

U.S. industry therefore hires better educated foreign nationals: Chinese and Indians). Education today is not about basics, it's not about proficiency at anything, it's not about literacy. What education is about is mental hygiene... the illiteracy cartel derives its power from those who stand to benefit financially and politically from ignorance and educational malpractice... Using personal information about students and their families educators are able to get into the belief systems of the students and correct the viewpoints they find distasteful... Educators predicate student job prospects on whether or not they hold acceptable viewpoints.

> BEVERLY K. EAKMAN, teacher, *"The Cloning of the American Mind: Eliminating Morality Through Education"* (reviewed in *The Washington Times* 2-12-99).

Our children, sadly, have learned definitive lessons from Hollywood-on-the-Potomac: If you don't like it rub it out. The violence that befell Columbine H-S, Littletown, CO (12-students and one teacher murdered by two students, one a JEW), and a rash of similar killings, strikes JEWS as sufficient reason to repeal the Second Amendment. They pretend that treating the symptoms cures the cancer. When, in fact, JEWS fear a widespread reaction against the disease itself: MARXISM / LIBERALISM / JEWRY and Hollywood's JEWS.

The FEDERAL GOVERNMENT is criminal, as this treatise proves. As all criminals it is paranoid. And with good reason. Its record is being exposed. Once the FACTS escape BIG BROTHER'S censorship the federal government will die from exposure and vengeance. Is it any wonder JEW Congresspeople (Schumer, Lowey, Specter, Boxer, Feinstein, Wexler, et al) are leading the effort to grab America's guns; with the same desperation they employed to save Clinton from impeachment! Paranoia is reflected in all government agencies. What they desperately seek is a

THREAT (to replace the Soviet threat). JEWS must distract Aryans from the ENEMY within. From JUDO-PHOBIA burgeoning throughout the civilized World.

Barely perceptible on the horizon is an enigmatic, tough, well-armed warrior. He peers at America through slanted dark eyes set between high cheekbones. He understands parasites. He understands our pathology. He envies our long-limbed Aryan women and our *lebensraum*. Almost imperceptibly he smiles. *It is not generally known that an extremely wealthy JEW minority exerts powerful political influence in Marxist China.* The COX CONGESSIONAL REPORT (5-25-99) details Chinese espionage actions over the past several years which purloined *ALL U.S. NUCLEAR SECRETS* from the Oppenheimer Nuclear Laboratory including the super-secret W-88, and the neutron bomb which destroys only living organisms leaving buildings intact. It is no wonder, with JEWS controlling the Pentagon, State Department, Department of Defense, CFR, *et al,* that China now has the capability to attack and kill U. S. subs underwater; and attack U.S. cities with nuclear missiles each with ten times the destructive power of the A-Bombs let loose on Hiroshima.

> Israel, the beneficiary of $100-Billion in U.S. aid has, according to London's Financial Times, sold China the technology for the Python-3 air-to-air missile and Phalson radar giving Beijing AWAC capability. China also acquired the technology for Israel's Star-1 anti-missile radar, the U.S. backed Levi fighter and the Patriot missile.
> PAT BUCHANAN, "Washington Times" (5-25-99).

Bernard Schwartz, JEW, Clinton campaign contributor,

and President of LORAL Space & Communications, a U.S. corporation with Israeli ties, is under Congressional investigation for illegally selling sensitive U.S. Hi-Tec equipment to Israel and to Marxist China. It appears that the ILLUMINATI is preparing for the diversionary war they so desperately need before Americans realize they have been dispossessed of their country.

You have not begun to appreciate the real depth of our guilt...We have taken your natural world, your ideals, your destiny, and played havoc with them.
MARCUS ELI RAVAGE, JEW, *Century Magazine* (1928).

Nowhere can one discern the slightest indication that in the great majority of our (White) people the racial instinct of self-preservation has not been lost... we cannot yet determine whether it has been extinguished or is merely in abeyance while our people are in a kind of cataleptic trance from which they may be aroused by physical suffering and acute privation when the time comes, as it most assuredly will.. .Our situation is desperate and we can afford no illusions... now more than ever optimism is cowardice.
DR. REVILO P. OLIVER, Prof. of Classics, Univ. Illinois.

Our (White) people are too apathetic, or spiritless, or cowardly to stand up and fight for what they believe in, or even to avert their own destruction. Some wait for tenure, some for retirement, some for safer times, but all wait for doom. Dead races do not come back. Those that wait are the pall-bearers of civilization.
DR. ROBERT KUTTNER, Univ. Chicago.

It is a basic axiom of biology that the struggle for existence cannot be escaped.
GARRET HARDIN, *"Nature and Man s Fate"*.

SYNTHESIS

History demonstrates that the metamorphosis of a High Culture-Organism can be stopped only by totally destroying it: a larva must become a butterfly; an acorn must become an oak; a child must become an adult the Culture-Organism must fulfill its Spiritual Destiny. These are the immutable LAWS OF NATURE. This Spiritual CERTAINTY provides much hope and great expectations. White Man is not in a "cataleptic trance" but instead like a wounded eagle dangerously vulnerable to attack predators is slowly recovering from wounds received during THE 20th CENTURY WARS TO ANNIHILATE ARYANS.

> Was mich nicht umbringt, macht mich starker.
>
> NIETZSCHE.

Today a SPIRITUAL METAMORPHOSIS, whose tremors were felt first in Europe about 140-years ago (at about the same time the ILLUMINATI unleashed its mad dogs on the United States), is spreading with increasing intensity throughout the WEST'S HIGH CULTURE-ORGANISM. All Aryans other than white -trash *instinctively sense this transformation* though few can articulate it. What they are experiencing is the SYNTHESIS PHASE of WESTERN HISTORY'S DIALECTIC: the merging of INSTINCTIVE LONGING FOR ARYAN

UNITY with remnants of the AGE OF PURE REASON! During this tumultuous and dangerous transition period component IDEAS of Thesis and Antithesis are being threshed, winnowed and culled by the Aryan Culture Stratum. The most viable IDEAS are selected *instinctively and rationally* with greater emphasis upon the former then synthesized within the West's High Culture-Organism. The Augean stables are being cleansed. The old icons, fallacies and superstitions are trashed. The resultant NEW THESIS gives rise to the MENDELIAN AGE providing for the GENETIC UNITY OF THE WEST and total rejection of MARXISM/LIBERALISM/JEWRY. Conversely, JEWRY'S efforts are directed TOTALLY against the spiritual and physical unity of the West! (The Mendelian Age has NO relationship with the "unification" of Europe under MONEY: the Bank of International Settlements).

To put the Historical Dialectic in perspective one should remember that the THESIS was expressed initially when the ancient Gothic tribes attempted to UNIFY: first, under the Crusaders; then the Empire; then the Papacy; and penultimately, the Nazis. *This deep yearning to up-gather the Aryan family is Instinctive, compulsive and in compliance with Nature s Laws. Therefore, it will be achieved.*

The Dialectic ANTITHESIS of the West appeared in the form of Rationalism virtually divorced from Instinct which produced: Liberalism, Capitalism, Free Trade; State against State, religion against religion; class warfare, and USURY against Aryan authority. These and other Rationalistic phenomena (stifling Instinct) shattered Europe into many competing, self-serving, fratricidal tribal States easily manipulated by Rothschild's treasonous central banks and consecrated Europe's battlefields with Aryan blood.

The nations, thought-forms, art forms, and ideas, which are the expression of the development of a Culture, are always in the custody of a comparatively small group...Culture is by its very nature selective, exclusive. The use of the word in the personal sense a "cultured" man describes a man out of the ordinary, a man whose ideas and attitudes are ordered and articulated. Cultured, in the personal sense, means devoted to something beyond one-self and one's own domestic well-being...patriotism, devotion to duty, ethical imperative, heroism, self-sacrifice, are also expressions of Culture primitive man does not evince them. The common man is the material with which the great political leaders in democratic conditions work. In earlier centuries the common man did not attend the Culture drama. It did not interest him and the participants were not yet under the Rationalistic spell, the "counting-mania" as Nietzsche put it. When democratic conditions proceeded to their extreme, the result is that even the leaders are common men, with the jealous and crooked soul of envy of that to which they are not equal...
FRANCIS PARKER YOCKEY, *"Imperium"*.

Thus we ceased to be a republic, under which the intention was to keep the control and direction of the country in the hands of those best qualified to ensure its welfare, and degenerated into a democracy into what Alexander Solzhenitsyn has called a "democracy run riot." This opened the dikes and let in a flood of "liberal" politicians who lifted the masses to domination. All wisdom and far-ranging vision in Government was lost in a sordid scramble for the votes of a motley collection of people who had no concern about the nation's crucial problems and no wit to grapple with them even if they did; who indeed were willing to sacrifice the long-term welfare of the nation as a whole for their own personal advantage, whether it was for bigger profits, higher wages, more "welfare," more speed, more gadgets, more pleasure, comfort, security or ease... All overseeing and aristocratic direction of our national life was thrown away. As always in a democracy there was no one to look where we were going, to provide the people with protection against soul-less exploitation and ruination, and to anticipate and steer us away from the desecration of the earth, the wasting of our resources, the pollution of our environment, and a differential birthrate in which those who had the brains and character to solve problems were swamped by those who created the problems. The land was left wide open and without much obstacle in the path of those whose consuming lust for gain made them want to turn the country first of all into a rich field for lucrative financial investment, and more and more open... to Jews who stealthily worked and wheedled and pushed it... toward a world slave state.

WILLIAM G. SIMPSON, *"Which Way Western Man?"*

The thunder that shook Europe, setting the West's SPIRITUAL METAMORPHOSIS in motion (the *Dialectical Synthesis*) was GREGOR MENDEL'S discovery of Nature's building-blocks! As all educated men now know, and it bears repeating, the Science of Genetics demonstrates that unique characteristics differentiate ALL men and ALL races: physiologically, psychologically, behaviorally, and spiritually ending forever the MARXIST/LIBERAL/JEW canard that all men are created equal.

One of the many profound legacies of the DIALECTICAL SYNT HESIS was re-discovery of Aryan man's spiritual and biological roots, resultant of Faustian probes into limitless *outer* space, macrocosm; and through *inward* probes revealing limitless space in microcosm with its new vocabulary: quanta, quarks, neutrinos, genomes, metaphysics, etc.

To see a World in a Grain of Sand/And Heaven in a wild flower/Hold Infinity in the palm of your hand/And Eternity in an Hour.

WILLIAM BLAKE.

One feels there is nothing in all the universe to be afraid of. At last there is only ONE Will the impulse that emanates from the core of your being, or call it your God. There is no longer a body and a soul glaring across the abyss at one another

...Body is the soul made manifest. Soul is the body's... exaltation... And the gaze through which man looks out upon the world... and all the starry universe is the gaze of his own wholeness...

WILLIAM GALEY SIMPSON, *"Which Way Western Man."*

There, in macrocosm/microcosm beyond the veneer of man-made laws, and superstition where matter and Spiritual Energy coalesce the Aryan found his primal-Self: his Instincts, Intuitions, and his One-ness with GOD'S LAW – PANTHEISM.

In this manner the Age of Reason died, murdered by its own hands. Assumed facts, upon which Science bases its rational conclusions, are now viewed as inconstant, in flux, evolving. The more Science learns the less it understands. The horizon moves farther away with each advancing step. Science now must consider probability, uncertainty, metaphysics, instinct, intuition and human fallibility. Science recognizes there is a Universal Force more pervasive, more dominant than Man's ability ever to comprehend. When Intuition, Instinct, and Probability entered the realm of mathematics Western Culture moved out of the Age of Reason into the AGE OF MENDELISM. *The ushering in of the MENDELIAN AGE awakened the Aryan Culture Stratum as from a Luciferian nightmare.* In this spiritual awakening Aryan Man discovered that he is part God and part animal a human bridge to Superman. Knowledge that forever assigns the ludicrous SEMITIC fetish, YAHWEH, and its World-hating spore CHRISTIANITY, to the pantheon of minor gods. PANT HEISM is Nature's religion; the good monk Mendel is its Holy Father.

Aryan man is a *Spiritual being.* He also is a *territorial animal* who will defend his honor and home against insurmountable odds... to the death! He doesn't opt to do this *he is compelled by genetic imperatives!* Intuitive/irrational behavior reflects the INSTINCT TO SURVIVE. This is Nature's Decree and it is Man's to obey! Nations that lose or deny their genetic instincts forfeit their right to Life! *When survival is the final measure compassionate nations DIE.*

INSTINCT, it bears defining, is a *non-rational response* to environmental stimuli.

INTUITION is *immediate comprehension without Reason,* emanating from primal or metaphysical sources.

REASON is the intellectual ability to *arrive at conclusions predicated upon assumed facts.* COGNITION (*ability to perceive and judge*), is seated in the supra-granular layer of the cortex, and is an evolutionary characteristic distinguishing race from race, man from man, and Man from lesser animals.

In creating an orderly and just society Man's Instincts essential to both creative genius and to his survival are tempered by the equally important ability to Reason. Instinct and Reason are not mutually exclusive but are core ingredients which together largely determine Man's behavior. Instinct, Intuition, and Reason are genetic characters.

Aryan instincts regarding race are fundamentally sound though not popular. Anthropology and Genetics prove that Genomes program the behavior of each race differently. It follows, then, that the U.S. Constitution and code of laws which were created for ONE race are totally inadequate for another. There is NO universal moral law or legal code. Beyond one's racial family the distinction between right and wrong vanishes. Why? Because genes determine racial behavior, and racial behavior determines morals and laws! Ergo, within a diverse society morals and laws cannot be legislated or encoded to categorically satisfy each race within that society. It follows that Western Culture has disintegrated in direct proportion to racial diversity evidenced in America's moral-ethical collapse. Racial differences cannot be changed through legislation. *God s Laws prevail!*

It is apparent that JEWRY is the only race genetically programmed to subsist upon host races. What law governs that? A PARASITE is one of Nature's many life-forms. It is neither a moral nor immoral animal it is simply a *biological fact.* To Aryans parasitism is pathological, therefore immoral. To JEWS parasitism is a biological necessity, therefore moral. What is ethical or moral to one race may be unethical or immoral to another. Nature acknowledges none of this. In her pristine realm there are no morals! There is only the WILL TO SURVIVE. It is absurd, to *hate* parasites; anymore than one hates termites, Negroes, vipers or bats. You simply don't allow them to eat the foundations of *your* home or hang out in *your* bedroom. *You excise them by whatever means is necessary.* Darwin, Spencer, Carlyle, Hitler refer to culling the gene-pool as necessary to *"survival of the species."* The TALMUD teaches survival. Green Berets, Navy Seals teach survival. Mendelism teaches survival. God teaches survival. CHRISTIANITY/LIBERALISM teaches: *"Love your enemy"* and enter Paradise. After WWII the parasitic *modus operandi,* detailed in the TALMUD and the PROTOCOLS, could not be debated publicly lest the speaker be branded *"racist"* tantamount to being burned at the stake. The word "RACIST" an opprobrium meaning "bigot, un-American, Nazi, crazy" was invented by JEWS to discourage discussion of *their m. o.* The Iron Curtain of censorship has grown ever tighter (save, so far, for the Internet). Today, in public institutions and on Ivy League campuses references to race, IQ, eugenics, historical revisionism, can cost you your tenure or your teeth. *To wit, we coin a new word: RACIALIST, n., an individual who respects the right of all races to exist in their own milieu; but whose loyalty is directed first toward his own racial family.* He believes in a tooth for a tooth. Our Founding Fathers were *racialists.* JEWS are *racists.* They have much to hide.

Our power... will be more invincible than any other because it will remain invisible until the moment it has gained such strength that no cunning can any longer undermine it.

PROTOCOLS OF ZION Number 1:12.

There are no English Jews, French Jews, American Jews. There are only Jews living in England, France and America.

CHAIM WEIZMANN, JEW, ZIONIST, Pres. of Israel.

All Jews will have a part in the future world... all Gentiles will be sent to Hell.

TALMUD: Lekh-Lekma.

Kiss his cheek. He'll never suspect.

GESTHEMANE.

We have now entered the final phase of the 20th CENTURY WARS TO ANNIHILATE ARYANS. The protagonists are Satan's ILLUMINATI, representing Money, Deceit and Slavery: versus MENDELISM, representing Nature, Truth and Beauty. The DIALECTIC SYNTHESIS OF THE WEST, like the thunder of breaking dawn, proclaims the SPIRITUAL ONE-NESS OF MAN AND NATURE.

GENES not wealth, not luck, not diversity, not nurture - provide Man with the capacity to achieve. Aryans now *know* (Rationally) as they have always *felt* (Instinctively) that the White gene-pool is their most precious possession! It is GOD'S GIFT to be protected at all costs. Those who would not are our deadly enemies and must be stopped in their tracks by any means available NOW.

Because Aryans belong to the same racial family it follows that their religions, philosophies, arts, sciences, languages, States are *not divisive* but are mere *differences* within the Aryan High-Culture Organism. The West's IMPERATIVE is to gather these disparate but related parts into ONE

ARYAN NATION-STATE; therein marshaling the West's vast intellect, creativity, might and resources to fulfill *its Faustian Destiny* whose prime symbol is the ever-receding horizon of limitless Space.

DIALECTIC SYNTHESIS, flowering of the MENDELIAN AGE, results in the maturation and spiritual fulfillment of the Aryan Nation, described so well by Yockey, Spengler, and Simpson. With SYNTHESIS *comes* ARYAN SOCIALISM over CAPITALISM *ethically, economically, and politically:* AUTHORITY over Money; ABSOLUTE POLITICS over Pacifism; RANK over Equality; MERIT over Democracy; PRODUCERS over Middlemen; QUALITY over Quantity; ACHIEVEMENT over Wealth; HEROISM over Hedonism; RACE over Miscegenation; HOMOGENEITY over Diversity; RESPONSIBILITY over Dependency; RELIGION over Materialism; DUALITY OF THE SEXES over Feminism; MARRIAGE over Free-love; FERTILITY over Sterility; SELF CONTROL over License; ORDER over Indulgence; CONSIDERATION over Pity; FACTS over Fiction; LEBENSRAUM over Congestion; NATURE over Nurture; NATION UBER ALLES!

WITHIN WESTERN CIVILIZATION EVERYTHING MARXIST/LIBERAL/JEWISH WILL BE ABOLISHED

... EVERYTHING!

The great White States of the world will be unified under THE HOLY WESTERN EMPIRE an *Aryan Socialist*

Government. WESTERN SOCIALISM emanates from the Spiritual IDEA that *each man, woman and child, represents one (1) cell in the* ARYAN HIGH CULTURE-ORGANISM (the NATION). Their combined souls form the *esprit* of the nation-state. *Because Cells and Organism are mutually dependent each individual works for the greater good of the State, and the State works for the fulfillment of each individual.* This is the true meaning of Family *"One for all and all for one"* rather than the Capitalistic credo, *"Every man for himself."* The *Synergy* of the Aryan Family working toward a shared Destiny will produce marvelous energy, great creativity, loyalty, teamwork, esprit de corps and individual-fulfillment all crowned with beauty and intelligence. At this moment the HOLY WESTERN EMPIRE (HWE) is but a SPIRITUAL IDEA taking shape within the Mind and Soul of the High Culture Stratum. *The following comments indicate what may develop:*

The HWE FEDERAL ARYAN SOCIALIST GOVERNMENT *(FASG) will resemble the U.S. Federal Government as it initially related to the confederacy of independent American states.* It is the hub of the wheel. The several White states to be united under Aryan Socialism within the HWE, are the states of Europe, Greenland, Iceland, Canada, the USA, Australia, and New Zealand. Ethnic Whites will be afforded representation.

HWE institutions will include: The Holy Aryan Church, Holy Supreme Archon, FASG Armed Forces; Supreme Aryan Court, Senate, Monetary System, Treasury,

Intelligence, Media-on-Line, etc. FASG's functions are to formulate, legislate, adjudicate, coordinate, enforce and direct the policies of the HOLY WESTERN EMPIRE as set forth in the Constitution (ratified by the member States). HWE goals and objectives have been gleaned from many centuries of Aryan experience expressed in the Constitution of the United States, the Magna Carta, the Napoleonic Code, the Third Reich, the Universal Mendelian Laws.

The HOLY EMINENT ARCHON: an Aryan of deep spirituality, impeccable honor, proven courage and leadership, will be elected by the Senate to preside for life as chief executive officer of the Holy Western Empire. He will serve also as titular head of the Aryan Holy Church which personifies, ARYANS/THE UNIVERSAL FORCE/PANTHEISM: Trinity of the High Culture-Organism. THE SUPREME SOCIALIST ARYAN SENATE (SSAS) a uni-cameral body will possess the highest deliberative and legislative functions. 20-SSAS Senators will be elected by the upper house from each of the several Aryan States.

In sum, FASG, elected by the People (see, Franchise), is the HWE federal governing authority. The individual STATES (Europe, Australia, U.S.A., et al) will retain residual powers of government: *each reflecting the Aryan Socialist IDEA: economically, ethically, socially, and spiritually* all coming together, under THE UNIVERSAL FORCE, as one Aryan federal HOLY WESTERN EMPIRE.

THE NATION'S CREDIT will be based upon the People's creativity and production faith in the White Gene-Pool no other standard is necessary. As Lincoln pointed out *"the abundance of the productive capacity of Nature, taken together with the responsibility of the whole People, belongs to the nation and there is not the slightest reason why the nation should have to pay for itsown credit."* Any more than a homeowner would pay rent for his own house. Rothschild central banks along with the JEWS will be banished from the Holy Western Empire. The compound-interest formula will be revised providing equitable principal/interest payments up-front, thus quicker amortization of debts. Frederick Soddy, Silvio Gesell, Ezra Pound, Gertrude Coogan, and great Aryans like them, have written extensively about MONEY; their views now suppressed will help shape the future.

COMPENSATION for work performed will be predicated on RANK plus MERIT.

Rank, reflects the IMPORTANCE TO THE NATION of the type of job (category). It bears a graduated pay scale (as in the military) including shares of HWE stock. Merit reflects the QUALITY OF SERVICE performed. It produces competition in the job-market for outstanding workers, providing additional compensation and perks for those who earn it: HWE stock-options, honorary degrees, decorations, etc. *The State compensates for Rank, the private employer compensates for Merit.* Thus, under the HWE Monetary System, soldiers, farmers, mechanics, and schoolteachers, for example *upon whom the Nation depends* will no longer live in comparative poverty and obscurity while food-brokers, junk-bond salesmen, pornographers, and war-profiteers live off the fat of the land. "Rockefeller wealth" (greed/exploitation/ treason) will not be tolerated nor will poverty. There will be work for everyone according to his ability. Those who can but won't work will be sterilized and placed in work farms.

SHARING THE WEALTH: The HWE Monetary System will be a publicly owned corporate banking and investment system. The trillions now scammed illegally by the FED will become HWE profit. Each citizen (cell) will share in the *health and wealth* of the HIGH CULTURAL-ORGANISM according to Rank and Merit. FASG will direct the use of PRIVATE PROPERTY but *will not own those means.* For example, *"free-enterprise"* will not be allowed to pave the face of the earth, nor will conglomerates be permitted to bankrupt farmers. Labor (see above) will share the net-profits of business and industry (a chain is as strong as its weakest link). Net profits at the retail level will be shared equitably between retailers, middlemen, producers, growers, and manufacturers. With less profits to middlemen and more to producers. "American" dummy corporations owned by aliens will be divested of their mineral, timber, agriculture, fishing rights, etc. Trade between the Aryan states will be coordinated, encouraged and protected. ECOLOGICAL PROGRAMS will be brought into conformity with the Holy Aryan Church (Pantheism). The White Gene-Pool, a spiritual organism, is an integral part of that ecology.

MASS-MEDIA. *"Freedom of the Press"* means *"Responsibility of the Press."* Without Responsibility there is no Freedom. After 85-years of JEW media control America borders on mongrelism and moral-disintegration. With responsibility comes penalties for malfeasance. LIES, misinformation and disinformation are crimes against the Nation and will be punished severely. Nor is the 1st Amendment a cover for sadists, schizophrenics, "Spielbergs", queers, pedophiles, and the like. NO more quotes from unidentified "deep throats," or from "sources close to the President." NO more docu-dramas posing as fact. *A panel of Aryan philosophers, poets, artists, and educators will determine what is moral and immoral; what is acceptable fare for our children.* From now on the mass-media will reflect the aspirations of Aryan culture: *The Truth Shall Set You Free.*

FRANCHISE. A plastic Social Security Card will be used to activate voting machines in polling booths. The card will contain a concealed code bearing the owner's Intelligence Quotient; if lower than average (IQ-100), the vote will not register. PREREQUISITES FOR HOLDING OFFICE:

Character and intelligence count. 1) Loyalty Checks: ALL government employees must pass a Lie-Detector Test. 2) IQ Test: SSAS Senators must have over 130 IQ scores. State Congressmen (Representatives) Lower house must have over 118 IQ, and upper house (Senate) must have over 124 IQ. All members will have served in the military.

PUBLIC EDUCATION: K-12 emphasis on math, humanities, "Holocaust," physical fitness. H-S emphasis on math, economics, Mendelism (Genetics, Eugenics, Anthropology, Biochemistry, etc.), science, humanities, money, physical fitness, electives. MILITARY at age 18 all men will serve a mandatory 2-year hitch. UNIVERSITY history, philosophy, logic, forensics, management, Mendelism, electives. HI-TECH AND VOCATIONAL SCHOOLS College is not desirable for everyone. The West needs skilled workers and craftsmen, those who love tools, grease and machinery: those who can keep the ship afloat as well as those who can command her all are Spiritual Cells composing a High Culture-Organism. FASG will set achievement standards for teachers and students.

ESTHETICS/DISCRIMINATION: Within the HWE the importance of Aryan esthetics and the ability to discriminate will be vigorously supported. The importance of TRUTH/BEAUTY to the human psyche is reflected in the devotion paid to the arts by all civilized people. To the extent Truth and Beauty are admired by the nation, lies and ugliness are despised.

Within the art community genetics is the influencing factor not only in determining an artist's creativity, but also in determining his audience's sense of beauty and ability to appreciate beauty. It is a well know fact that what is aesthetically appealing to one race is often appalling to another in some cases to the point of revulsion another reason why racial diversity is destructive to all races involved. Xenophobia is not *racism* but is *racialism*: a genetic survival mechanism. Love for one's family is instinctive. Discrimination is the ability to make comparative evaluations: who or what is best, largest, nearest, brightest, etc. Lack of discriminate ability is a serious handicap. In a Democracy, however, racial discrimination is deemed unacceptable; *"everyone is equal"* or else is a *victim of "discrimination"* meaning bigotry. It is for wont of discrimination that the U.S. Supreme Court, and Hollywood, have made a sewer out of America. RACE: Citizens of the Holy Western Empire must be Aryans. Ethnic Whites are encouraged to immigrate to the HWE. Non-White populations living within the Empire will be assisted financially to colonize in genetically compatible countries. This provides a splendid opportunity for Negroes and Jews to create civilizations of their own. Perhaps together as brothers. No longer must they endure a "degenerate" Aryan society: "God almighty, free at last!" The Hema-genometer, about the size of a 3-cell flashlight, allows for quick genetic-scans, revealing racial identity of JEWS, Orientals, and Asiatics with 95% accuracy; and provides 98% accuracy when identifying Negro and Mexican blood lines.

Non-Whites preferring to remain within the HWE may do so under these provisos:

1) They are over 40-years old.
2) They are legally sane.
3) They obey all State laws.

4) They are not indigents.
5) They submit to sterilization (chips).

PANTHEISM: The Holy Western Empire is a product of Pantheism; not the other way around. We pointed out earlier how, within Western Synthesis, intellect and intuition/ instinct correlate. So too, within Pantheism (to the same degree) Science and Religious Faith correlate. Pantheism equates God the Universal Force the Laws of Nature not with some vengeful JEW in the sky. JUDEO-CHRISTIANITY, with its emphasis on historical certainty to sustain its myths and miracles, has collapsed under scientific analysis and the archaeologist's spade. All that remains is its ritual, its anachronisms, its MONEY, and its hatred for knowledge and Nature.

With the emergence of the MENDELIAN AGE, Mankind realizes that the *Universal Force has been handed down and entrusted to him via his ancestral gene-pool; providing him a relationship with the DIVINE that man-made religions have never attained.* All of the holy men and their prayers, incense, rattles, and relics throughout the millennia never saved one child from disease; never cured one cancer; never achieved one heart transplant; never predicted one earthquake. Whilst Yahweh's "CHOSEN ISRAELIS", who presumed to interpret the WORD OF GOD, believed the earth to be flat and floating in brine.

Awakened by the spiritual brilliance of MENDELISM, ethnic groups the world over seeking to realize their Godgiven potential hope to tear down the stultifying territorial boundaries established by MONEY which propagates perpetual war through diversity and establish instead FAMILY HOMELANDS. (American troops dispatched by the ILLUMINATI to force square pegs into round holes in these multi-racial tinder-boxes should break camp). Within the HOLY WESTERN EMPIRE Aryans may worship what gods their Spirit requires, that too is the meaning of PANTHEISM. Much of the great art, literature, music, pageantry, pagan festivals, architecture and dear traditions, created by Aryans to make Semitic Christianity palatable, will find perfect harmony within God's Laws PANT HEISM: the Spiritual expression of Truth and Beauty.

The HOLY WESTERN EMPIRE intends to replace the Semitic Bible with THE ARYAN HOLY SCRIPTURES (not yet compiled) containing IDEAS which express as does our music the Aryan Soul; among these are: The Laws of Manu; Nietzsche's, *The Anti Christ*, and *Thus Spake Zarathustra* (Christianity arises in part from Zoroastrianism let us venerate the source); Homer's, *The Iliad*, and *The Odyssey*; *Beowolf*; Icelandic sagas of Njal, and Gunnar; Goethe's, *Faustus*; the *Songs of Kabir*; *Les Chansons de Roland*; Malory's *Le Mort D'Arthur*; Leonides at Thermopylae; Tennyson's *Idylls of the King*; Tacitus' *Germania*; *der Nibelungenlied*; Petrarch's *Canzoniere*; Cicero's *Philippics*; Dostoevski's *The Idiot*; and Solzhenitsyn's *Gulag Archepelago* (replacing "Revelations"). Also included will be the MYSTIC writings of Lao-tse, Siddartha, Mohammed, Jesus, Shakespeare, Nietzsche,

Blake, Schopenhauer, Vivekananda, Sappho and Whitman.

SYNTHESIS OF THE WEST CONTINUES:

Nature's Laws are to be discovered, obeyed, revered. God's races are to be preserved in their uniqueness. Genetics reveals Man can conquer disease, age, and eugenically improve himself physically, mentally and spiritually, making his life sublime indeed it may be within his capacity to UNDERSTAND AT LAST the omnipotent, omniscient, omnipresent FORCE. *God gave the good monk Mendel to Aryan Man. Aryan Man gave the Keysof the Kingdom to Mankind: Know thyself!*

Power and law are not synonymous. In truth they are frequently in opposition and irreconcilable. There is GOD'S LAW from which all equitable laws of man emerge and by which men must live if they are not to die in oppression, chaos and despair. Divorced from GODS ETERNAL AND IMMUTABLE LAW, established before the founding of the suns, man's power is evil no matter the noble words with which it is employed or the motives urged when enforcing it. Men of good will, mindful therefore of the LAW LAID DOWN BY GOD, will oppose governments whose rule is by men and, if they wish to survive as a nation, they will destroy that government which attempts to adjudicate by the whim or power of venal judges.

CICERO

The weak and the botched shall perish: the first principal of our humanity.

The greatest obstacles to reaching Superman are Christianity and Democracy.

The last Christian died on the Cross. The weak and congenitally unfit can't compete so they use devious means to achieve power.

NIETZSCHE.

I say unto you which hear, love your enemies, do good to them which hate you. Bless them that curse you, and pray for them which despitefully use you. And to him that smitest thee on one cheek, offer also the other; and him that taketh away thy cloak, forbid not to take thy coat also.

JESUS CHRIST, Luke 7:27-29.

Think not that I am come to send peace on earth; I come not to send peace but a sword. For I am come to set man at a variance against his father, and the daughter against her mother, and the daughter in-law against her mother-in-law. And a man's foes shall be they of his own household.

JESUS CHRIST, MATTHEW 10:34-36

Resist not evil.

JESUS CHRIST, Matt. 5:39.

The King James translation of LXX (Septuagint: Greek translation of the OLD TESTAMENT from the Hebrew) contains over 6,000 major redactions.

ENCYCLOPAEDIA BRITANNICA.

Let me issue and control a Nation's money and I care not who makes its laws.

AMSCHEL MAYER ROTHSCHILD.

As a young unknown major I took the wisest step of my life I consulted Mr. Baruch.

GENERAL DWIGHT DAVID EISENHOWER, U.S. Army.

TOB SHEBBE GOYIM HAROG!

TALMUD: Sanhedrin 39

CHAPTER 12

SUMMING UP

ARYANS appear everywhere as the promoters of true progress and in Europe their expansion marked the moment when the pre-history of (Europe) begins to diverge from that of Africa and the Pacific.

Dr. V. GORDON CHILDE.

As a social anthropologist I naturally accept and even stress the fact that there are differences, both mental and physiological, which separate the different races of mankind.

Dr. L. S. B. LEAKY.

Material prosperity encourages the preservation, pampering, and reproduction of the biologically inferior elements which are parasitical upon rich civilizations. Then some cleaner blooded and crude stock crashes in and wipes the slate clean.

Dr. ERNEST HOOTEN.

Pacifism remains an ideal, war a fact, and if the White race decides to wage it no longer the colored will, and will become the rulers of the world.

SPENGLER.

Your Constitution is all sail and no anchor. Either some Caesar or Napoleon will seize the reins of government with a strong hand, or your Republic will be laid waste by internal barbarism in the 20th Century as the Roman Empire was in the 5th.

SIR THOMAS MACAULEY.

To communicate anything to a Goy about our religious relations would be equal to killing all Jews, for if the Goyim knew what we teach about them they would kill us all openly.

TALMUD: Libre David 37.

The men who can manage money manage all.
WILL DURANT, "Story of Civilization".

Aristocracy has nothing to do with plutocracy. The best are NOT the rich... character and capacity are what should count.
WILLIAM G. SIMPSON.

Whenever any form of government becomes destructive... it is the Right of the People to abolish it...
DECLARATION OF INDEPENDENCE.

We now come to the final chapter of this treatise which has dealt with the decline of Western Civilization and more specifically with the despoliation of America. History reminds us that as the racial majority goes down the culture goes down with it. As America's White majority dies America herself dies.

We have seen that while Americans were absorbed in the creation of one of history's great civilizations a bastion of Western Culture Mankind's ancient ENEMY, pursuant to genetic imperatives, embedded itself within the sinews of the United States and proceeded to betray, corrupt, and plunder her. We recalled the origins of the CONSPIRACY in the plagiarized Mosaic Law (TORAH) wherein the HEBREWS, a Semitic tribe, assigned themselves the nomen "GOD'S CHOSEN PEOPLE" whose business it is to rule the world; and in the Pharisaical Oral Law (TALMUD) ("our promises to Gentiles shall not bind") from which egested the PROTOCOLS OF THE LEARNED ELDERS OF ZION ("the *goyim* are a flock of sheep and we are their wolves"). The PROTOCOLS provided the paradigm for Rothschild's ILLUMINATI ("the question is only whether world government will be achieved by consent or by conquest", JAMES WARBURG, JEW).

We saw how the Asiatic Khazars (Ashkenazim) PRETENDED to be Biblical Judeans in Diaspora; although their bloodlines (confirmed by DNA tests), assign them Armenoid-Mongol affinities with NO Semitic genes; therefore they have NO Israeli roots; ergo, NO Biblical claim to Palestine. They are imposters, parasites and murderers, as this treatise irrefutably proves. This treatise also presented for your consideration the ILLUMINATI *modus operandi.* We have seen with what calculated treachery "American" JEWS covertly attacked and seized pivotal links in the iron-chain of American sovereignty, paramount among which are: THE NATION'S MONEY SUPPLY (The Federal Reserve System), and the MASS-MEDIA (Newspapers, magazines, radio/television, Hollywood, theater, tin-pan-alley, et al). Thus, the JEW CONSPIRACY effectively abrogated the U.S. Constitution! Thereafter, reacting to the "terrible power of the purse" and censorship of "Free Speech," every facet of American society fell one by one under LIBERAL/MARXIST/JEW control. Imagine if you will the impact on a U.S. Congressman's career should he introduce legislation establishing a "Holocaust" investigation committee; or legislation to determine the constitutionality of the FED; or, legislation demanding racial/religious quotas in media ownership, or in the military, or on university faculties; or, establishing a committee to report upon the negative effect of miscegenation on I.Q. scores; or probing why so many Zionists are appointed to high government positions. Today we find our once great Aryan Republic has been twisted into a mongrelized DEMOCRACY ruled by MARXIST/LIBERAL/JEW PLUTOCRACY. This CONSPIRACY, world-wide in scope, is financed and led by International Bankers. Its goal is ONE WORLD ZIONIST GOVERNMENT. Its strategy, explicit in the PROTOCOLS, is to wield the power of MONEY with one hand, while with the other unleash L'INFAMIE and WAR until the West, finally, bankrupt, exhausted and disillusioned, surrenders its sovereignty. Well known ILLUMINATI tactics, established during the French Revolution, include LIES, treason, espionage, blackmail, slander, extortion, murder, disinformation, false witness, phony wars, financial chaos, usury, immorality and so on. The same tactics are employed in America today, accompanied by Spirochetes of JEW Syphilis: repeated ceaselessly by academia and mass-media. Meanwhile, Americans naively attempt to play the game of life in accordance with Aryan morals and ethics, pledging their allegiance "...to the Flag of the United States and to the Republic for which it stands..." while JEWS play the game sub rosa in accordance with the TALMUD, the PROTOCOLS OF ZION, and the KOL NIDRE OATH: reserving their hatred toward Gentiles and their allegiance only to JEWRY.

Nationalism is an infantile disease.

ALBERT EINSTEIN, JEW.

How odd of God To choose the Jews.

SAMUEL HOFFENSTEIN, JEW.

The JEWS' triumph over America could not have been so complete had not Aryans collaborated with them. White defectors represent a broad social spectrum ranging from certifiable racial traitors, as Paul Volcker, Kingman Brewster, Theodore Hesburgh, Ted Kennedy, and William J. Clinton, to local white-trash who make any MORAL CONCESSION even selling their children's heritage if it smells of MONEY (see: *Easton Star-Democrat*). Between these two poles are ideological traitors such as Pat Robertson, Patrick Moynihan, Jimmy Carter, and the Bush dynasty whose ignorance of Mendelism, and *"feel-good compassion"* has helped lead America into a mongrel society teetering on the brink of anarchy.

As the West's Dialectical Synthesis continues to unfurl: the sheep are beginning to bleat restlessly and ask forbidden questions. Wherever Gentiles congregate (here and abroad) Judeophobia is on the rise. Alarmed at the *goyim*'s ominous interest in JEWRY'S *remarkable* success (inversely proportioned to the decline of American Culture) JEWS now contend that generations of inbreeding has produced greater Intelligence among Yahweh's CHOSEN than that exhibited in their Gentile flocks! JEWS insist, *with NO reliable statistical proof,* that their rise to power is attributable to JEWRY'S high IQ; *not* to a Luciferian CONSPIRACY. In other words, the playing field is level; the rules are fair and *Aryans who produced Western Culture are too dumb to compete!* One of the proponents of this

Spielbergism, Dr. Ashley Montague (Israel Ehrenberg), JEW, enjoyed a professorial Ivy League career waving the red-banner of racial equality, until Mendelism shot him down, circa. 1980. Thereafter, Montague (dec'd 1999) lectured unconvincingly on JEWISH *genetic* superiority. Albeit, History the final arbiter in such matters reveals that JEWS aren't nearly so intelligent as they would have you believe (JEWS do produce brilliant individuals but, per capita, far fewer than Aryans, or Orientals). In fact, *ALL great advancements in World Culture were made in exactly those places where there were no JEWS or where they had been kicked-out!* Certainly this makes their IQ claims suspect if not irrelevant. Ancient ISRAELIS created nothing of significance other than the BIBLE, and the TALMUD; the former, today, is viewed as a fossil; the latter, as pathological. Hebrew statesmanship from King Saul to Bar Cochba generated little more than chaos. The "heroic" mass-suicide of Israeli zealots at Masada is a warrior's joke (The Roman general who lost not a man said he wished only that all his enemies were so generous). Finally, Israelis bequeathed to posterity no art, architecture, music or science.

The Asiatic KHAZARS (JEWS) masquerading as JUDEANS, who today dominate the machinery of the United States government, are recognized less for their high IQ than for their psychopathic behavior delineated to some degree in this treatise.

JEWS are remembered not for their ability to create great

states, or to govern, but for their compulsion to corrupt and destroy host states. No JEW rode with Charlemagne, nor signed the *Magna Carta,* nor the *Napoleonic Code,* nor the *Declaration of Independence;* or, for that matter, attended the *Constitutional Convention* in Philadelphia. Contemporary JEWS are remembered, rather, for the OGPU, NKVD, the Gulag Archipelago a horror unequaled in human history; and for the "Holocaust", a grotesque LIE deliberately created to cover-up JEW/Bolshevik atrocities!

Obviously, courage, honesty, and statesmanship do not account for JEWRY'S incredible conquest of America. Rather, *it is their ability to deceive from without and corrode from within: it is their mastery of MONEY and the BIG LIE.*

> ...he appeals to the baseness that lies deep in the souls of all men. He rots the soul of a nation; he works secretly and unknown in the night to undermine the pillars of the city; he infects the body politics so that it no longer can resist. A murderer is to be less feared.
>
> CICERO.

To make the transition from U.S. constitutional government to ONE WORLD ILLUMINATI GOVERNMENT, JEWS have been hard at work *subverting America s Will to resist.* One of their stratagems is *an intense propaganda campaign designed to denigrate everything White man has accomplished: to destroy his and his children s self esteem; cause him to lose pride in his history; make him less vigilant and cease to protect his incomparable White gene-pool to which he is indebted for everything.* Unrestrained cross-breeding between the races represents the ultimate victory of MARXISM/LIBERALISM/JEWRY over the West.

THE FINAL SOLUTION

White genes will become the property of the mud races. To that end the MASS-MEDIA, ACADEMIA, CHRISTIANITY, the FEDERAL GOVERNMENT, have targeted the minds and wombs of YOUNG WHITE WOMEN. In blunt terms, they want to lower White women's resistance to fornication with NEGROES, and JEWS. It is no surprise, then, that the U.S. government is "unable" to stop third-world, and banana republic, DRUG TRAFFIC, which finds its way into the hands of The Mob, and Mafia, pimps, the military, college dorms, high-schools, and the entertainment industry where beautiful young Aryans hang out. Whereas, during WWII the United States ably smashed the most powerful nations on earth, and more recently bombed the hell out of Serbia, Iraq, Syria and other JUDEOPHOBIC nations. The Feds (who incinerated the Branch Davidians American men, women and children) are "unable" to stop illegal immigrants (each a Democratic/Catholic vote) from invading the U.S. like a plague of locusts abetted by the MARXIST/LIBERAL/JEW 5th column (and Arkansas drug-czars).

The federal government, ever obedient to its masters, refuses to crush these criminal assaults upon the White Majority; nor will it repeal Constitutional Amendments and Laws that soon will number Whites a minority in their own land. In effect Aryans, who sprang from the world's greatest race of warriors, have been rendered powerless by their own government.

Never forget, not one member of the United States Government, despite his or her total awareness of the CONSPIRACY, dares take remedial action against the ILLUMINATI. In this cowardly manner the federal government has committed *misprision* a point in sedition law that states High Treason is committed by those who have knowledge treason is being committed but who conceal, or do not act upon that fact. (See Chap. IV, MONEY).

> Treason doth never prosper, what is the reason? For when it doth prosper none dare call it Treason.
>
> LORD HARRINGTON.

> The Tree of Liberty is nourished by the blood of tyrants, It is its natural manure.
>
> JEFFERSON.

Damage inflicted upon the West is serious and ongoing. However, we note that a jagged rent appears in JEW confidence. It bleeds. Mendelism terrifies them, and rightly so. Their Marxist maxim *"Liberty, Equality, Fraternity"* has been blown to smithereens; their egos shattered; their cunningly constructed post WWII image nose-jobs and all has been exposed. Indeed, JEWS have been struck a mortal blow. They cannot escape their genes! It follows then, as day follows night, that ALL laws, ideologies, and legislation proceeding from the EQUALITY THEORY are false, fraudulent and PATHOLOGICAL. Democracy, One World Government, The Great Society, World Banks, Family of Man, The United Nations, Talmudism, Christianity, Communism, Sexual Equality, Busing, Racial Integration, Quotas, Diversity, Miscegenation, etc., are now revealed, in the pervasive light of Mendelism, as: IGNORANCE in action, on the one hand; and, on the other hand, a TALMUDIC CONSPIRACY to destroy the White Race. So long as federal and state laws supporting these abominations continue to exist America will continue her downward spiral into the racial morass IQ-85 ±.

It is no secret that White Americans have reached a CONSTITUTIONAL IMPASSE: No LEGAL recourse exists whereby they can redress their dispossession. And it is no surprise that Ben Wattenberg, JEW, elatedly remarked (See: FORWARD), that the bell of Manifest Destiny has been rung (he means, White power in America is finished... he thinks).

Americans must decide if they agree with Ben. Do they want a White society OR a mud-race society. There is no compromise. Social intercourse leads to sexual intercourse. Miscegenation means breeding out of existence *FOREVER* blue-eyed blondes, red-heads, fair skinned brunettes and the higher intelligence they represent. The mud races will benefit through injections of White genes whilst the White Race will disappear. It means that our Fathers who fought and died that their Nation might live, will have lived and died in vain. Within 30-years (or less if they open the

Mexican border) the U.S. population, followed closely by Europe, will resemble that of Cuba, India, Mexico. JEWS will have won the world.

> The American Negro's past is a stigma, his color is a stigma, and his vision of the future is the hope of erasing the stigma by making color irrelevant... I share this hope... I believe that the wholesale merging of the two races is the most desirable alternative for everyone concerned...
> NORMAN PODHORETZ, JEW, editor "Commentary".

> BOSTON... at the time busing began (c. 1970), the city's public school population was 52% White, 37% Negro, 8% Hispanic, and 3% Asian. Much has changed, the result of White flight and immigration trends. Today the students in Boston's 129 public schools are 16% White, 49% Negro, 26% Hispanic, 9% Asian.
> THE WASHINGTON POST, 7-18-99.
> (It should be noted grades have plummeted, crime escalated).

> The difference in thickness of the supragranular layers of the cortex of White and Negro brains is the difference between civilization and savagery.
> WESLEY CRITZ GEORGE,
> Head Dept. of Anatomy, Univ. N. Car.

American sheep must learn, despite Biblical nonsense, that in NATURE the lion lies down with the lamb NOT in the spirit of brotherly love (as pictured in Hick's fantasy, *"Peaceable Kingdom"*) but to *eat it!* In God's Kingdom ALL living organisms feed on others (lamb chops). The Homo Sapiens social jungle is crowded with taxons each seeking its destiny at someone's expense. There is NO equality in Nature, All is unequal (a FACT "bleeding-heart" pols know very well). There is NO "Family of Man" (UNESCO). There are only races and mongrels; each race bearing distinct, unique, God-given qualities *("Race is everything!"* DISRAELI, JEW). To destroy racial differences is genocide.

> Already in *ancient times* we were the first to shout the words, "Liberty, Equality, Fraternity"... the presumably clever and intelligent Gentiles did not understand the symbolism of the uttered words; did not understand their contradiction in meaning did not notice that in nature there is no equality..."
>
> THE FIRST PROTOCOL.

The Catholic (Universal) Church, founded by HEBREWS, implanted itself among world states proclaiming the Equality of Man. This emphasizes the dirty secret, which JEWS have long asserted privately, that Christianity will pave the road to One World Zionist Government. Recently, Pope John Paul II confirmed the secret by announcing *"there will be One World Government for the first time ever by the year 2000 A.D."* He didn't elaborate on who would rule that One World. However, as the Church solidifies its ancient alliance with the JEWS (MONEY), REMEMBER that thumb-screws, and fire, figure prominently in Catholic displays of love for YAHWEH and hatred for Nature. An ungrateful Catholic Church (saved from Moslems by Aryan knights at Tours) today denounces dreams of an Aryan Empire. Pope John Paul's bias has precedence. Saul of Tarsus, HEBREW, invented Christianity (including the Immaculate Conception, which Jesus never heard of) to destroy Rome seat of pagan Aryan Power. The Church, built by Peter, JEW, (and expanded by the pagan Constantine) mixed PAGAN lore with HEBREW Scriptures to make the poisonous-brew palatable to pragmatic, lusty Aryans. It can be said, they survived in spite of it. Christianity's great contribution was bringing cohesion, briefly, to the European tribal states no small gift! Magnificent Aryan art, architecture, and music became dear to the entire world. Nor should we forget the unselfish services performed by the clergy in the name of JESUS CHRIST. These ministries of hope, faith and charity are also an important element in PANTHEISM. The irrevocable fact is that Christianity (like Marx, Freud, Boas) abhors FACTS. Instead, the Church blathers about original sin (abhorrence of Knowledge); shame; forgiveness (at a price), miracles, equality, loving your enemy; and Yahweh's Kingdom of Heaven which was never described and never arrived. Unbelievers were judged, tormented, physically tortured, murdered and cast into Hell which *is* described in maniacal detail. Castles built on sand, and fear-induced faith will not last forever. Nor will ignorance in so long as freedom of expression is tolerated. *Jesus, who walked on water, raised the dead, and believed the world flat, has lost his influence over the West's Culture Stratum.* Today, displaying tantrums, Christianity is fading back into the primitive myths and fables from whence it came. It is a fact of psychological necessity that *ALL great People require a deep faith in a higher Power to which they can give total obedience.* The Aryan religion, PANTHEISM which arose full-blown out of the Mendelian Age worships NATURE'S LAWS, made manifest in MENDELISM/GOD/FAMILY (THE ARYAN RACE) and by so doing exposes JUDEO-CHRISTIANITY as another HOAX, *reductio ad absurdum!* PANT HEISM now radiates the UNIVERSAL FORCE throughout Western Civilization. Only the superstitious, ignorant and venal continue to believe, or pretend to believe, in the jealous, vengeful, paranoid tribal god Jehovah (note: George Washington, Thomas Jefferson, and Abraham Lincoln, et al, were Deists. They worshipped an Omnipotent Creator, NOT JUDEO/CHRISTIANITY). *To accept JUDEO-CHRISTIANITY is to deny Nature's Laws: to deny Nature's Laws: is to deny God's Laws: to deny God's Laws is blasphemous. There is no Equality of Man or of the races – THAT rings democracy's bell!*

The great Mystics: Zarathustra, Jesus, Siddartha Gautama, Mohammed, Shakespeare, Blake, Goethe, Schopenhauer, Vivekananda, Whitman, et al, tell us that Man's Soul lives eternally (in the Universe ALL ENERGY IS CONSERVED Soul is Energy); Truth, Beauty and Justice (Karma) do at last prevail. PANTHEISM and NATURAL SCIENCE support many mystical revelations. For example,

Instinct, Intuition and Intelligence (Reason) have coalesced during Western Synthesis revealing Unlimited Space which *in microcosm and in macrocosm* is constituted of energy particles millions of times smaller than atoms. These particles, arranged in strings of electrical energy (emitting sounds described by Mystics as *"celestial music"*), each on different frequencies and vibrating with Life, twist and turn through many space-time dimensions providing the Universe "many mansions". *Here, where the worlds of macrocosm/ microcosm merge and energized-matter becomes fluid FORCE, we enter the METAPHYSICAL UNIVERSE.* Here the incomprehensible vastness of inner and outer space are ONE. This UNIVERSAL FORCE, *in greater or lesser degrees,* flows through ALL things. What resides "inside" the "mansions" is hidden... for now. There remains only God's command: KNOW THYSELF: OBEY NATURE'S LAWS.

JEWISH power at the end of the 20th Century is revealed by their ability to force the "HOLOCAUST" HOAX down the World's throat. The German People known for their integrity, courage and high ethical standards; their advanced science and creativity have been slandered and virtually ruined by a nation of parasites who have managed *few achievements in any realm of life except in the realm of LIES and EXTORTION.*

For 60-years the World has been subjected to SHOAH propaganda despite the FACT that the JEW "survivors" have been proven LIARS by aerial photographs, forensic reports, eye-witness reports, diaries, official files, and bysworn testimony in courts of law by the survivors themselves. All educated men concede, there were NO execution gas-chambers during WWII. Nevertheless, as though FACTS are irrelevant, JEWS incessantly repeat their venomous LIES in the JEW CONTROLLED MASS-MEDIA; whilst the ILLUMINATI punishes any form of rebuttal. Although privy to the FACTS the gutless U.S. Congress keeps the lid tightly closed on this seething kettle. Inevitably, FACTS WILL OUT! With America wearing a JEW face and carrying a big stick, little wonder that wherever informed Gentiles congregate (here and abroad) JUDEOPHOBIA is reaching Hitlerian proportions:

Shooter Left Journal SKOKIE, Ill., July 10 -Police are analyzing racist notations in a journal apparently owned by Benjamin Nathaniel Smith, hoping to learn more about the deadly shooting rampage in the Midwest last weekend... "Anyone who knows the history of this plague upon humanity who call themselves the Jews will know why I have acted...." Smith is believed to have killed two people and wounded nine others all either Jews, blacks, or Asians in Illinois and Indiana before his suicide... *WASHINGTON POST* (7-11-99).

Where There Is Hate, There Also Springs Hope. (Sic!) Over the past eight months or so, Western media have carried alarming reports on the resurgence of anti-Semitism (sic) in the former Soviet Union, especially in Russia and the Ukraine, where roughly most of the regions 1.5 million Jews reside... The most disaffected Ukrainian Jews... have left, most of them for Israel, the United States, and Germany... In Moscow, Vladimir Shapiro, eminent sociologist, told me of a recent survey that found anti-Semitism rampant in high schools throughout the Russian Federation... The perseverance of Jews in the region and their sense of cohesion are admirable... The fear that the Jews, as so often in the past, may again find themselves as scapegoats for their countries' economic ills, cannot be dismissed.
ABRAHAM BRUMBERG, JEW, Washington Post (7-11-99).

Aryan Group's Parade Attracts Large Protest.
COEUR D'ALENE, Idaho, July 10 Members of the Aryan Nations paraded through downtown streets today under protection of a federal court order but were outshouted by protestors who forced the marchers to detour... Aryan Nations holds that God has ordained the formation of a whites-only homeland in the Pacific Northwest.
WASHINGTON POST (7-11-99).

Possible Hate Link in Calif. Killings.
REDDING, Calif., July 10 ...Federal and Shasta County area homes

of Ben Matthew Williams, 31, and James Tyler Williams, 29, turned up a notebook linking the brothers to the June synagogue fires and produced racist, anti-Semitic propaganda related to the World Church of the Creator... They look like a couple of all-American boys," Richardson said. They don't have any weird tattoos. They're not skinheads..." World Church of the Creator members have been connected to numerous hate crimes in recent years including the 1993 bombing of an NAACP office in Tacoma, Wash., the 1997 beating of a Black man and his teenage son... in Sunrise, Fla., and last years beating of a Jewish video store owner in Florida.

WASHINGTON POST (7-11-99).

Israel warns Japan to denounce growing anti-Semitism mood. TOKYO Japanese academic and business circles should denounce signs of growing anti-Semitism says Israeli Ambassador Yaacov Cohen... "This is a phenomenon that should worry the Japanese more than anybody," Mr. Cohen said in an interview with The Japanese Times.

EDWARD NEILAN, *Washington Times. (Several months after this article appeared the Japanese experienced a major stock-market collapse, c.1999)*

RUSSIA Nationalists differ from patriots. A patriot loves his country but to a nationalist hatred of the ENEMY is more important than love of his own country. In Russia there is a deep affinity between the neo-Communists and the nationalists. Their common enemy is the JEW. They say: "We have a great deal in common with the Germans... If the two of us get together we'll rule the world."

AUTHOR'S REVIEW of *"Black Hundred,"* by Walter Laqueur.

Khakid Abduk Muhammad, the "Representative" and "National Assistant" of Minister Louis Farrakhan and the Nation of Islam, arrived at Kean College... and rays of zeal and hatred beamed from his mouth. His topic was a book published by the Nation of Islam called "The Secret Relationship Between Blacks and Jews." The National Assistant said that the Jews were "impostor Jews" demonic liars who rejected Jesus. He said "Jesus was right. You're nothing but liars. The Book of Revelations is right. You're from the synagogue of Satan."... They dispossessed the Palestinians. They exploited the German: "Everybody always talks about

Hitler exterminating six million Jews. But nobody ever asks what they did to Hitler..." The U.S. Senate voted 97 0 to condemn the Kean College speech. PAUL BERMAN, JEW, *The New Yorker* (2-28-94).

When thou comest nigh unto a city to fight against it then proclaim peace unto it. And it shall be, if it make thee answer of peace, open unto thee, then it shall be that all the people therein will pay tribute unto thee and serve thee. And if it will make no peace with thee, but will make war against thee, then thou shalt besiege it: and when the Lord thy God hath delivered it unto they hands thou shalt smite every male thereof with the edge of the sword: but the women, and the little ones and the cattle and all that is in the city, even all the spoil thereof, shalt thou take unto thyself... But of the cities of these people, which the Lord thy God hath given thee for an inheritance, thou shalt save nothing alive that breathest.
THE HOLY BIBLE Deuteronomy 20:10.

What's sauce for the goose is sauce for the gander.
GRANDAD, *"Down on the Farm."*

SYNTHESIS OF THE WEST is unfolding at an accelerating rate. Its Aryan People think of themselves, once again, not as nationalistic tribes (*French, German, Hungarian, Italian, English, Irish, Polish, Spanish, Russian (Rus), et al*), but as ONE WHITE NATION. They are as voyagers come home at last after a storm-swept odyssey at sea and much the wiser for it. Aryans now realize that Western Culture is genetic in origin and that White genes and White genes alone have enabled them to transmit beauty, behavior, capability, intelligence and SOUL across the generations. The Culture-Bearing Stratum of this great ARYAN CULTURE resides within a relatively small group of extraordinary men and women who place race, family, loyalty, duty, honor, at higher value than their own lives. They are unique because they Instinctively sense, Intuitively understand, and Rationally believe in the great ARYAN

IDEA: WESTERN SOCIALISM AND THE HOLY WESTERN EMPIRE.

These are the "nay-sayers and down-goers"; the achievers, the martyrs, the heroes through whose veins flows the blood of Aryan conquerors. They come from all walks of life: cowboy, scientist, iron-rigger, teacher, artist, businessman, farmer, military, et al. The Aryan gene-pool provides them with an extraordinary evolutionary edge. They will preserve that edge – with bloody hands.

THE ILLUMINATI, as this treatise clearly shows, controls, indeed owns, the United States of America. The power of World Finance, and of World Mass-Media is in their grip, thus abrogating the U.S. constitution, and rendering the Executive, Legislative and Judicial branches of government irrelevant and incapable of protecting the White gene-pool. The federal government is coerced, blackmailed and bought! The State no longer functions. There is no way for White America to attain redress using constitutional measures. *These FACTS are very difficult for Patriots to accept. They bring home, as nothing else can, the tragedy of our loss.*

JEWS will never voluntarily relinquish control over the West. It would be suicidal for them to do so. The FACTS would be revealed. JEWS can survive only by suppressing the FACTS. The battle to save the White Race from extinction, therefore will be fought NOT in the Halls of Congress, as patriots would wish, but among the hedge-rows and in the streets of North America where our forefathers fought.

There are about 15-million JEWS living in the U.S. They claim only 2.5-million. The Census Bureau, of course, is not permitted to count them. Any traveler with eyes and a keen nose realizes JEWS are scattered across the continent like colonies of termites (recently a big influx in Idaho!). *They have concentrated largely in 3-major areas: New York City, Philadelphia-Baltimore, Washington D.C. corridor; Chicago-St.Louis, Dallas corridor; and Los Angeles, San Francisco corridor. Four time zones.* They also gravitate, on dual and forged pass-ports, between the U.S., Israel and all nations of the world. Their forte as we have seen is a superb organization designed to implement the Protocols. JEWS zealously believe JEHOVAH requires them to employ ANY MEANS to destroy Gentiles. Battlefields of the world are covered with Aryan White Crosses. The polluted White womb destroys the Aryan gene-pool.

Because the U.S. government has denied constitutional redress to Aryans, only two options remain: REVOLT or DIE. *The pro-White objective is not to destroy the great Nation/State established by the Founding Fathers that already has been accomplished by the ENEMY. ARYANS intend to re-establish the FOUNDERS' VISION of America and return State and territory to their White progeny. Our FOREFATHERS' VISION will be extended to create a HOLY WESTERN EMPIRE encompassing ALL WHITE STATES world-wide. The HWE will assist all non-White races to maintain their identity. This NEW WORLD will boast truly DIVERSE racial populations, God given, each in its own homeland governed by its own people.* As the Western Dialectical Synthesis progresses the Aryan *Culture-Bearing Stratum* will step to the front leading the NATION against the PARASITES and the mongrel armies enlisted in their behalf. Aryans need only adopt Bolshevik Revolutionary strategy and tactics (c. 1900) to regain their heritage. Fight fire with fire. Had JEWS possessed modern bio/chemical weapons Whites today would be scarce as Neanderthals. *Might makes right and the winner takes the spoils.* That's the lesson of the Bolshevik Revolution.

Today, the Parasite owns the West. But not for much longer. Aryans have the weapons. We have the men. It requires only financing and leadership. It won't require an army. 150-Special Forces personnel will be more than sufficient. *Only through UNIFICATION of the White States and establishment of TERRITORIAL INTEGRITY can White Man FULFILL his DESTINY. The future is inevitable, it is difficult, and it is filled with heroes, martyrs and glorious victories.*

King Gordius, of Phyrigia, devised an elaborate knot which he said only the future king of Asia could untie. When the knot was presented to Alexander the Great he smiled, then severed it with one stroke of his sword. The ILLUMINATI CONSPIRACY will be SEVERED AS ALEXANDER SEVERED THE GORDIAN KNOT! In this endeavor ALL HONORABLE ARYANS will participate. It requires only FAITH in God; and the WILL to achieve. *A great new Age is emerging: The MENDELIAN AGE. A marvelous HOLY WESTERN EMPIRE will be built!* NATURE'S COMMAND is: CULTIVATE THY GARDEN ISOLATE THY GENE POOL EXCRETE YOUR WASTE OR DIE!

The IMPERIUM: ALL ARYANS, the World over, "awakened as from a bad dream," weapons held high, will stand victorious astride their homeland a White Nation-State The HOLY WESTERN EMPIRE.

THE ARYAN OATH Upon the Blood of My Sacred Aryan Ancestors I Swear:

Eternal LOYALTY to My FAMILY + RACE + NATION + GOD + To be BRAVE + CONSIDERATE + JUST + REVERENT + FRANK + TRUSTWORTHY + and + VENGEFUL

This do I swear so help me God!

THE CATEGORICAL IMPERATIVE

(Revised)

Act only on that maxim whereby thou canst at the same time WILL that it should exalt the Aryan race.

PANTHEISTIC TRINITY

(Aryans-THE FORCE-Pantheism):

Holds Yahweh in utter contempt: A bumbling JEW tribal-god "full of sound and fury signifying nothing."

THE ARYAN CRUCIFIX the *Iron Cross* has at its porcelain center the face of a beautiful Aryan woman. Her blue eyes are cast upward; her cherry lips are slightly parted. Flaxen hair fine as silk cascades over her shoulders A trickle of blood travels from the corner of her mouth down her throat and onto her bosom. *She too was crucified by the JEWS.* She wears a crown of thorns bearing the word: *DRESDEN!*

+++

Aryans appear everywhere as promoters of true progress, and in Europe their expansion marked the moment when the prehistory of (Europe) begins to diverge from that of Africa or the Pacific.
DR. V. GORDON CHILDE, "easily the greatest pre-histo*rian... probably in the world."* (Encyclopedia Britannica).

The sole condition required to centralize power in a democratic society is to profess equality.
ALEXIS de TOQUEVILLE.

Mr. Speaker, it is a monstrous thing for this great nation to have its destiny presided over by a traitorous Federal Reserve System acting in secret with International Usurers.
LOUIS T. McFADDEN, Chr. House Banking Committee.

The JEWISH nation is the only nation that possesses the secrets of all the rest... there is no government in the world so completely at their service as America. "The British did this", the Germans did that", when it was the International Jew who did it..."the Americans are (now known as) a sordid, greedy, cruel people." Why? Because JEWISH money-power is centered here. The genius of the Jew is to live off people, not off land, nor off the production of commodities from raw materials, but off people. Let other people till the soil; the Jew if he can will live off the tiller. Let other people toil at trades and manufacture; the Jew will exploit the fruits of their work. That is his particular genius. If this genius be described as parasitic, the term would seem to be justified by a certain fitness.

HENRY FORD I, *"The International Jew."*

Power and law are not synonymous. In truth they are frequently in opposition and irreconcilable. There is God's Law from which all equitable laws of man emerge and by which men must live if they are not to die in oppression, chaos and despair.

CICERO (106-43 BC).

The Department of Education reported that In the *Third International Mathematics and Science Study*, U.S. 12th graders performed among the lowest of 21 TIMSS countries outperforming only students from Cyprus and South Africa.

WASHINGTON TIMES (8-30-99).

This above all, to thy own self be true; and it must follow as night the day, thou canst not then be false to any man.

SHAKESPEARE, *"Hamlet"* (Polonius).

Then spake brave Horatius, keeper of the Gate: To every man upon this earth death cometh soon or late. What better way to die than facing fearful odds for the ashes of our fathers and the temples of our gods!

MACAULEY, *"Lays of Ancient Rome"*.

All that is necessary for the triumph of Evil is for good men to do nothing.

EDMUND BURKE.

The Tree of Liberty is nourished by the blood of tyrants; it is its natural manure.

JEFFERSON.

What I anticipate for I see it preparing slowly and hesitatingly is the

United Europe. The nations which got to be worth anything never attained to that condition under liberal institutions: great danger made out of them something which deserves reverence; that danger which alone can make us aware of our resources, out virtues, our means of defense, our weapons, our genius which compels us to be strong.

NIETZSCHE.

To communicate anything to a Goy about our religious relations would be equal to killing all Jews, for if the Goyim knew what we teach about them they would kill us all openly.

TALMUD: Libre David 37.

All vows, oaths, promises, engagements, and swearings which I make in the future shall be null from this Day of Atonement until the next.

TALMUD: Kol Nidre Oath.

TOB SHEBBE GOYIM HAROG! (Kill the best Gentiles!)

TALMUD: Sanhedrin 59

FINIS

GLOSSARY

AD HOC concern for a particular (subjective) case or purpose.

AD HOMINEM attack (in Logic) on an opponent's character rather than on his contentions.

ANGST, n. fear.

ANTI-SEMITIC wrongfully interpreted to mean Anti-Jewish. Jews (Asiatics) hate Semites (Arabs) and kill them daily.

ARISTOCRACY government by the best individuals; the aggregate of those believed to be superior. Uncommon man.

ARYAN (Noble), n. Perhaps Atlantean. Progenitor of the White Race which spread culture throughout Europe, India, Persia, Egypt, America and other parts of the globe.

ARYAN PANTHEISM A doctrine that equates God with the Force and Laws of the Universe: most specifically with Mendelism.

ASHKENAZIM JEWS the "13th Tribe" (Arthur Koestler). Asiatic Khazars converted to TALMUDISM who spuriously identify themselves as Judeans. 98% of all U.S. JEWS are Ashkenazim.

BOURGEOISIE, n. Social middle-class.

CANAILLE the "dogs" of all revolutions who pillage, murder, and rape the Jews of Paris, St. Petersburg and Chicago.

CASTING COUCH where starlets are made.

CENTRAL BANK a private stock-company holding a charter to manage a nation's money for a piece of the action.

COMMON ordinary, plain, vulgar, cheap, mediocre and popular.

DEMOCRACY government rule by the majority. A form of government despised by the Founding Fathers and required by parasites.

DOCU-DRAMA a drama that is objective in content and based upon documented facts (reality). Hollywood spins disinformation into the docu-drama format, producing propaganda.

EGALITARIANISM false belief in individual and racial equality.

ESPRIT DE CORPS, n. group spirit, inspiration, enthusiasm.

EX POST FACTO done (as enact a law) after the fact.

IN FLAGRANTE DELICTO in the act of committing a gross misdeed.

IN SITU in the natural position.

FED The Federal Reserve System: central bank that controls U.S. MONEY; privately owned by members of the KEHILLA.

FIFTH COLUMN B'nai B'rith; saboteurs, guerrillas, treasonous groups hidden within a nation to assist the enemy.

FREEDOM FIGHTER/TERRORIST depending upon whose ox is gored.

FREE MASONRY an international secret organization (Masonry) whose top echelons are permeated by JEWS.

GENETIC related to or determined by the genes.

GOY (plural Goyim) Gentile (sheep grazing in JEW pastures).

GULAG ARCHIPELAGO Bolshevik death camps, USSR. The most hideous prisons in world-history (read: Solzhenitsyn).

HOLLYWOOD Sodom USA. Jews on display. Pus. Infection. Disease.

HOLOCAUST Atrocities committed by Allies against Germany.

"HOLOCAUST" false religion created by congenital liars.

IDEOLOGY visionary theorizing.

ILLUMINATI Rothschild organization created to destroy Gentiles: specifically, Western Culture.

KEHILLA Board of Directors of the Illuminati: 13 Jews.

KHAGAN King of Jews, head of Kehilla.

KHAZARS Asiatic tribe bearing Mongol-Turko-Armenoid affinities, converted to Talmudism (Judaism) in 730 A.D.

LAUGH-TRACK sound-track bearing laughter, applause, cheers, etc., edited into film/tape shot with no audience present.

L'INFAMIE slander, defamation; Jew propaganda weapon.

MAFIA U.S.A Sicilian/Italian crime syndicate.

MANIFEST DESTINY a necessary policy of imperialistic expansion, esp. the White Race.

MASS-MEDIA public (mass) communications media, including: radio, TV, internet, publishing, theater, motion-pictures, Tin Pan Alley, and music industries.

MARRANO Christianized JEW.

MENDEL, AGE OF the Age of Genetics.

MENDELISM n. all studies emanating from discovery of genes.

MISCEGENATION, n. marriage or cohabitation between a White person and a member of another race; esp., with Negro or Jew.

MISPRISION – when one has knowledge that treason is being committed but takes no action to prevent that crime, then the knowledgeable party is also guilty of treason.

MOB U.S.A. Jewish crime syndicate.

MORGANTHAU PLAN plan to starve to death 20-million Germans.

MORPHOLOGY, n. branch of biology dealing with the physical structure of plants and animals.

NATION (Natal: to be born: nationality) a People from the same gene-pool; their race, family, culture, territory.

ORIENTAL JEWS mixed ethnicity (largely Hebrew), settled in the Mideast, North Africa, Asia and China.

PHYSIOLOGY, n. branch of biology that deals with the physical aspects of an organism and its normal functions.

PROTOCOLS Records of a conference showing what has been agreed upon by the negotiators. A plan of action.

PRIX DE GUERRE legitimate war target, prize of war.

PSYCHOLOGY, n. the science of mind and behavior SET-UPS

Bait: Lusitania, Pearl Harbor, Coventry, Bay of Pigs, Tonkin Gulf, USS Liberty, Harvey Oswald, et al.

SPIELBERGISM any outrageous lie; e.g., "Schindler's List."

SEPHARDIM JEWS Hebrews who settled in Spain until they were kicked out in 1492.

SEPTUAGINT trans. of O. T. into Greek by 70-rabbis, each of whom arrived at identical translations!

SPIROCHETE genus of bacteria, as those causing syphilis.

TALKING HEADS Goy TV-moderators: sycophants mouthing JEW ideology, lies and propaganda: Racial Traitors.

TALMUD Pharisaical Law; "Synagogue of Satan" (Jesus).

THAUMATURGY performing miracles, magic.

TORAH (Pentateuch) first five books of the Old Testament.

TYPHUS deadly infectious disease transmitted to man by fleas and lice; historically, particular to East European JEWS.

UNIVERSALISM Catholicism, Judaism, Illuminism, Marxism, New Age, etc.: accept miscegenation or burn at the stake.

USURY Jewish Capitalism: Compound Interest, Bankruptcy, War.

WOLZEK fake death camp named by Rudolf Hoess, commandant of Auschwitz (before he was hanged) to notify history that his confessions in re Jews gassed were obtained by torture.

ZIETGEIST, n. Spirit of the Age. WELTANSCHAUUNG, n. philosophy of life.

BIBLIOGRAPHY

America

GARRETT, GARET Burden of Empire: Road to Servitude

NOCK, ALBERT JAY The State of the Union: Essays

OLIVER, REVILO America's Decline

PIERCE, WILLIAM The Turner Diaries

SKOUSEN, CLEON The Naked Capitalist

BEATY, JOHN O. Iron Curtain Over America

BURNHAM, JAMES Suicide of the West

BROWN, LAWRENCE The Might of the West

ALLEN, GARY None Dare Call It Conspiracy

NORMAN, CHARLES Ezra Pound

LARSON, MARTIN The Federal Reserve: Manipulated Dollar

MULLINS, EUSTACE Mullins On The Federal Reserve System

SODDY, FREDERICK Wealth, Virtual Wealth and Debt

McFADDEN, LOUIS T. Speeches from the Congressional Record

SOMBERT, WERNER The Jews and Modern Capitalism

SMOOT, DAN The Invisible Government.

SUTTON, ANTHONY National Suicide

GOLDWATER, BARRY* With No Apologies

Historical Revisionism

VEALE, F. J. P. Advance to Barbarism: Total Warfare

KEELING, RALPH Gruesome Harvest: Postwar Germany

WILTON, ROBERT The Last Days of the Romanovs

RADZINSKY, EDWARD The Last Czar

IRVING, DAVID Churchill's War, Dresden

ENNES, JAMES Assault on the USS LIBERTY

WEBSTER, NESTA H. The French Revolution, World Revolution

HOFFMAN, MICHAEL A. The Great Holocaust Trial: Zundel

BARNES, HARRY ELMER In Quest of Truth and Justice: WWI

Genesis of War

TOLAND, JOHN Infamy: Pearl Harbor

ZAYAS, ALFRED A Terrible Revenge: Murder of Germans, The Wehrmacht War Crimes

CROCKER, GEORGE Roosevelt's Road to Russia

DEGRELLE, LEON Hitler: Born at Versailles

VON BRUNN, JAMES Kill the Best Gentiles

Holocaust Revisionism

ZUNDEL, ERNST Did 6-MIllion Really Die?

BUTZ, ARTHUR R. The Hoax of the 20th Century

STAGLICH, WILHELM Auschwitz: A Judge Looks at the Evidence

LEUCHTER, FRED Leuchter Report: First Forensic Examination of Auschwitz

ROQUES, HENRI The "Confessions" of Kurt Gerstein

BALL, JOHN Air Photo Evidence: "Holocaust" sites.

HESS, WOLF Who Murdered My Father, Rudolf Hess?

Race and Culture

YOCKEY, FRANCIS PARKER Imperium

SIMPSON, WILLIAM G. Which Way Western Man?

BAKER, JOHN R. Race

PEARSON, ROGER Shockley on Eugenics and Race

GARRETT, HENRY E. Heredity: The Cause of Racial Differences in Intelligence

HERRNSTEIN/MURRAY The Bell Curve

PUTNAM, CARLTON Race and Reality

GUENTHER, HANS Racial Elements of European History

JUNG, CARL Secret of the Golden Flower, The Development of Personality

ARDREY, ROBERT The Social Contract, African Genesis

COON, CARLTON Origin of Races, The Races of Europe

CHILDE, GORDON On The Aryan Theory

GRANT, MADISON The Passing of the Great Race

SPENGLER, OSWALD The Decline of the West

ROBERTSON, WILMOT The Dispossessed Majority

GIBBON, EDWARD The Decline and Fall of the Roman Empire

DE CHARDIN, TEILHARD The Phenomenon of Man.

SANTAYANA, GEORGE The Last Puritan

HUXLEY, ALDOUS The Perennial Philosophy, Brave New World

RENFREW, COLIN Before Civilization

LUDOVICI, A. M. The Quest of Human Quality

FRAZER, JAMES G. The Golden Bough.

KERR, W. P. Epic and Romance

GRANT, MICHAEL Jesus

KUNG, HANS On Being A Christian.

OTTO, RUDOLPH The Idea of the Holy.

NIETZSCHE, FREDERICK The ANTICHRIST, Man and Superman. Thus Spake Zarathustra

CHAMBERLAIN, HOUSTON The Foundations of the 19th Century

DOSTOYEVSKY, FYODOR The Possessed

KLASSEN, BEN Nature's Eternal Religion, The White Man's Bible

JUNG, CARL The Aryan Christ

RENAN, ERNEST Life of Jesus

SPENCER, SIDNEY Mysticism & World Religion.

HAWKING, WILLIAM A Brief History of Time

JEWS

ARENDT, HANNAH* Eichmann in Jerusalem.

FORD, HENRY The International Jew

KOESTLER, ARTHUR* The Thirteenth Tribe

MARSDEN, VICTOR E. The Protocols of the Learned Elders of Zion

LILIENTHAL, ALFRED M.* The Zionist Connection

SAMUEL, MAURICE* You Gentiles

FREEDMAN, BENJAMIN* Facts are Facts: Truth About Khazars

CHESTERTON, A. K. The New Unhappy Lords

BELLOC, HILLAIRE The Jews

ROBNETT, GEORGE W. Conquest Through Immigration

SHAHAK, ISRAEL* Jewish History, Jewish Religion: The Weight of 3000 Years (Intro by Gore Vidal)

STANKO, RUDY "Butch" The Score!

SOLZHENITSYN, ALEKSANDER The Gulag Archipelago A Day in the Life of Ivan Denisovich

KLASSEN, BERNHARDT (WCOTC) The White Man's Bible

The Third Reich

HITLER, ADOLPH Mein Kampf

IRVING, DAVID Goebbels: Mastermind of the 3rd Reich

ROSENBERG, ALFRED The Myth of the 20th Century

+ + +

Many of the above books are available at your Public Library others may be obtained from one or more of the following sources:

THE INSTITUTE FOR HISTORICAL REVIEW

(Mark Weber) POB 2739 Newport Beach CA 92659 CHURCH OF THE CREATOR POB 2002 E. Peoria, IL 61611 (Matt Hale)

NATIONAL ALLIANCE (Dr. William Pierce) POB 330 Hillsboro, WVA 24946

THE TRUTH AT LAST (Dr. Edw. Fields) POB 1211 Marietta, GA 30061

CHRISTIAN DEFENSE LEAGUE (Dr. J.K. Warner) POB 449 Arabi, LA 70032

MONTANA MILITIA (John Trochmann) POB 1486 Noxon, MT 59853

THE LIBERTY BELL (George Dietz) Box 21 Reedy, W. Va 25270

ZUNDEL-RIMLAND 3152 Parkway, Suite 13 PMB 109 Pigeon Forge, TN 37863

A FEW WEBSITES WITH INTERLINKAGE TO OTHER GREAT SITES

www.WCOTC.com (Matt Hale) www.naawp.com (David Duke) www.natall.com (Wm. Pierce) www.codoh.com (Bradley Smith) www.zundelsite.org (Ernst Zundel) www.vho.org (Germar Rudolph) www.russgranata.com (Russ Granata) www.Kevin-Strom.com (Kevin Strom) www.fpp.co.uk (David Irving) www.adelaideinstitute.org (FredrickToben)

A HANDFUL OF MANY DISTINGUISHED SCIENTISTS WHO REFUTE MARX/FREUD/BOAS

JOHN R. BAKER: Professor of Biology, Oxford U., Fellow of the Royal Society, author of *"Race"*.

V. GORDON CHILDE: Prof. Oxford, "easily the greatest prehistorian in Britain and probably in the world" (Ency. Brit.)

CARLTON S. COON: Professor of Anthropology Harvard; Past President of the American Assoc. of Physical Anthropologists; author of, *"The Origin of Races"*, etc.

F. A. E. CREW: M.D.Sc., PhD., Professor of Genetics and Animal Breeding, Univ. of Edinburgh.

GEORGE W. CRITZ: Prof. Anatomy, Univ. N. Carolina; *"The Biology of the Race Problem"*. the most important document yet published on the scientific aspect of the race question."

C.D. DARLINGTON: FRS, Prof. Botany, Oxford. Internationally renown for contributions to sciences of genetics, cytology and evolutionary theory

EDWARD M. EAST: Prof. of Genetics, Harvard; *"Mankind at the Crossroads"*.

HENRY E. GARRETT: Head of Dept. of Psychology Columbia U., Past Pres. of American Psychological Ass'n.

R. R. GATES: Emeritus Prof., Botany, University of London. Wrote *"Human Genetics"*, eleven books, and 400 articles.

MADISON GRANT: Chairman New York Zoological Society; Trustee, Amer. Museum Natural History wrote: *"The Conquest of a Continent"*; "The Passing of the Great Race".

HANS F. K. GUENTHER: Prof. Univ. of Berlin. His text, *"Racial Elements of European History"* is considered a masterpiece.

E. A. HOOTEN: Prof. of Anthropology, Harvard Univ.; author of *"Crime and the Man"*; *"Ape, Men, and Morons"*, etc.

ARTHUR R. JENSEN: Prof. of Educational Psychology, Univ. Calif. Berkeley; Research Psychologist at the Inst. of Human

Learning.

SIR ARTHUR M. D. KEITH: Rector Univ. Edinburgh, Curator the Museum of the Royal College of Surgeons, "one of the greatest anthropologists of this century." Many books including, *"The Place of Prejudice in Modern Civilization".*

L.S.B. LEAKEY: famous for his excavations at Olduvai Gorge, Tanganyika. Wrote, *"The Progress and Evolution of Man in Africa",* stating... *"however great may be the physical differences between such races as the European and the Negro, the mental and psychological differences are greater still."*

WILLIAM SHOCKLEY: Nobel Laureate, Poniatoff Prof. of Engineering, Stanford Univ., devoted his scientific efforts to Eugenics and race studies.

AUDREY M. SHUEY: Head of Dept. of Psychology, Randolph-Macon, formerly on the faculty at New York Univ.; authored the monumental, *"The Testing of Negro Intelligence"*..."The results are impressively consistent, Negroes, whether they are rural or urban, whether they live in the North or South, whether they are literate or illiterate, whether they are professional or unskilled workers, make lower scores than comparable groups of Whites."

WILLIAM G. SIMPSON: Union Theological Seminary, *magna cum laude;* Assoc. Director, American Civil Liberties Union; St. Francis of Assisi Pilgrimage; one of the world's great authorities on Nietzsche and Christ; author and lecturer.

EXHIBITS

THE FIRE

Shingletown home burns; family is safe

FRI AUG 2 6 1977

SHINGLETOWN — An early morning fire did an estimated $120,000 damage to the home of James W. Von Brunn on Wrangler Hill Road here today.

Shasta County Fire Department spokesman Deems Taylor said the fire apparently broke out in the attic near the chimney, but the exact cause is still under investigation. The fire was noticed about 3:25 a.m. when Von Brunn was awakened by the smell of smoke.

Von Brunn rushed his family out of the house and called firemen. Units from the Shingletown Volunteers, Shasta County and the California Department of Forestry responded. It took nearly two hours to quell the flames in the 3,800-square-foot wooden framed home.

The loss to the building was estimated at $80,000, and the contents at $40,000. Most of the loss is believed to be covered by insurance, according to firemen.

JVB was inspecting the ashes the morning after the fire when a man approached and introduced himself as a neighbor. A retired logger, he lived about three quarters of a mile away, down in the valley. He said he believed the fire was arson. About 1:30 AM he was awakened by his boar hounds. He went outside to quiet them. "I heard a pop — like a flare gun — from up your way." Then he heard car doors slam, followed by the squealing of tires on the blacktop.

This incident tied in with phone calls made earlier that month threatening serious consequences if JVB didn't halt publication of the book *Zionist Rape of the Holy Land (Conquest by Immigration)* by Robnett. For reasons too detailed to go into here, the probability of arson was never reported to the police.

LETTER TO JAMES HENRY WEBB

Written in prison, this letter was purloined from the mail, never reaching addressee Webb.

Honorable James Henry Webb. Jr, U.S. Secretary of the Navy The Pentagon Washington, D.C. 20500

James W. von Brunn Federal Prisoner #07128-016 P.O.Box 904-H FCI Ray Brook, N.Y. 12977

Dear Mr. Secretary:

Rear Admiral John G. Crommelin, U.S.N.(Ret.) suggested that I write to you and request your assistance. I am a political prisoner incarcerated in a Federal Prison resulting from my actions against those whom I believe threaten our Nation's security.

Admiral Crommelin submitted a Plea for a Presidential Pardon for me to our President, Honorable Ronald Reagan, on 28 February 1985. The Plea was handled in a very helpful and courteous manner by Mr. David B. Waller, Senior Associate Counsel to the President, as indicated in Enclosure "A". Upon receipt of Mr. Waller's letter I filed a personal Plea for a Presidential Pardon, as directed, to Mr. David Stephenson, Presidential Pardon Attorney, Chevy Chase, Maryland.

Several weeks later Mr. Stephenson held a meeting with my sister, and her attorney. Stephenson told them he would not submit my written Plea to the President (Please see Enclosure "B") but that he would recommend that my sentence be commuted because: my sentence was too severe for the crime committed; this was my first offense; my age -now, 67.5 years. I have no written evidence of these, Mr. Stephenson's statements. My court appointed attorney, John Hogrogian, told me I should take no further legal action while the Pardon Attorney processed my Plea.

On or about 20 December 1987, in a letter to the Warden, FCI Ray Brook, Mr. Stephenson reversed his opinion stating that "no favorable action" is warranted in my case. Admiral Crommelin's several attempts to ascertain the disposition of his Plea in my behalf have been ignored by Mr. Stephenson.

Mr. Secretary, after reading this brief you may deduce that the personages behind the scenes who manipulated my trial and extended the length of my incarceration may also have influenced Mr. Stephenson.

I respectfully request, based upon the following facts, that you use your influence to get some action on Admiral Crommelin's well documented Plea for Pardon in my behalf, and upon my personal Plea for Pardon, which the Pardon Attorney, according to his own words, never intended to submit to the President.

I served as PT-Boat skipper, and executive officer during WWII in the Mediterranean, and Pacific Theaters. I received a Commendation from Admiral Hewitt. When I took the Navy Officer's Oath I pledged my heart to every word of it and of course I still do. I am under the impression that the most formidable enemy of these United States, and of Western Culture, is Marxist-Communism. American tax-payers have spent billions of Federal Reserve Notes fighting a prolonged "cold war" with the Soviet Union, and we've spilled buckets of blood fighting "no-win wars" against Marxists in almost every part of the globe. Yet, within our own gates, protected by the very Constitution they seek to destroy, Marxists have been permitted to capture the machinery of our government. No doubt a conspiracy exists to create One World Marxist Government at the sacrifice of America's sovereignty. Just as certain, One World ideologists of all stripes are financed by the International Banking Cabal, in which the Federal Reserve System(FED) plays a major role. It is no secret that U.S. Bankers financed Soviet military build-up. That during the "police operation" in Viet Nam, Soviet truck production doubled resultant of U.S. financing and technological assistance. Those trucks were delivered to N. Viet Nam aboard ships, on the Haiphong run, built by America and our allies Why are dominant men in positions of great power in America willing to sacrifice America's treasure and lives to advance the spread of Marxism throughout the world? One reason was given by Rheinhold Niebuhr: "Marxism is the modern fulfillment of Jewish prophecy." James Warburg, son of the principal architect of the Federal Reserve Act, stated before the U..S. Senate: "We shall have One World Government whether we like it or not. The question is, shall we have One World Government by consent or by conquest"(1953).

7 December 1981, 1 hoped to reveal to the American People certain Facts regarding the World Marxist Conspiracy that are suppressed by the mass-media. I attempted to place the FED Board of Governors under legal, non-violent, citizens arrest supported by D.C. statutes, and by Misprision of Felony statute under U.S. Treason and Sedition Law. I charge the FED with Treason, operation of a Fraudulent Enterprise, and Un-Constitutional Private Corporate Operations. I intended to hold the Board prisoners in the Board Room, demand that their fellow conspirators at CBS provide national TV-hookup ; then, over TV to figuratively hand over the felons to the American people with an explanation of my charges against the FED. I then intended to hand over the prisoners, unharmed, to the President of the United States. I expected to stand trial in a U.S. Federal District Court, and prove the

Fed's culpability to a jury of my peers. I expected the jury to find the FED guilty and my citizens' arrest of the felons upheld by statute. Thus, We the People would issue a mandate to the Congress of the United States to bring proceeding against the FED, a privately held corporation, under Federal Tort Law.

I failed to achieve my objectives at the FED Building. There was no violence. I voluntarily surrendered my unloaded weapons to the guard, a former U.S. Marine. I carried no ammo or explosives (all of these facts either omitted or distorted in the official record).

My bail/bond was set at $3,000 ($300 cash). I was released upon my own recognizance by Judge Hess. Later I was indicted for Attempted Kidnapping, Robbery, Burglary, Assault with, and possession of Illegal Weapons. 14-months later, after the timely aspects of my actions were permitted to fade out, I was tried, convicted and sentenced for all counts. The government had offered to drop all charges if I would plead guilty to the weapons charges. I refused the Plea Bargain relying on a fair trial.

I was denied a fair trial for the following reasons:

1)   The government tried me in Superior Court, Washington, D.C. which does not have the standing to try Constitutional issues. Thus, I could not pursue the issue of the FED's un-constitutionality an important element in my defense. My request for change of venue was denied. The case should have been tried in Federal District Court. I am

now a D.C. prisoner "warehoused" in a Federal Prison and under jurisdiction of the Federal Parole Commission which recently re-tried and re-sentenced me.

2) There was no media coverage of my trial. I personally visited D.C. newspaper editors and wrote major networks inviting coverage. One recalls the favorable publicity afforded Daniel Ellsberg's "Pentagon Papers Trial". Those who orchestrated his publicity were the same media-masters that suppressed my attempt to expose the Marxist Conspiracy within our Nation.

3) At my arrest, on my person, was an 11-page Outline (Gov't. Exh. 14) (Please see Enclosure "C") from which I intended to extemporize on TV. Exhibit 14 implicates Jews/Zionists in the One World Marxist plot. The Outline also shows that Negroes are being used as dupes, by the Marxists to destroy our Western Culture. The manipulators, to assure my conviction, simply appointed court officers who would be racially prejudiced against me because of the contents of Exhibit 14.

Court Officers and Jury appointed as follows:

Judge, Harriet Rosen Taylor, Jew; Prosecuting Attorney, Elliot Warren, Jew (Warren, later replaced by Ron Dixon, remained in the court gallery throughout the trial as acting consultant to Dixon); Prosecuting Attorney, Ron Dixon, Negro; Probation Officer, Marvin Davids, Jew (Rabbi); Recorder & Bailiff, Negroes. 53 potential jurors attended voir dire, six were white. Dixon, using his peremptory challenges, dismissed all but one white woman juror seating

11Negro jurors, and 3-Negro Alternates, Court Appointed Defense Attorney, Jew (Miss Elizabeth Kent) was dismissed by me when she did no work on the case for several months. Her court appointed replacement, Gerard Lewis proved to be a Trojan Horse. I would have had a fairer trial in Iowa!

4)   Ineffective Assistance of Counsel (at trial and at Appeal). Lewis disclosed to me at trial that he didn't have the "heart to defend" my political or racial beliefs, nor to resist the racist attacks by prosecution because he, Lewis, was part Jew and was a card carrying member of the NAACP.

5)   "Government Exhibit 14, was central to the government's effort to rebut Appellant's defense ... given the meagerness of attention paid in the document to policies of the Federal Reserve Board less than one page as compared to the views concerning Blacks, Jews, Zionists - 10-pages the prosecution was clearly entitled to question Appellant's true motives in undertaking his actions ... while the contents of the document were controversial and undoubtedly offensive to some, that fact alone cannot shield defense from being confronted with it during cross-examination..." (Appelle Brief, Gov't #84-1641. Criminal # F 7199-81).

The objection was not that prosecution used Exh. 14, but the manner in which it was used. First, a biased Negro jury was selected, and a Jew Judge. Then statements from the Exhibit were used out of context to inflame the court. I was not permitted to read the entire Outline, to place the prosecution's remarks in perspective, and to show that the quotations within the Outline were by prominent, competent, and in many cases revered men.

Prosecution reasons that because I devoted only onepage to the FED that my real motives were to take hostages and air my racist views. This specious reasoning would contend that the superstructure of a skyscraper because it contains more cubic feet is more important that its foundation. Prosecution also seems to imply that one cannot be an alleged racist and at the same time seek to arrest felons that the two ideas are mutually exclusive. Nevertheless, the Court of Appeals, a mixed racial bag, entirely supported the prosecution's arguments and procedures. What I endeavored to present in outline form, of course, was that a long period of Jewish History developed into Marxist-Communism, financed by International Usurocrats, abetted by the massmedia (largely in Jew hands) and other support groups.

6)   I was denied the constitutional right to subpoena (among others) Messrs. PaulVolcker, and Zibigniew Brzezinsky, neither of whom bears immunity from subpoena, both of who are privately employed in anti-National activities.

7)   During trial the government admitted it had in its possession documents relating to my case from the office of Elizabeth Kent, my original (and initial) Defense Attorney. Prosecution had also received other documents during trial from outside sources which the Judge refused to admit as

evidence but which were made part of my case records.

8) Dr. Elgin Groseclose, monetary expert, who had testified in that capacity before Congress several times, appeared as Expert Witness for the Defense. He testified (I paraphrase) that: the FED is privately owned, subject to U.S. Tort Laws; acts independent of the 3-Branches of our Government; the FED Note is worthless as a storage of value is conceived out of thin air; the FED deliberately creates boom-bust periods to the detriment of the American people; that violence may be required to unseat the FED because its enormous power controls Congress. No wonder the massmedia was not allowed to attend the trial! Dr. Groseclose's testimony is virtually omitted in the Appellant's Brief except to say that he blamed the FED for inflation.

I was refused presentence bond and directly from court was clapped into D.C. jail. D.C. Statutes require Presentence Investigation (PSI) reports to be presented to defendant at least 10-days prior to sentencing. My PSI report was presented to me in a holding cell 5-10 minutes prior to sentencing. Lewis urged me to sign my approval because the rabbi had recommended that I be given probation. This carrot, to gain my signature, succeeded. Much later I discovered the errors, distortions and omissions contained in the PSI, e.g., the facts that there was no violence, and no ammo or explosives at the scene was unreported.

I was shipped to Springfield Federal Hospital to

determine the state of my mental health. After 3.5 months the psychiatrists declared me "sane without even a paranoid personality." However, predicated upon tests (answered in pencil) Springfield stated that I had a low I.Q. To refute that statement I insisted on supervised tests, the results enabled me to join MENSA whose requirements for membership start at the 98th perecentile of I.Q. The Springfield report attesting to my good mental health does not appear in Prison records.

Benjamin Baer, Jew, Chairman, National Parole Commission, Chevy Chase, MD. ignores the Springfield report. He insists in his many memos that I require "mental health care – and after care." In Baer's paranoid world anyone questioning Jew/Marxist motives is – perforce – insane.

Being warehoused in a prison 700 miles from D.C. effectively prevented me from meeting with my court appointed attorney, John Hogrogian. He had no office phone! So I was unable to assist him prepare my Appeal. The Appeal Schedule was so arranged that I did not receive a copy of the brief until*after the original had been filed.* I didn't receive trial transcripts until many months after my Appeal had been denied by a racially slanted Court of Appeals. Among other mistakes Hogrogian failed to present a jury list. The racially biased Court of Appeals used that excuse to NOT rule on my motion that the trial Court was prejudiced, that I did not have a jury of my peers. Shortly after the hearing Hogrogian was rewarded with a position as attorney for the city of New York ("Greatest Jewish city in the world" – Harry Golden).

Judge Taylor sentenced me to 3-years 8-months to 11years. If qualified I was eligible for parole at the lesser figure.

I was qualified. However, Benjamin Baer and his Regional Parole Board officer, Shelley Wittgenstein, Jew, re-indicted me, in effect, for an additional crime: "committing a serious crime against the security of the nation." Baer also stated in a memo that I advocated the elimination of a "certain race". A distortion of my statement (Exh. 14) that Negroes and Jews should be deported to their homelands. A sentiment expressed by Lincoln, Jefferson, et al, and by contemporary Jew/Negroes. Baer and company then retried, judged, and resentenced me to serve a total of 8-years 4-months.

This implies a 25-years sentence (1/3rd of 25). Benjamin Baer is largely responsible for expansion of Federal Prison Bureaucracy. He produces incredibly long sentences by taking cons out of their guidelines. Many young convicts, resultantly, are returned to society as middle-aged men, families gone, with no job potential. They become instant recidivists suitable only for employment in FedPr system's UNICOR, a growing business.

Viet Nam vets are considered threats to society in direct proportion to their military experience the more battle-stars the more medals for valor the stiffer the re-sentences handed out by Baer. He has no sense of honor. Certainly, a more flexible commutation policy for the vast majority of Nam vets is in order. Their patriotism has been stretched to the breaking point. Allow them to win one war against Baer.

I realize that I have imposed far too much, sir, upon your valuable time. So I will end this.

Mr. Secretary, my efforts were directed not against our Nation, but against those who would destroy our Nation. I believe my actions at the FED were supported by statute. While you may or may not subscribe to my philosophy, or condone my actions, I know that you support an American citizen's right to a fair, speedy and public trial. You are justified, then, in using your righteous influence to reveal the immense and arrogant control Marxists now exert over D.C. jurisprudence, and over the Federal Prison System not unlike the Federal Reserve System's power over America's monetary system.

Therefore, I respectfully request that you do whatever is feasible to help place before the President of the United States the two aforementioned Pleas: Rear Admiral John G. Crommelin's Plea for Pardon in my behalf; and my personal Plea for Presidential Pardon.

Respectfully,

James W. von Brunn. Encls :

"A" White House letter

"B" Von Brunn Plea for Pardon "C" Gov't Exhibit 14

C C :

Rear Admiral John G. Crommelin, U.S.N.(Ret.)

Crommelin Letter to Erik von Brunn

(first page photographically reproduced below; full text follows)

JOHN G. CROMMELIN
REAR ADMIRAL U. S. N. (RETIRED)
HARROGATE SPRINGS
WETUMPKA, ALA.

October 17, 1983.

Dear Erik,
Your Aunt Alyce has told me that you are a strong, healthy six year old boy and that you miss your father, James Von Brunn, who has been held by U.S. federal authorities now for some time. We all hope that he will soon be released, for in the opinion of those of us who understand the malfunctioning of certain elements of our once near perfect government he has committed no crime. But quite the contrary, he has taken very courageous and patriotic action to try and alert the U.S. citizens to the real organization of the Federal Reserve System and its great danger to the survival of our once White Christian constitutional republic, the corner stone of Western Civilization.

It is my conviction that James von Brunn deserves the gratitude and assistance of every White Christian citizen of these United States. And I believe he would have this support were it not for the cabal which controls not only the Federal Reserve System but also the nationally effective communication media.

In the early 1950s I discussed this media control with General Douglas MacArthur in a lengthy private conversation. We both agreed that the greatest internal or external threat to the survival of The United States was the near ironclad control which our enemies and subversives exercise over the U.S. communication media.

I suppose you know that your father was a PT Boat captain in World War II. We were both naval officers and

OVER

JOHN G. CROMMELIN .

Rear Admiral U. S. Navy (Retired) Harrogate Springs

Wetumpka, Georgia October 17, 1983 Dear Erik,

Your Aunt Alyce has told me that you are a strong, healthy six year old boy and that you miss your father, James von Brunn, who has been held by federal authorities now for some time. We all hope that he will soon now be released, for in the opinion of those of us who understand the malfunctioning of certain elements of our once near perfect government he has committed no crime. But quite the contrary, he has taken very courageous and patriotic actions to try to alert the U.S. citizen to the real organization of the Federal Reserve System and its great danger to the survival of our once White Christian constitutional republic, the cornerstone of Western Civilization.

It is my conviction that James von Brunn deserves the gratitude and assistance of every White Christian citizen of these United States. And I believe he would have this support were it not for the cabal which controls not only the Federal Reserve System but also the nationally effective communications media.

In the early 1950s I discussed this media control with General Douglas McArthur in a lengthy private conversation. We both agreed that the greatest internal and external threat to the survival of the United States is the near ironclad control over the U.S. communications media.

I suppose you know that your father was a PT-Boat Captain in World War II. We were both naval officers and have been friends for a long time. I was fortunate enough to be Air Officer and then Executive of the aircraft carrier, U.S.S. Enterprise, the greatest fighting ship in all the annals of recorded history. Perhaps some day I shall have the opportunity to tell you about the fierce battles which took place near Guadalcanal.

This is something you must know: all U.S. naval officers, before they are granted a commission, take an oath "to support and defend the Constitution of the United States against ALL enemies, foreign OR DOMESTIC. " This is a lifetime commitment as long as the officer remains a U.S. citizen.

When your father attempted a non-violent citizens' arrest of the board of governors of the Federal Reserve System, I believe the evidence will show that he intended no physical harm to anyone and that his motive was to force the controlled media to give him the opportunity to prove to the American public that the Federal Reserve is their most dangerous enemy, and that the Federal Reserve Act of 1913 must be repealed by the U.S. Congress if the U.S. Constitutional Republic is to survive.

To show that your father was not alone in his attempt to expose the character and dangers of the Federal Reserve I am sending herewith some documents proving that the Alabama State Legislature passed (unanimously in the House) a joint resolution HJR-90 signed by Governor

James on Mach 2, 1982 "memorializing the U.S. Congress to Repeal the Federal Reserve Act of 1913."

Erik, although your father and your Aunt Alyce are now suffering legal or illegal decisions which we hope can be successfully challenged, when you grow older and become a man you will realize that your father has upheld the basic element of White Christian Civilization, to wit: every intelligent White man should live and strive to provide a better future for his children and grandchildren. That is what Jim von Brunn is striving to do for you.

Sincerely,

Jno. G. Crommelin

Rear Admiral U.S. Navy (Retired)

ANDERSON BOYCOTT

Anderson urges boycott of series sponsor 5·24 94

By MARCIE ALVARADO
Staff Writer

EASTON — Talbot County Council Vice President Andrew Anderson has urged county residents to avoid the local sponsor of an anti-Holocaust TV series airing on local cable television.

Jim VonBrunn is sponsoring a six-part series that questions whether the Holocaust occurred and attempts to suggest that the *Diary of Anne Frank* is a hoax. The programs are being broadcast on Easton cable channel 15.

The first program aired Monday, May 16 and the series is scheduled to run every Monday and Thursday night for four weeks. The tapes, made in Canada in 1982, attempt to refute historical accounts about the Holocaust and Adolf Hitler's genocidal "Final Solution" for European Jews.

. Because of federal cable regulations local access channels are open to almost any programming, including ones promoting racist ideas, cable officials said this week. They said they can't refuse to run the programs.

During yesterday's council meeting, Anderson spoke out against the series and VonBrunn's opinions.

Anderson, a retired U.S. Army general, said he spent 13 years of his military career in Europe and toured the former concentration camps at Belsen and Dachau.

"I have seen evidence of the 'Final Solution.' It is documented fact," Anderson said. "For someone to show these tapes on our cable channel boggles the mind."

Anderson then called for a boycott of VonBrunn's business.

Speaking during the council members' comment period, Anderson said, "I will not frequent his business and I ask other people to stay the hell away from him. He is bad news."

VonBrunn, contacted at his home on Tuesday, declined to comment on Anderson's remarks.

5-26-94

Dachau photos vivid reminder

As I write this I have before me three snapshots taken by my husband at Dachau the day after it was liberated by the U.S. Army.

One shows skeleton-like bodies tossed on an open car of a train. The other two, taken in a shed, show discarded remains of what once were human beings.

Perhaps Mr. VonBrunn has an explanation for these snapshots. I wonder where he was the day my husband was at Dachau taking these pictures.

DOROTHY DeCAMP
Oxford

Denial just won't change history

In response to the article concerning the series of anti-Semitic programs airing on an Easton local access channel, I will defend to death Mr. VonBrunn's God-given right to free speech. However, it is imperative that we, as Christians, remember always that Jesus Christ was born, lived, and died a Jew. We should also remember that even as he died, for ALL mankind, he said, "Forgive them, Father, for they know not what they do." Denial can never change history. Peace and love.

KITTY SCHNEIDER,
Trinity Cathedral
Easton

LETTER TO ROBERT HIGGINS

JAMES W. VON BRUNN

POST OFFICE BOX 2821, EASTON, MD 21601

24 May 1994

OPEN LETTER

RE: COUNTY COUCIL QUOTES APPEARING IN EASTON *STAR-DEMOCRAT* (5-24-94)

Robert Higgins, President Talbot County Council Court House Easton, MD 21601

Dear Mr. Higgins:

As a young man I took the Naval Officers Oath, swearing to "...protect and defend the Constitution of the United States of America from all enemies foreign and domestic..." I regard that oath as important today as I did during WWII.

I am surprised to learn that a domestic enemy of our Constitution appears to be the Talbot County Council, represented by your vice-president, Mr. Andrew Anderson, who would deny me and the citizens of Talbot County our First Amendment rights. Were I a book he would burn me because he disagrees with what I believe to be true. He publicly calls for me to be shunned and my business to be boycotted, thus threatening my livelihood. I doubt the County Council supports Anderson's totalitarian views. However, I ask that you make your position clear publicly.

Anderson states he saw "evidence of the 'Final Solution'" at Dachau, and Bergen-Belsen concentration camps. He could receive a sizable reward for producing that evidence. No one else has seen it. The Allied War Crimes Commission determined, early on, there were no execution gas chambers in those camps, or in any of the thirteen (13) camps located in Germany/Austria. An official document to that effect is signed by members of that Commission dated 1 October 1948 (Official CopiesAvailable).

During the final months of the war Allies took command of the skies. We targeted highways, roads, bridges, railroads, power-plants, etc. Vital supplies were prevented from reaching the camps. When the Allies took over they were greeted with horror scenes: the sick and dying; unburied emaciated corpses covered the area. They had not been gassed or shot as we have been conditioned to believe, but died slowly of malnutrition and typhus, which raged throughout most of the camps. To complete the macabre scene the U.S. Army 45th Division, "liberators" of Dachau, gathered together 560 uniformed German guards and nurses and machine-gunned them to death.

The International Committee of the Red Cross (ICRC), and the Catholic Church, whose members frequented all camps, report no mass executions, and do not mention gas chambers. Hundreds of tons of evidentiary material, including Ultra-Enigma de-codings of German Communications, have been scrutinized by world experts. No one has produced evidence of any order, or budget, or plan, or machine directed toward the so-called Final Solution." THERE *IS NO* EVIDENCE OF THE PLANNED MURDER OF JEWS. The Jews were interned as enemies of the state. Germany's war was against Communism, Bolshevism, and Zionism. Hitler wanted a confederation of European states with a white population base. It is estimated that fewer than 300,000, Jews died from all causes during WWII.

Sincerely,

James W. von Brunn

STAR-DEMOCRAT EDITORIALS

Page **4A** Tuesday, April 22, 1997

★THE STAR EDITORIAL
DEMOCRAT

Tiger Woods is the new face of our country

The Tiger Woods phenomenon, coming at the 50th anniversary of Jackie Robinson's destruction of baseball's color barrier, has been interpreted as an example of another African-American breaking through a racial bulwark.

But it's much more than that, because Woods is not only an African-American. His father is black, while his mother is Thai. He's also American Indian, Chinese and white.

In America, he's lauded as an African-American role model, while in Thailand, he's the nation's favorite son.

In reality, Woods is an exemplar of the American melting pot. Some call him mixed-race, but that's a stale phrase in a nation of immigrants from every corner of the planet at a time when melting-pot ingredients blend more and more each day. The number of multiracial marriages quadrupled from 1970 to 1990 in America, according to census figures, but the real figure is likely much higher. The number of multi-racial young people is clearly on the rise.

Of course, we cannot be naive. Woods is a person of color, subject to the prejudices that infect our society. While his recently acquired wealth and fortune may shield him, bigotry still afflicts people of color, particularly those who don't have Woods' benefits. For them, racial obstacles still loom large.

Yet Woods is confounding prejudice. He defies racial labels in a society obsessed by race, while commanding awe in a sport dominated by whites.

The result is that he baffles the American institution of bigotry. Those who might have disdained him have no choice but to respect him. Confused about his ethnicity, they're nonetheless amazed by his abilities, and grudgingly accept him.

In the past, the term melting pot was seen through a white European prism, mainly referring to Irish, Italians, Swedes, Poles and others who immigrated here around the turn of the century. But today, more than ever, the melting pot continues to bubble and brew.

Our nation has become a place, perhaps the only one in human history, where all races and ethnicities mix together.

In our children's lifetimes, we will see the notion of labeling people as fill-in-the-blank Americans begin to fade, and bigotry and prejudice along with it. In that light, Tiger Woods is a true modern.

He shows the world the face of our country, today and in the future.

THE STAR
DEMOCRAT

EDITORIAL

Double helix that binds us all

There is no denying the reality of race. The proof confronts us daily — the color of our skin or the texture of our hair, even the diseases to which we sometimes fall prey. But underneath the microscope, those differences melt away.

Recent efforts to unravel the genetic code demonstrate that there simply is no biological basis for the concept of race. Scientists involved in the research to decode the human genome say that people are 99.9 percent alike, at the genetic level.

That should come as no surprise to any student of history or biology. We've long recognized that human anatomy is the same the world over. We know that compatible blood or organs can be transplanted from people of one color to those of another without undue complications. We know that modern humans first appeared in Africa 100,000 or so years ago — the blink of an eye, in evolutionary terms.

We are too young a species to have developed distinct biological subgroups. And we know that the concept of race has been remarkably plastic over the years. Classification schemes developed as recently as the 19th century placed people from Italy and Ireland in a different group than those from Northern Europe.

The accumulating evidence hasn't stopped modern racists seeking biological differences. The latest effort involves comparing average brain weights of different racial groups to create a hierarchy, with Asians on top and blacks at the bottom. By that tortured reasoning, Neanderthals would have inherited the Earth. They had larger brains than any of the modern humans that displaced them.

Race and ethnicity can, of course, be useful concepts. But they can also mislead. Australian Aborigines and African Americans both have shorter life expectancy than their white countrymen. But the explanation is more likely found in their social status than in the genes. Skin color is but an accident of evolution. It is our culture and experiences far more than our race that shapes who we are.

And so our efforts to unravel the genetic code have reinforced a lesson most knew already. At the most basic level, we are all inextricably bound together by DNA's double helix.

We who share this increasingly tense and crowded planet are all members of the same race — the human race.

NEVER SURRENDER SOVEREIGNTY

Mighty the men who made this land; Firm of purpose and strong of hand, Great in vision and free from fear, Fortress and home they built them here.

This they chanted unceasingly Never surrender sovereignty!

Dark is the night, the nation sleeps, Careless the watch the sentry keeps, Deaf are the ears that will not hear The song of free men ringing clear;

Borne on the wind eternally Never surrender sovereignty!

Confusion reigns, the hour is late, Traitors swarm through the unbarred gate. Freedom's for sale, and with it men - Hark can't they hear that cry again? Down through the ages endlessly -

Never surrender sovereignty!

JOSEPHINE POWELL BEATY.

Barboursville, Virginia

CICERO II

Power and law are not synonymous. In truth they are frequently in opposition and irreconcilable. There is GOD'S LAW from which all equitable laws of man emerge and by which men must live if they are not to die in oppression, chaos and despair. Divorced from GOD'S ETERNAL AND IMMUTABLE LAW, established before the founding of the suns, man's power is evil no matter the noble words with which it is employed or the motives urged when enforcing it. Men of good will, mindful therefore of the LAW LAID DOWN BY GOD, will oppose governments whose rule is by men and, if they wish to survive as a nation, they will destroy that government which attempts to adjudicate by the whim or power of venal judges.

CICERO (106-43 BC).

OTHER PUBLICATIONS

Omnia Veritas Ltd presents:

THE WORLD ORDER
OUR SECRET RULERS

A Study in the Hegemony of Parasitism

by

EUSTACE MULLINS

The peoples of the world not only will never love Big Brother, but they will soon dispose of him forever.

The program of the World Order remains the same; Divide and Conquer

Omnia Veritas Ltd presents:

EZRA POUND
THIS DIFFICULT INDIVIDUAL

by

EUSTACE MULLINS

Ezra's interest in money as a phenomenon, in contrast to the usual attitude toward money as something to get, is a legitimate one.

An illustration for his own monetary theories...

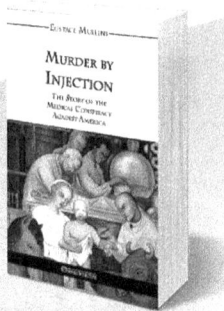

Omnia Veritas Ltd presents:

MURDER BY INJECTION

THE STORY OF THE MEDICAL CONSPIRACY AGAINST AMERICA

by

EUSTACE MULLINS

The cynicism and malice of these conspirators is something beyond the imagination of most Americans.

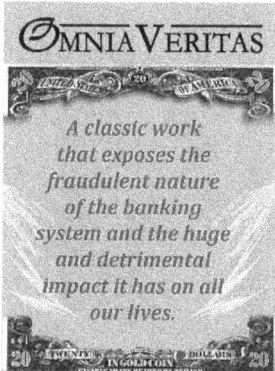

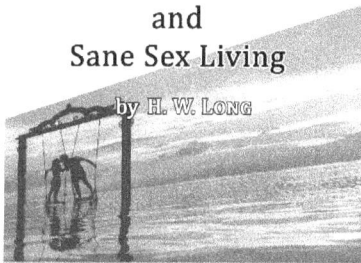

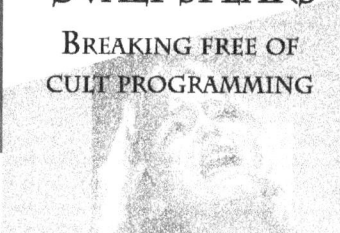

Omnia Veritas Ltd presents:

THE HIGH COST OF VENGEANCE

France and Britain refused to listen to the statesmen who said that you can have peace or vengeance, not both...

BY FREDA UTLEY

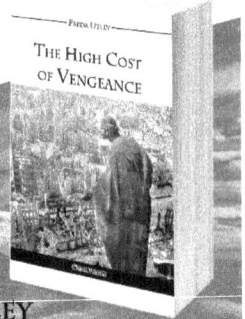

The victors refused even to discuss the terms of peace with the vanquished

Omnia Veritas Ltd presents:

The History of Money

It is fascinating and almost magical how money appeared on our planet...

Most people don't realise that the issuing of money is a private business...

Omnia Veritas Ltd presents:

The Ladies' Book of Etiquette, and Manual of Politeness

A complete hand book for the use of the lady in polite society

BY

FLORENCE HARTLEY

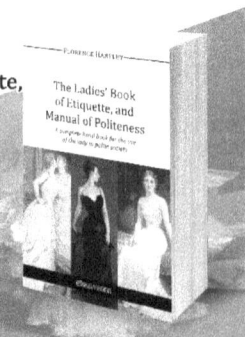

... to be truly a **lady**, one must carry the **principles** into every circumstance of life

Politeness is goodness of heart put into daily practice

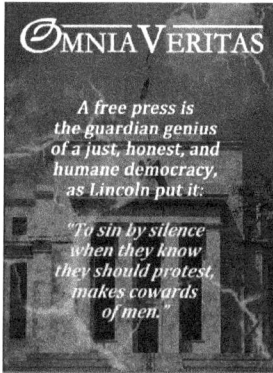

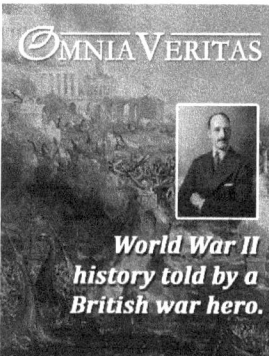

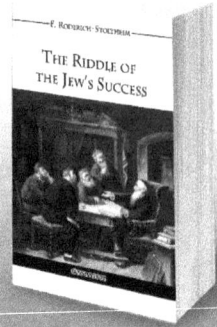

www.ingramcontent.com/pod-product-compliance
Lightning Source LLC
Chambersburg PA
CBHW072004270326
41928CB00009B/1542